LOVING ANIMALS

LOVING ANIMALS

Toward a New Animal Advocacy

KATHY RUDY

University of Minnesota Press
Minneapolis
London

Published by the University of Minnesota Press
111 Third Avenue South, Suite 290
Minneapolis, MN 55401-2520
http://www.upress.umn.edu

Library of Congress Cataloging-in-Publication Data

Rudy, Kathy.
    Loving animals : toward a new animal advocacy / Kathy Rudy.
    p. cm.
    Includes bibliographical references and index.
    ISBN 978-0-8166-7468-8 (hardback)
    1. Animal welfare. 2. Animal welfare—Moral and ethical aspects.
3. Animal rights. 4. Animal rights activists. I. Title.
    HV4708.R83 2011
    179'.3—dc23
                                    2011015734

Printed in the United States of America on acid-free paper

The University of Minnesota is an equal-opportunity educator and employer.

18 17 16 15 14 13 12 11   10 9 8 7 6 5 4 3 2

This book is dedicated to my parents, Rosamond and Frank Rudy.

CONTENTS

A CHANGE OF HEART

THE WORLD OF "ANIMAL RIGHTS" IN THE FIRST PART of the twenty-first century is busy, perplexing, and extremely uneven. Sometimes, people who call themselves animal rights activists simply mean they don't eat meat or wear leather; sometimes they eat fish, cheese, or eggs, and sometimes they don't. Sometimes, these activists break into scientific research labs and steal animals used in experiments. Sometimes they kill animals in "shelters." Sometimes, the term animal rights refers to people who rescue injured wildlife for rehabilitation and release them back into the wild. Sometimes it means people who run permanent sanctuaries for retired entertainment animals or exotic pets; at other times it refers to people who believe wild and exotic animals should not be kept at all and work to shut such sanctuaries down. Sometimes, people who say they're into animal rights mean they really love animals and share a large portion of their lives with them, even trying various sound and unsound methods to communicate with them. At other times, being an animal rights activist means holding a strict abolitionist policy toward all animals, and condemning zoos, pet ownership, and all other venues in which humans come into intimate contact with nonhuman animals.

It's not easy to make sense of all these conflicting viewpoints and issues. Indeed, other than the fact that all these projects have something to do with animals, there aren't transparent ways to articulate what holds all these agendas together. It's even more confusing when the general public uses a kind of shorthand to classify all animal rights interests as extremist food police; when I try to convince my women's studies majors to take one of my animal classes, for example, their response is almost always, "I can't take that class because I'm not a vegetarian." It reminds me of the way people used to equate all feminism with lesbianism in the 1970s: "I can't be a feminist because I like men." The public discourse concerning feminism has certainly changed, and I think it's time for things to change with regard to animal rights as well.

This book argues that animal advocates should undertake and attend to significant emotional shifts concerning animals for animal rights to become a more mainstream movement. In other words, to hold all these competing agendas and ideas together, we must work toward building a shift in public thinking about nonhuman animals such that animal advocacy can become more accepted by wider sectors of society. "Women's rights" does not mean the same thing in every pocket of feminism, nor does "gay rights" or "civil rights." These terms point to orientations toward social change, not specific agreed-upon agendas. Indeed, inside each of these other movements, arguments and conflicts abound; what holds them together in the public eye, though, is a fairly general cultural acceptance. The same thing needs to happen for "animal rights." We need to explain animal advocacy agendas, and the variety of approaches they take up, in a different way such that animal issues become more accepted by a wider public.

Loving Animals asks us to step back from the rational principles employed by many animal advocacy philosophies to examine the emotional and spiritual connections that, for many, produced the desire for change in the first place. Stepping back allows us to ask a whole range of different questions about animals and our relationship with them: What mechanisms of language sorted all living things into only two categories called "humans" and "animals"? What practices in capitalism rendered the bodies of some animals as killable commodities? What religious practices gave only some of us souls? What scientific data render some animals as wild and others as domesticated? What stories support the view that animals could and should be exploited for human benefit? And what, exactly, counts as exploitation? How do we interact with and connect with real animals, and how do those connections reflect (or not) current ethical thinking about animals? How well are our relationships with animals reflected in culture today? Do these stories adequately portray the way we feel with and about animals? When and under what circumstances do we get our relationships with animals "right," and how can those examples serve as a model for treatment of other animals? Examining the ways that emotion, connection, and stories have constructed our current world, I believe, can lead to new strategies for change.

Although this book is informed by my training and work in theological ethics and women's studies, it begins, really, with the passions that are closest to my heart. It would not be an overstatement to say that most of the important and successful relationships I've had in my life have been with nonhuman animals. The vast majority of them have been dogs, a half-dozen cats, a few birds, one horse, and most recently two pigs. Almost every picture of me as a kid is taken with a dog or a kitten or a horse; if there's no animal in the picture, chances are pretty high I am not smiling. It's very hard to explain, but I am most "myself" when I am with animals, they alone "speak my language" (and not all of them, just some); without them around, I feel just a little bit invisible. The connections that shape my own life, then, form the heart of this book. I start with a dog by my side and go from there.

This sort of self-revelation is important up front because—in addition to the general confusion around the theoretical stakes of animal advocacy—there is often a fairly large disconnect between much of the theory of the movement and the experiences of many people who call themselves animal advocates. Most of the people I encounter in my daily life who self-identify as animal advocates truly love animals. Like me, they have special connections to certain nonhuman animals. Some articulate it as a spiritual bond, others say that animals have purer hearts or are easier to live with than humans. Many of these folks would sell their last possessions to help an animal in need; and some have done just that. For them, no sacrifice is too great. Yet, very little of this love or emotion is reflected at the level of ethical theory around animals. Many writers speak about the animal as a distant other, a creature that needs our consideration but not necessarily our love. Very few ethicists write about their pets; indeed, some, as we shall see, believe pet ownership is wrong. They implore us to take animals' interests seriously, but not necessarily to be involved with them at the most fundamental bodily and emotional levels. I believe that emotional connections with real animals, connections based on love and shared lives, need to be included in the discourse of animal advocacy in order to maintain and model a better world for them.[1]

This new approach to animal advocacy strives to develop a way of seeing the world where animals are subjects, agents, and actors in their own right. Through their relationships with us, they can gain more of a voice in public debate about the conditions of their existence. Inside the connections we share with all kinds of animals, a new sense of subjectivity emerges where humans and animals are not separate entities, but creatures inextricably attached to one another through emotional bonds. Put differently, this approach to advocacy is not only about humans loving animals but also about animals loving us back. It recognizes that animals have choices, and one of the choices many of them make is to become loving, to be loving animals. They transcend the boundaries of their bodies and their species by trusting, caring for, and communing with us. Thus, "loving" is both a verb and an adjective, something both humans and animals do, but something both of us also are. Inside these attachments, animals can fully be seen as subjects rather than objects.

When I think about other social movements, it is not only principles that made them viable but a whole host of other things as well. Many of those tools found their stage in the realms of emotion and connection, and specifically in the registers of language, stories, identification, and love. What I call for in this book is the inclusion of emotion—and in the way that connections can change culture—in the theory and practice of animal advocacy. Social movements all started somewhere, usually from a few voices crying out not only for better treatment but also for a different outlook on the world. The first time we heard Dr. Martin Luther King speak, or watched Cesar Chavez march on television, or knew someone who died of AIDS, our world shifted just a little to let in this new reality. A deep change in the way we act and think almost always starts with a change of heart, and our hearts are usually changed by hearing, seeing, feeling, and sensing something different. Thus, although I think ethical principles are critical in defending any new vision, those of us who are border crossers, who have intense emotional bonds with specific animals, bear a particular burden right now to share our world-view. Only when we understand better how to change people's hearts will animal advocacy become a more viable social movement. The current animal advocacy movement can and will gain even more legitimacy in the next generation if those of us who love animals can think and talk and write about those connections; we all then need to extrapolate those relationships to the twenty billion or so animals that have no advocates, those creatures that never see sunlight or grass, that never know the touch of a kind hand. What I call for in this book is a more sophisticated understanding of the role of affect and emotion in the building of a contemporary animal advocacy movement.

Each of the chapters that follow addresses one realm in which humans use animals; in each chapter I try to think not only about animal suffering but also about venues in which good relationships between humans and animals exist. My goal in each of these settings is to explore the power structures that landed us in a world where abuse is accepted. It's not the case, I believe, that all humans are inherently destructive toward nonhuman animals; rather, social structures such as gender oppression, capitalism, Western religion, and scientific objectivity obscure the realities of animal suffering. My aim in this book is to dig out the problems involved with such institutions. In each chapter, I ask questions like the following: Why do we kill so many unwanted pets in shelters across the country? How did we move from the small family farm to animal agribusiness? Are there alternatives to keeping wild animals in zoos? What kinds of dualisms support our ability to cut nonhumans open to better develop human medicines? How did we come to live in a world that does such things? And can we intervene to construct our relationships with animals differently? The thinking in this book implicates larger institutions in animal oppression; it's rare, I believe, that individual humans torture animals. Most of the torture is done by larger structures, and I name those throughout.

But there's more to the story than what is done wrong and how we bought into systems that perform such atrocities. That's the reconstructive part of this book. In each of these chapters and settings I ask: Is the human use of animals in this setting ever done right? Is deep connection with animals possible in environments where we use them? What does it look like, and how will I know it when I see it? Are there spaces where animals seem happy, where they aren't mutilating themselves, where they aren't engaged in obsessive behavior, where they seem (to my eyes) to be fulfilled? What kinds of cultural artifacts might help better represent these successful connections? How can we construct a different kind of society in which connection with and affection for animals becomes the norm?

This kind of assessment is difficult, for we can't actually ask the animals what they're thinking or feeling. I'll speak more fully about the problems the language barrier produces (and offer ways of seeing around it) in later chapters, but suffice it to say right now that the strategy I have chosen to mark connection is really based on my own experience of living with animals. While we may not be able to access the deep structures of their thinking or the precise contours of their emotions, I think most observers can tell when animals are miserable and unhappy. They act in a way that seems wrong. They bite themselves or pee where they're not supposed to or pick on animals bigger than they or spin or cry or just lie unnaturally still. At the same time, I believe most observers can tell when animals are filled with pleasure and joy, when they run and seem to dance and act as if the world were wholly designed especially for them. They cuddle and laugh and lick their young and turn their faces to the sun and smile. These are the markers I used in evaluating animal happiness. I could be wrong on many counts, but finally I believe that the communication problem between humans and animals is not different in kind from the communication issue between two humans. We don't all speak the same language, and, yes, people and animals can lie about what they experience. But in the final count, if (as evolution tells us) we're all made of the same "stuff," some impressions about happiness can be discerned across species lines.[2]

Many theorists of animal advocacy begin their thinking by valorizing the wild animal.[3] For them, animals in the wild function as a representation of the beauty of nature over the tameness of culture and domestication. This book flips that paradigm around and looks toward domestication as a new location for a cultural shift concerning the human-animal relationship. Put simply, I begin my thinking with the animals that are closest to us, our pets, and move out from there to examine human relationships with farm animals, exotic animals in zoos and sanctuaries, and animals in science labs. I am not at all interested in making stark contrasts between nature and culture, but rather in seeing how the "natureculture" worlds we inhabit with other animals can become healthier and happier spaces for them—and for us.[4]

Consequently, this is a very different kind of animal advocacy book. What the reader will find in the chapters that follow are analyses about human oppression of the animal as well as lots of narratives about animals that aren't suffering, animals that are thriving, animals that have reached across the species divide and chosen to connect with humans. These are the stories that I believe can provide guideposts to help us into a new form of animal advocacy.

Chapter 1 reviews current philosophical approaches to animal advocacy by examining the competing methodologies of rights, utilitarianism, welfare, and animal studies. The first three methods comprise the vast majority of the thinking behind animal advocacy today. All three are based, in one way or another, on Enlightenment philosophy; each deploys a different method for bringing animals into the circle of protection. Rights-based strategies move a limited catalog of rights out into the world of (some) animals; utilitarianism extends protection to animals based on their ability to suffer; and welfare orients advocacy toward animals as a function of human sympathy. Each of these methods is limited in its ability to truly serve animal advocacy. I argue instead for a different approach toward animal advocacy, one based not solely in rights or sympathy but in the revolutionary power of love many of us feel toward animals.

Chapters 2 (pets), 3 (food), 4 (entertainment), and 5 (science) display what emotional connections do or could look like in each of the areas where humans live with and use animals. In each of these chapters, I display what real connection brings to the table. While I recognize that animal rights, and to a lesser degree welfare and utilitarianism, are operating in political settings that seek legal change, my aim in each of these chapters is to show how a strategy based on transformative love differs from these established approaches. I want to show how connection with animals can bring us to different conclusions. Over and over in my research, I found some humans living in harmony with some animals in ways that established ethical methodologies simply cannot account for or endorse. This is not to say that my observations and experiences with real animals in connection render philosophical theories wrong; it's more like they are just incomplete, especially at the task of capturing what goodness can come from sound human-animal connections. Many readers will call this approach particularistic, a soft method for reform at best. After all, we can always find exceptions that prove a rule, but those exceptions can't form the basis of public policy, right? My argument rests on the hope that with a little prompting, human culture could do much more work to make connection with animals the norm. Emotional connection has transformed our lives in relation to every other social movement, and it needs to be engaged more fully in animal activism. What I found in my research are many models of humans connecting with animals that—if we could extrapolate them into wider social norms—would produce a much better world for animals. This is not, then, a book that calls immediately for policy change (although we certainly need that as well). Rather, I want to think about the possibility that change happens in many ways at many different levels, and altering the hearts and minds of many people through affective shifts will lead to an easier job for philosophy and policy, and mostly to a better world for animals.

Chapter 6 of this book uses the metaphor of "clothing"—the final way humans use animals in daily life—to introduce the concept of affect. I use the word affect because it differs slightly from emotion; where emotions can be too easily manipulated, affect includes a sense of reason, but not a freestanding or objective reason. Rather affect recognizes that reason and emotion are inextricably intertwined; like two sides of the same coin, you can't have one without the other. They affect each other, and we are made through and in that interaction. Through processes of development and identification, we form various habits that help give expression to our emotional bonds; these bonds are not without reason, but they often do not entirely depend on reason either. The creation of the self emerges through attachments and disattachments, identifications, disidentifications, and misidentifications. We are part what we love, part what we think, part what we feel, and part what we believe. The term affect captures the almost liquid nature of subject formation and allows for a different sense of self to emerge. It helps us understand how we proceed in the world by affecting both hearts and minds.

While focusing entirely on emotion can quickly lead us to an impoverished sentimentality, the concept of affect tempers that by intermingling emotion with reason. Affect symbolizes the fluid and interconnected nature of life itself. In other words, we change things as we bump up against them, and are similarly changed through these interactions. It is through affect that all lives become animated; we learn to cope with and live in the world by performing different feelings and sensibilities. Through those performances we become visible to ourselves. Affect signals our entire orientation to the world around us; while it may at times include the sentimental, it is not bound by it. Thus, my use of the term affect marks the fact that our realities are made for us in part through the worlds and meanings available to us, as well as by who and what we are attracted to and love (or don't love).

The concept of affect focuses on emotions like love, inclination, tendency, and desire, coupled with their interaction with reason, to argue for a new mode of subjectivity production, a new model of how we become "selves." Put simply, we become who we are by being involved with—affected by—the people, places, things, and ideas that draw us in. Our world is made by the constant interplay of our environments with our bodies, our reason, and our emotions. What drives us forward is the desire to connect with the world in an endless stream of different ways. The engine of that change is affect.

The concept of affect is also deeply rooted in material, corporeal bodies; it is about the way bodies live near each other, inside each other, with each other. Whether a tree, or a vegetable, or an animal, or a human, affect attends to the ways bodies move through life relying on other material beings, using living things to make houses and food and clothing and meaning. Affect is not only about the ways reason and emotions are linked together but also about the specific ways they are embedded in real bodies. Who gets to exploit what or whom, who gets to eat what or whom, who gets to love what or whom are central concerns in the agenda of affect. Thus, the concept of affect forces us to focus on competing claims for scarce resources; it pushes us to think inside the limitations of the material world. On the shrinking planet we all currently inhabit, this corporeal aspect of affect is perhaps most salient, especially when it comes to animals.

In many ways, I will suggest, affect is also about a certain notion of spirituality or sacredness. I use these terms not to signal organized religion but rather to attend to the fact that as bodies crash up against and change each other, something sacred happens, something that cannot be contained by the concepts of reason or emotion or even corporeality. Affect, for me, points to the mystery that accompanies us through our daily lives, namely, how our attachments and enmeshments transform us in ways that sometimes seem magical or otherworldly. Other terms could be substituted here: animism, pantheism, vitalism, enchantment, and process thought, for example. But I use the terms spirituality and sacredness because they open up the possibility that the sharing of scarce resources, the crashing together of all kinds of bodies in this material world, requires a sustained attention to larger meanings. It demands that all of us (and really every living thing) make sacrifices in order to cohabit this planet together. Who and what are forced to make those sacrifices and under what conditions is the work of advocacy, ethics, and politics. But without a sense of spirituality and sacredness, sacrifice has little value.

In his famous 1967 essay "The Historical Roots of Our Ecological Crises," Lynn White wrote, "More science and more technology are not going to get us out of the present ecological crisis until we find a new religion, or rethink our old one."[5] White was not really interested in finding a new religion in his writing, and I am certainly not interested in that here. Indeed, I'll display the differences between religion and a spiritualized concept of affect in chapter 6. Rather, I think both of us are pointing to the kinds of excessive meaning that often accompany deep interconnections with animals and the natural world. What White and I are both calling for is a shift that reorients our attention to the more-than-human world. Reason, emotions, and bodies produce things that are greater than the sum of their parts—ecstasy, peace, tragedy, fulfillment, wholeness, brokenness, hope, grace, to name a few. These are the kinds of things I want the concept of affect to capture, things beyond simple emotions, things that open our hearts, minds, and bodies to new realities and new possibilities of worldmaking.

The language of sacrifice, sacredness, and spiritual embodiment haunts the margins of many thinkers in animal studies; for me, the concept of affect helps bring these (almost) otherworldly realities into sharper relief. It is because we are embodied, emotional, rational creatures that attention to these matters is required. Donna Haraway's work, for example, is often peppered with spiritual metaphors, especially when she discusses both human and animal suffering: "My story ends where it began . . . when the logic of sacrifice makes no sense and the hope for forgiveness depends on learning a love that escapes calculation but requires the invention of speculative thought and the practice of remembering, of rearticulating bodies to bodies."[6] I understand Haraway to mean that human and nonhuman animals are enmeshed in a world that requires sacrifice on both parts, and that the nature of that sacrifice depends upon the idea that such interconnection, even when it causes suffering, is sacred. Susan McElroy locates and identifies a transcendent power associated with human-animal interconnection:

> Indigenous people look upon wild animals as living incarnations of special powers, traits, or virtues that humans might learn from if we watched closely and with reverence. Early priestesses and magicians donned animal skins and masks to call in specific virtues and abilities inherent in particular animals. Rituals and ceremonies in which people acted out or danced the essence of animals have been practiced since human time began. For centuries, animals have served as our bridge to the natural and supernatural.[7]

In keeping with Haraway and McElroy, I want to suggest that sacredness and spirituality are central themes that need to be taken more seriously in animal advocacy. I propose in this book that a broad definition of the concept of affect can help us attend to these realms more substantially. Spiritual and sacred experiences of and with animals are not limited to indigenous peoples, or to priestesses and magicians, or rituals and ceremonies. They surround all of us who live with and are connected in any way to the world of animals. We only need better eyes to see them rightly. Such a sacred dimension resides in pet owners who keep the ashes of their beloved departed friends on their mantels, in the world of good hunters who keep a few bones of their prey around the house to remind them of sacrifices made on their behalf. This kind of spiritual, affective connection rests in stories of animal love from John Grogan's *Marley and Me* to films like *Babe* and *Black Beauty*. It lives inside human-animal relationships that are based on kindness, kinship, and reciprocity. What if we could, for just a moment, imagine that animals possessed different kinds of powers from the ones we can now measure? What if we assume that animals serve as our bridge to the natural and to the supernatural? What if their different biologies hold the key to healing the wounds we humans have inflicted on this earth and the animals that inhabit it? Thinking about animals like this, in the realm of spirituality and affect, can offer us new forms of relationship with them, new methods of creating reality together.

I have purposely placed my fuller explication of the concept of affect at the end of this book for several reasons. While it might make sense to tell you up front exactly what affect is and how it replaces or revises theories of rights, utilitarianism, or welfare, I want to signal instead that the concept of affect is operating in a completely different realm from that of principled reason. An affective approach is not about finding the right rule and applying it; it's about examining the greater meanings and attachments that construct our lives. More important, placing my theory at the end of the book signals the fact that affect can only be displayed through narrative. In chapters 2 through 5, you will find emotional animal stories—lots of them—that collectively show us how to become better humans through our love for animals. It's only through reading those stories, stories filled with joy, grace, sorrow, despair, loneliness, happiness, fulfillment, and many other emotions, that we can fully comprehend the work of affect. Through these stories, I will show that change comes from the heart as much as from the head, and that the powers that trivialize emotions and dismiss them as mere sentimentality always function to reinforce the sole superiority of reason. This book begins in the conviction that human reason is not big enough to bring about the changes animals need. Thus, in using narrative and affect to change the conditions that oppress animals, theory follows the practices that can only be displayed in narrative, or put more correctly, theory and practice emerge together as a new approach to advocacy. Placing my theory chapter at the end signals the fact that I am not offering a new principle for animal advocacy but a new way of living based on the revolutionary power of love.

The conclusion to this book offers one final personal story that highlights the role of affect, narrative, sacrifice, spirituality, and sacredness in our relationship with animals. Loving animals, and being loved by them, is not always an easy or blissful proposition. While a sentimentalized view of animals makes loving them seem easy, the reality of their corporeal existences means that attaching to and with them is often sad, painful, and heartbreaking. They do things we don't like, they hurt each other, and us, and they don't always know how to get along. The conclusion displays the fact that animals are not always or often cuddly playthings that acquiesce to our desires; they are beings with their own worldviews, ideas, and affects. And sometimes their realities crash harshly into our own. But, just as with humans, the work of love knits us together and forces us to endure and move forward, even during the harshest of times. Receiving their love, I will suggest, changes what it means to be human. These are difficult lessons, and in the conclusion, I will pull together all the reasons why I think love, as hard as it sometimes is, may be the only way to break through to a new reality.

I firmly believe that given the right opportunity, most humans can connect with animals, can look in their faces and see the spirit of a fellow being, and can make the changes necessary to improve their lot in life. It's the structures of our world that impede this process, structures that could be organized differently. Few people really want to see another being suffer. The problem is always either that they don't see the suffering (in factory farms or labs, for example) or they don't understand that an animal's life is made of the same "stuff" as yours or mine. Sustained attention to love, and the stories that produce that love, can help us address both of these issues. Good stories about animals can entertain us and educate us and help change the nature of humanity. I believe such transformation is possible. This book calls us to dismantle the arrangements that allow the unnecessary mistreatment and torture of animals to continue. By speaking about our deep connections across the species divide, we can call forth the goodness in even the most hardened human heart.

We must embark on this project of advocacy by first noting that the world is messy: it's filled with bad attitudes toward animals but also with grand and positive relationships. An orientation toward animal advocacy that chooses only to see only a world full of agony pushes us to the premature conclusion that all human intervention with animals is deeply flawed, that nothing can be saved. Such a strategy misses the goodness that happens when things are done well. When the abandoned puppy finds a new loving home, when the single guy looks forward all day to coming home to his cats, when the cow plays chase with the butterfly in a field of sunshine, when the orphaned chimp puts her arms around Jane Goodall's neck, when my dogs sense I am just about to finish writing and start to get excited about their walks, when the lonely teenage girl finds delight in galloping on her horse, and when that horse anticipates that girl's daily return from school with joy: These are things we simply can't give up. In a funny twist on the Velveteen Rabbit's story, these are the things that make us (humans) real.[8]

ONE WHAT'S BEHIND ANIMAL ADVOCACY?

I'T'S IMPORTANT TO UNDERSTAND THE ABSTRACT ETHI-
cal theories that underpin any social movement because those theories form a foundation for the various directions a movement takes. The
easiest way to see this is in retrospect with other social movements, movements that are perhaps more self-reflective about their foundations than
animal rights is today. The women's movement, for example, spent many
years debating different strategies for the eradication of sexism. Some
feminists sought equality and worked for change within existing political and economic structures; other feminists sought ways to celebrate
women's differences and focused on cultural changes to valorize women
and the feminine aspects of many different spheres. Still others sought
to correct economic hardships for women and children in poverty, while
many found ways to build coalitions with different kinds of women across
national and cultural boundaries. Forty years into the movement, feminists have become pretty adept at figuring out how these agendas differ
and even sometimes conflict, and how we can all work together to build
a better world for women. The same kinds of differences exist in all contemporary social movements from civil rights to gay rights to environ-
mentalism to Latino liberation to union building; competing goals are

evident, such as assimilation versus separation, equality versus difference, extremism versus moderation. The animal rights movement is no exception, and a rudimentary understanding of the terrain of these strategies is essential.

The map that follows is in no way intended to offer an exhaustive discussion or review of the philosophical literature concerning ethics and animals. Rather, it is simply intended to show that most of the philosophies and strategies associated with animal advocacy pay very little attention to things like identity, affect, culture, emotion, or narrative. This map examines the principles that stand behind current animal advocacy, in part to see how competing principles lead to competing practices, and in part to show how a different orientation could add to and legitimate the movement as a whole.

Animal Rights

Although the term "animal rights" is often inaccurately used to refer to the whole movement of animal advocacy (in much the same way that "women's rights" is sometimes used to mean everything feminist), for accuracy's sake we should start by thinking more precisely about what a right is and what kinds of rights are being advocated for animals. Put as simply as possible, a right is a legal way of protecting a particular interest, even when that interest may conflict with the interests of either what is perceived as the common good or more powerful agents such as governments or corporations. Humans are born with a catalog of rights that, in the United States, stems from the basic commitments to life, liberty, and property. According to this view of rights, we are free to pursue our interests in these three realms as long as our engagements do not compromise the rights (i.e., the interests) of other humans. We are free, for example, to purchase medical care to extend our lives or to purchase property and goods that will make us happy. We are free from being owned as property by other human beings or other entities such as corporations or nations. In this approach, we are thought to be agents of our own creation, protected from undue interference or coercion, free to become whoever we want to be. Animals, of course, have no such protection.

One form of animal rights advocacy works to secure specific rights for specific types of animals in specific conditions. Certain animals have a right not to suffer unduly, advocates claim; these animals have an interest in not being treated cruelly. Those who hold this position work to pass legislation that would prevent humans from, for example, keeping dogs on chains outside, keeping calves in veal crates, using pipes to force-feed ducks for the production of pâté de foie gras, selling pets for scientific experimentation, slaughtering horses for meat—the list goes on and on. Stated differently, in most existing laws pertaining to animals, the animal in question is protected only as a form of property. Although some states do currently have anticruelty laws in place, the vast majority of laws protecting animals do so under the rubric of property. If I beat my neighbor's dog, for example, I may be found guilty of damaging his property; it is the neighbor's interests that the law protects, not the dog's. Animal rights advocates in this first sense want to change that and argue that the animals themselves have an interest in not being beaten. In a sense, they want the animals themselves to have a certain agency in relation to their rights as living creatures. Even when those interests conflict with the interests of more powerful agents, rights (in this first sense) function as a protection that trumps everything else. So even though a farmer may have made a substantial portion of his income off veal, if confining young male calves to crates is outlawed, the calves' interests in not being treated cruelly trump the farmer's interests in making money. These types of protections are rights in the weak sense because each case and issue must be addressed in separate legislation. That is, animals have no blanket rights, only the particular ones stated in that specific law.[1]

This is not to say that laws such as these are ineffectual or unimportant. For example, the passage of the 2008 Prevention of Farm Animal Cruelty Act in California (Proposition 2) prohibits the confinement of certain farm animals in a manner that does not allow them to turn around, lie down, stand up, or extend their limbs. Sponsored by the Humane Society of the United States, Prop 2 effectively wiped out veal crates, battery cages, and sow gestation crates in the entire state of California. This is clearly a great victory for animals. The Animal Legal Defense Fund (ALDF) similarly works to pass legislation in local communities to limit and close puppy mills and animal hoarders; the organization's recent victory in North Carolina against hoarder-breeder Barbara Woodley marked a historic shift in the process for legal advocacy; prior to the Woodley case, only state prosecutors could bring forth animal cruelty cases in North Carolina. The ALDF win set a precedent for allowing private citizens to bring charges. The group People for the Ethical Treatment of Animals (PETA) has also enjoyed many local legal victories, especially with regard to limiting the production of fur in many states. These are just a few examples. There are more than eighty registered animal advocacy groups in the United States, and the vast majority of them are or have been involved in some aspect of specific legislation of rights in this weak sense. These efforts, no matter how modest or local, are crucial in the ongoing protection of animals.

But there is another sense of animal rights that makes a much stronger claim. Animal rights in the strong, abolitionist sense is not invested in protecting specific interests (such as the right not to be confined to a veal crate or perpetually chained outside), but argues instead that all animal interests can best be addressed if we extend to them the primary human rights of life and freedom. Philosophers and political theorists have different ways of describing what these rights look like and why they are warranted. Philosopher Tom Regan, the first to extend the tradition of rights into the realm of animals, speaks of animals as "subjects of a life" who have an overriding interest in the continuation of their own lives.[2] Legal theorist Gary Francione states, quite simply, that the right not to be the property of others serves animals' best interests.[3] For animal rights in this strong sense, the interests of animals stem from the fact that they are conscious, sentient beings, that is, beings capable of perceiving the surrounding word and having feelings about that world. This strong version of animal rights, especially in the United States, relies on our common American sensibility that slavery (i.e., owning another human being) is morally repugnant.[4] While many people in the wider public find this comparison of animals to dark-skinned humans troubling, animal rights advocates want to capitalize on that discomfort to get us to reevaluate our practices toward animals. From this perspective, many white Americans once believed that slaves and dark-skinned humans were similar to animals, but thinking about these humans changed, progressed, developed; our thinking about animals should follow the same path, according to animal rights advocates. For animal rights in this strong sense, it's not enough that we just call ourselves "guardians" rather than "owners"; we really shouldn't own them or inhibit them or use them or contain them in any sense at all. For these rights advocates, animals need to be set free much the same way slaves were set free. According to this strong rights view, animals are not ours to use for any purpose whatsoever.

Animal rights in the strong sense presumes a kind of self-determined nonhuman subject that can operate in the world uncoerced by culture, the state, needs, desires, identity, commitment, or the necessities of everyday life. One of the biggest gaps between theory and practice rests right here; those of us who live with animals (and many others as well) often do not ourselves enjoy the kind of freedom this theory prescribes for nonhumans. We make "deals" that inhibit our liberty; we need to eat, we work for money, we pay taxes, we live in houses with locks, and so on. The structures of our lives produce necessary compromises to these absolute freedoms. The "deal" that domesticated animals have made over time with humans is that some of their freedoms would be curtailed in return for food, shelter, belonging, and love. I am not suggesting that every dog deliberates on her specific arrangement, but rather that dogs over thousands of years found it evolutionarily beneficial to live near and with humans. The same is true for cows and horses and any other species that live close to humans. An exchange is going on between two or more species, and to renege on that deal would surely mean the extinction of those animals that could not return to the wild.

Stated differently, the most devastating long-term implication of the strong animal rights claim is that, other than wildlife, we would not have animals in our lives or in our worlds. The philosophers who advocate animal rights in the strong sense suggest that we should care for the animals we have here now, but that we stop breeding all domestic animals into existence for our use. No dogs, no cats, no horses, no pigs. No birds, no cows, no chickens, no fish. We wouldn't eat them or make them work for us or cuddle them or walk them or ride them or wear them. We couldn't use them to assist the blind or in search and rescue or to add joy to our lives. Hundreds of thousands of years of developing relationships with domesticated animals would cease. This position is taken up by many animal rights philosophers, including Tom Regan, Gary Francione, Lee Hall, and Steve Wise. They share a view of the world where animals would never suffer at the hands of humans, where the human experience of animals would be limited to wildlife observation.

I think about all the people in the world like me who find their identities intertwined with nonhuman animals. A world without their companionship seems very dark and uninhabitable. I look at my pack of pets, six dogs and three cats, watch them play with each other, comfort each other, learn to live together, and know in my heart that the world is a better place for having them in it. They represent for me all that is good about the world, all the grace and hope that make life worth living. Finally for me, it's a question of joy—mine *and* theirs—that demands we think through these animal issues from different and expanded positions. Advocating a future free of animals in order to save them from the suffering we may put them through seems unnecessary. Surely we can do better than that. Surely we can think more lovingly about our ethics and craft a moral world teeming with all kinds of life that is treated fairly and well.

While I know these strong rights theorists only want to end animal suffering at any cost, the very real connections we have with actual animals make this path problematic. To produce alternatives, we need to see the animal issue from other perspectives, particularly those in which humans and animals are living together happily and successfully. We need to add to the legal and philosophical discourses about rights the sense of urgency we feel about the necessity of sharing our lives with real animals. Another way to articulate this criticism is that in some ways "animal rights" are just not privileges that can be distributed by the courts. Rather, they are also interpretations of relationships, the outward symbol of recognition, respect, and acceptance that one animal does or does not have for another. In this way, I suggest, animal rights are not something we give, they are something we do. "Women's rights," "gay rights," and "civil rights" aren't simply legal artifacts handed down by the government; rather these terms represent shifts in culture as well, shifts whereby large numbers of people came to see these identities and oppressions in a different light. The same needs to happen for animals. In addition to philosophy and the law, we need a shift that better negotiates their best interests with our own.

There's nothing inherently wrong with animal rights in the weak sense, of course. Using the law to better the lives of certain animals in certain conditions is important and necessary work. Indeed, even in the frame of the wider affective shift I call for in this book, one might see this strategic use of rights as analogous to civil rights activists' using affirmative action as a temporary measure to ensure immediate fairness, while in the long run working for a world were things like affirmative action will be unnecessary. We should work now to legally abolish things like gestation crates and debeaking and sport killing, while at the same time working to shift the world so that—in the long run—people will not *want* to participate in such activities. Due to the urgency of many situations of extreme suffering or endangerment, this dual strategy is key.

In addition to this, we need a new way of seeing ourselves—and the earth and animals—as one collective entity wherein the health of "others" directly influences the quality of our own existence. In concrete ways, it is true that the well-being of future generations directly depends on whether or not we can learn to care for the planet and its creatures—soon. I argue in this book that we can learn to see the world with new eyes and change the world of animals through focusing on affect. We don't need to live without animals; we need to learn how to value them differently.

Let me give a concrete example of the kind of approach I'm talking about, and how it operates in a different register than rights discourse. One way to think of the significant work of early primatologists like Jane Goodall and Dian Fossey is not that their contributions changed science (although their work has revolutionized our understanding of primate behavior).[5] Rather, because Goodall and Fossey were not scientifically trained before entering the field, the methods they used to study their chimps and gorillas actually altered human relationship with these animals. They named them. They saw them as subjects with distinct personalities. They cared about their well-being. The field of primatology became more like anthropology as great apes emerged as fellow beings. Animal rights in the strong sense advocates the freeing of nonhuman subjects from the constraints of enslavement. I'm advocating, instead, a shift much more along the lines of what happened between Jane and Gremlin, between Dian and Digit. It wasn't the case that the wild apes were "owned" property before Goodall and Fossey started their studies and now are "free" subjects. The revolution that happened with their studies was about something else. Before Goodall and Fossey entered the field, the chimps and gorillas were in some ways unseen, invisible. We knew they were there, of course, and we had captured countless numbers of them to bring back to zoos and labs. Indeed, at least in Rwanda a few researchers had spent time there before these women, trying to understand the mountain gorilla in its native habitat, but with little success. It took the fresh eyes of two young women to tell stories about these creatures, and their love for them, in such a way that the rest of the world could learn to value them differently. Goodall and Fossey made us see them in the frame of love. It wasn't the fact that the gorillas and chimps were free that brought them into our grid of consciousness, it was the fact that they were loved. This, for me, is what all animal advocacy ought to be about.

Most domesticated nonhuman animals could not live in this extremely developed world without human assistance, and the number of species requiring human assistance is growing in our increasingly stressed environment. While I am not in favor of assigning animals the status of "property," if the only options available to us are "property" and "not property," it is only the status of property that can marshal for animals the kind of protection they require for continued existence. What I really believe, though, is that our language and categories are wrong. Why do animals have to be either "property" or "not property"? Why must we abolish them from our world in order to protect them? Our world, the human world, is increasingly the only world; soon there will be little "wild" left. Animals have been good friends to us throughout the millennia. Can't we find a place for them now? Can't we develop another way of thinking that embraces them and allows them to flourish? "Freeing" them is not like freeing human slaves; "freeing" these animals means their certain end. In this respect, it isn't just deforestation and factory farms that destroy our animals; our language and our categories kill them as well. Language has carved up our reality in a way that leaves no space for them, no reality for them to inhabit. Language now only leaves us two options: to own them as property and therefore have the right to abuse them however we want, or to set them free and watch them die out. I say we need to change the categories and create a better option—and a better world.

Animal Welfare

If animal rights in the strong sense wants to elevate nonhuman animals to the level of human rights, animal welfare as an ideology desires to leave everything in place, and simply appeals to humans to be kinder to animals. Much older, deeper, and generally better funded, an animal welfare approach asks humans to be more virtuous toward animals without changing the moral status of nonhuman animals or the categories that carve up the world. In general, animal welfarists oppose unnecessary cruelty toward animals, but they do not believe that using animals for human purposes, such as pets, food, clothing, or entertainment, is necessarily wrong. From their perspective, improving the lot of animals may improve conditions for humans as well.[6] The problem with this perspective is that humans truly do remain at the center of analysis: human exceptionalism reigns. If the strong animal rights project hopes to dislodge humans from their centered seat of power by extending the human construction of rights to other living creatures, welfare simply pleads with us to do a little better. Animal welfare means humans still hold all the power. This is not surprising because the animal welfare movement has gained legitimacy by aligning itself with certain modes of organizing and styles of corporate leadership. As it has functioned in the United States to date, middle- and upper-middle-class white people largely promulgate animal welfare, with little attention to other social movements or struggles. For good reason, it sometimes feels like an elitist enterprise. It's about reform, not revolution. Some theorists see a link between animal welfare and utilitarianism (discussed later in this chapter). My understanding of ethical paradigms differs from these interpretations. While utilitarianism is a method that *can* lead to a welfarelike outcome, by my lights animal welfare is informed much more fully by historical and often religious appeals to "charity." That is, self-identified welfarists do not often use the utilitarian formula "the greatest good for the greatest number"; rather they talk about and are driven by concepts such as charity, kindness, compassion, empathy, aid, mercy, and sympathy.[7]

Advocates of animal welfare are involved with animals because they simply feel bad for them. Whether it was horses beaten in nineteenth-century city streets, or fully conscious dogs cut open by experimenters in twentieth-century science labs, welfarists sympathize with the animals' pain. In some ways they don't have a grand theory about rights or value motivating their actions. Their campaign is much simpler: they care, and because they care they want the suffering to stop.

While I agree with welfarists that compassion and empathy are important, the kind of change I'm interested in is much more imbricated in affect. Think back to the Jane Goodall, Dian Fossey example; by falling in love with their apes, these women brought the plight of the great ape into focus for the rest of the globe. Something bigger than sympathy was operating in their projects, something that was centered in transformative love, rather than pity. Goodall and Fossey brought fresh, undisciplined eyes to the question of apes in the wild, as well as a sense of courage and adventure that pushed their connections into a new register. With *National Geographic* there to tell their story, we all were transformed. It wasn't just a fleeting emotion that made such an impact; with their courage, endurance, compassion, and sense of adventure, they taught us to think outside a box that had previously contained us. They produced an affective intervention that changed reality. It's this kind of process that this book advocates.

Transformation does not accept the world as it is, but looks around for ways to address root causes of animal oppression. In doing so, it helps us make links with other social movements to bring those members into the world of animal advocacy as well. That feeling of being transformed will take us much further in examining the structures of culture and language that oppress animals. For example, I think about people living at or below the poverty line, who have no extra income to spend on vet care for their pets, or on higher-priced free-range food products. A welfarist approach might see solutions to poverty in the realm of charity and education: offering low-cost spaying and neutering, for example, or teaching people about the health hazards of cheap meat. Transformation based on love can lead us down a different path. It can expand our concerns to oppressive institutions like capitalism and racism, and cause us to work to eradicate those problems, all because we love animals.

Whereas the discourse of animal rights in the strong sense is about humans' absolute obligation to liberate all animals, animal welfare is, in the final moment, quite optional. It's often not really about what we owe to animals but about helping ourselves become better people in relation to them. Indeed, due to the corporate structure of many kinds of animal welfare organizations, significant social change of the kind that would address, say, poverty is probably not an option; it may even be discouraged. Animal welfare leaves too much of the current power structure in place. It doesn't challenge the oppressive structures of the world itself, the very structures that lie at the core of animal suffering.

It's important to understand that most animal advocacy organizations deploy many different (and sometimes competing) kinds of ethical principles in their campaigns. In other words, sometimes PETA practices animal rights in the weak sense (discussed earlier), often advocates for animal rights in the strong sense of abolition, and sometimes marshals tactics that reflect a welfare-based approach. The same is true for most animal advocacy organizations. Traditionally, the American Society for the Prevention of Cruelty to Animals, along with its state-based organizations such as the Massachusetts SPCA, have been thought to be more welfare oriented than rights oriented. However, due to the inherent limitations of a welfare-based approach, even ASPCA and MSPCA have moved into legislative realms. Put simply, the abstract theories behind animal advocacy don't line up perfectly with the organizations involved in social change, as these groups strategize and campaign using whatever resources they think will make change. Virtually all animal advocacy organizations draw from a mixed and uneven tool kit of theories to advance animal interests.

Advocates of animal rights in the strong sense are critical of animal welfarists and, in some ways, for good reason. Theorists like Gary Francione claim that welfarists are essentially only invested in justifying their own use of animals, in convincing the public that something is being done about those animals living in horrid conditions.[8] Rightists deride welfarists for constructing a roadblock to progress. Treating some animal a little bit better is not an acceptable solution for them. What echoes in my mind when I think about this disagreement are early-twentieth-century conflicts between socialist union organizers who wanted the unions to overthrow capitalism and private ownership of the means of production, and union organizers who sought very small changes—like the right to go to the bathroom or to call in sick—in the grueling workday of the manual laborer. These two factions had to meet in the middle and form viable labor unions. In some ways, I am promoting a similar middle ground in this book, a way that does not promote animals as property or as nonproperty, a way that challenges us to think beyond the borders of our current reality and use the tools of affect and narrative to better the world for all animals. I want a union that works outside the debate about legal standing and pushes us humans to think about the best interest of animals. Where welfare promotes animal advocacy without calling for significant human change, I want us to recognize that significant change is necessary. The affective love that connects us to particular animals, and shifts in our stories about them, can help motivate us to transform the world for animals, not just give them our charity.

Utilitarianism

Utilitarianism is a concept that doesn't fit easily on this list. Although the "father" of the animal rights movement, Peter Singer, is in fact a utilitarian, and although I believe utilitarianism does to a large degree inform many aspects of the animal rights movement, few animal activists or advocates actually self-identify as utilitarians. Indeed, the debate between rights and welfare so dominates the world of animal advocacy that few scholars or activists seem to take utilitarianism seriously, which could be a mistake.

Utilitarianism was founded by Jeremy Bentham in the late eighteenth century and modified by John Stuart Mill in the early nineteenth century. Instead of focusing on rights and obligations, it centers on the consequences of an action as the site of moral judgment. In utilitarianism, actions are not wrong in and of themselves, but should only be evaluated in terms of their results, results that are expressed in a kind of cost-benefit analysis of good and bad (sometimes referred to as pleasure and pain). This calculation is most often expressed as *the greatest good for the greatest number*, and utilitarianism as a method attempts to maximize the good by giving "equal consideration" to all parties involved, regardless of rights. That is, where rights language grants immutable protections to individuals for life, liberty, property, and so on, utilitarianism weighs the good produced by different actions to solve moral dilemmas. If someone owns a bag of groceries and is surrounded by starving people, for example, a rightist would argue that the owner of the food has the right to do anything he wants with it; a utilitarian, conversely, would try to measure the value of allowing the owner to hoard the food (does he have an endless amount, for example, or is he saving the one bag to feed his own large family?) against sharing it with others in order to discern the most moral outcome. If it can be demonstrated that the food owner will not suffer for sharing his food, and that others around him will benefit from eating, utilitarianism would demand such distribution. It's not that all parties are granted equality, then, but rather that they are given consideration equal to their interests in avoiding pain and seeking pleasure; the starving person thus has a greater claim on the food than a man who has recently eaten. "Equal consideration" is not "equality"; it is an attempt to give attention to disparate levels of need when making choices. There are many different types of utilitarianism, some adhering more strictly to the concepts of pleasure and pain or suffering (sentience), some emphasizing the value of rules within the moral calculation, others highlighting outcomes only, while still others placing more weight on issues of freedom and choice; all types of utilitarianism, however, seem to provide a very simple way of measuring the morality of any action. In general, if the action produces more pleasure than pain, it is deemed morally right; if it produces more pain and suffering than happiness or pleasure, it should be considered wrong.

Peter Singer was the first to extend this apparatus into the realm of animals, and as such, he names the movement "animal liberation" (also the title of his first book) rather than "animal rights." Singer argues that the interests of all beings capable of pain and suffering ought to be taken into consideration when calculating the greatest good for the greatest number. For him, giving lesser consideration to beings based on their having wings or fur is no more justified than discrimination based on skin color. All animals should be valued in proportion to their ability to feel pain; an animal's capacity to suffer is what should guarantee its "equal consideration." According to Singer, we should make moral decisions that maximize the pleasure and minimize the pain of all animals, not just humans. Thus, animal rights in the strong sense wants to protect individual animals from harm by extending them the rights of life and liberty;

utilitarianism wants to protect animals in a different way, that is, by weighting social goodness in a way that includes nonhuman animals on a sliding scale. Thus, if the suffering and death of, say, ten scallops (an example Singer has used to illustrate his argument) would save the life of perhaps one chimp, utilitarianism would advocate the sacrifice of the scallops. However, if the suffering and death of, say, ten cows, only brings about the rather fleeting pleasure of one hundred human hamburger eaters, utilitarianism would here deem this killing immoral. Utilitarianism believes that not all animals have equal value, but that all animals do have some value, and that value can be calibrated by their ability to feel pain and pleasure, by their sentience.

Singer is most often criticized when addressing the relationship between higher-functioning nonhuman animals and orphaned infants and intellectually disabled humans. In particular, he argues that some nonhuman animals may show an increased capacity to experience pleasure and pain when measured against some severely impaired humans and most orphaned infant humans (the orphaned infant has no parents who will suffer if she is killed). Therefore, with the ability to experience pleasure and pain as the sole criterion of calculation, Singer argues that it would be morally appropriate to sacrifice orphaned and unwanted human infants and humans with intellectual and other disabilities over some animals such as the higher-functioning primates, if such a sacrifice would serve the greatest good. Of course, Singer is not actually advocating that we kill human babies or the intellectually disabled; rather he is provoking us to be more thorough in our moral orientation toward animals. However, if the rightist comparison of animals to human slaves draws a great deal of public criticism, this kind of calculation that blurs the boundary between higher functioning animals and lower functioning humans has led to public outcry.[9] Although I believe it was intended to help us think more clearly about animals and the harms we cause them, in some ways, especially when it's misrepresented in the media, these kinds of interventions ultimately serve to discredit efforts on behalf of animal advocacy.

Even more troubling to me, however, is the way this simple formulation of *the greatest good for the greatest number* misrepresents itself as objective when it actually relies on highly subjective evaluations. While it may on the surface look as if we're performing a simple mathematical calculation, how can we judge the personal experiences of pleasure and pain between any given group of individuals? While I completely agree with Singer and others who suggest we don't need to rely on language to witness such things as pleasure and pain (i.e., that joy, delight, fear, injury, aches, and so on can be discerned from indicators such as body language and eye contact), how can we know precisely how another experiences pain or pleasure? I have a friend who has had several injuries and subsequent surgeries in the past few years, and they don't slow her down in the least; she is up and working days earlier than her doctor recommends. Other folks (me included) need lots of time to rest and recuperate after pain and injury. Some people are on pain meds their whole lives, while others who have similar disabilities never touch the stuff. My point here is that pain is subjective, and so in fact is pleasure. It's not simply that what gives one person pleasure and happiness is different from what delights another; it's also true that how we experience these things varies widely. Some types of bliss are momentary, and other types provide grounding for years or even lifetimes. It all depends on who you are. As we'll see, the concept of affect attends to such difference.

Trying to calculate pleasure and pain on an objective scale overlooks the importance of affect and character in evaluating morality.[10] To judge the value of something like pain and pleasure, we need to hear or imagine something about what it feels like to the creature who experiences it. We can't measure these things with numbers, but need to flesh them out with stories. To take a somewhat silly example, let's look at three of my dogs and evaluate how much they like their walks. I could tell you that based on visible excitement, the time it takes them to get to the door, and their unwillingness to head back home, Duncan values his walks at an 8 (on a scale of 1–10, 10 being highest), Hattie at a 7, and Jerome at a 5. On this scale, according to utilitarianism, if I had a limited amount of time and can only walk one, it would be best spent walking Duncan, right? Unpacking the story more, though, might (or might not) lead us to different conclusions. Duncan is my alpha male, the big yellow lab whose only impulse in life is to protect his pack. He loves to walk more than anybody because he thinks his job in life is to guard us from all the evils of the world. On our walks, everything we meet, from squirrels to people to mailboxes (he's not very bright), is first perceived as a threat. Given time, he can get used to something, but the joy in his walks comes from barking and lunging at anything new. Hattie, a bloodhound mix, enjoys her walks for only one reason as well: smells. Her nose is to the ground every step of the way, as she fully inhabits a world I can only imagine in my wildest dreams. She bays loudly when (to my eyes and nose, at least) there's nothing there. She is very happy. The only reason I give her walks a 7 is because her other favorite activity in life is sleeping on my bed, so she is often a little reluctant to get up, even for the walk she knows she will love. Jerome is my pit bull, and he is the most contained member of my household. As the only bully breed dog in the house for years, I believe he senses his difference and looks to me for guidance on everything. It's not quite that he is unsure of himself (as dogs that are unsure of themselves tend to be anxious and fearful, and that does not describe Jerome), it's more that he never wants to do anything wrong and so holds back and waits for a clear command. He's devoted but not in the way a golden retriever is devoted (as in, please let me please you, please). Jerome is more reserved in his devotion, more staid with his emotions. I give his walks a 5 because I think he likes them, but only if I tell him he can. He is the only dog of the three that walks off leash soundly and that greets all other dogs and humans with perfect equanimity. As such, he is the easiest of the three to walk by far. However, if my gate were to be inadvertently left open, Jerome would *never* go for a walk on his own, but Hattie and Duncan would be gone before you knew it.

My point here is that the numbers I assigned to their walks obscured who they really are. Although the numbers were as accurate as I could make them, they didn't show you why the walks mattered or how they differed for each of these dogs. The assigned numerical values sort of missed the point. The same is true for my dogs' pain. Duncan will go outside in the middle of a raging storm to accompany any member of his pack that needs to pee; he would stand in the way of any perceived threat and defend any of us to his death. But when it comes to having his teeth or ears cleaned or his nails trimmed, he is a nightmare. Hattie, although she rarely gets off the bed, will jump at the chance to get cleaned because she perceives that as a sign of affection. And Jerome, although it's clear from his body language that he hates it, will endure anything at the hands of a human; last year he cut himself badly, and my vet was able to stitch him up without anesthetic because he is so calm and steady. So even if utilitarianism is not wrong in its intent to place animals on a continuum, it's incomplete at capturing the world as they live in it. We need something more.

In this book, I offer for your consideration a method that is distantly related to utilitarianism, but instead of basing its moral calculus on abstract sentience, it focuses on personal knowledge, expanded stories, individual experience, identification, love, and affect. Utilitarianism strives toward a kind of objectivity or public agreement on animals' value; the version I am suggesting argues that animal value cannot be formulated objectively. It is based on love and stories about that love. The stories told in everyday life render connection with animals legible and can serve as a new foundation for animal advocacy. While some philosophers and political theorists will reject this kind of approach as being too subjective, I suggest that if we begin our moral deliberations with those animals that we connect with and move out from there, a large cultural shift can follow. In other words, rather than shy away from affect, my strategy depends on it.

Returning to Singer, there is something of an internal conflict within his utilitarianism concerning the question of proximity. In most ways, Singer wants to maintain an objective consistency regarding the idea that all life-forms need to be measured on the same scale of pleasure and pain and given equal consideration in relation to their places on that scale. As he puts it, "If we make a distinction between animals and humans, how can we do it, other than on the basis of a morally indefensible preference for members of our own species?"[11] At the same time, however, he regards it as somewhat natural (if problematic) that in making our moral calculations, it is hard to give as much consideration to the stranger as we give to those close to us. He asks, "Can any of us really give equal consideration to the welfare of our family and the welfare of strangers?"[12] In other words, he wants us to examine all sentience from a distance, but he also understands that we can't help seeing those who are close to us as somehow more valuable than the distant, abstract stranger.

I suggest that we capitalize on the principle of proximity and use it to leverage more compassion for those animals that are closest to us, closest to our hearts. And I mean closest in every way possible from the great apes, who share high percentages of our DNA, to the dogs and cats who share our beds. We start with what we know, or what we think we know, and move out from there. In agreement with Singer, I think we should break open the moral boundary between humans and animals, but I suggest instead that we begin this process with the kinds of animals we know—and love—best. Starting with fuller accounts of the animals with whom we share our lives, we teach each other how to value animals differently, how to appreciate them and have compassion for them. Put differently, where Singer theorizes all animals—human and nonhuman—on an objective continuum according to sentience, I propose that all animals be placed on a subjective continuum based on our connection with them. This affective connection is constituted by the stories we tell about them, by our affection for them and theirs for us, and by the various ways their characters inspire us.

Think for a moment about the ways we treat other humans. Given the choice to save a close friend or a total stranger from drowning, most of us would instinctively save the friend. Those who are closest to us, with whom we have the most connection, demand our greatest respect. This is part of what it means to be a human animal rather than a machine, I think; the particular people around us matter. We can't treat others as universal or interchangeable, even if we subscribe to a moral theory that might want us to try. We struggle with notions of human rights and many of us would like to see all humans provided with conditions that will allow them to flourish, but for the most part we learn to care in a world where what is closest to us matters most.

I simply propose to start our thinking about animals by extending this principle of proximity to their realm. We start by disseminating the stories about how those that are closest to us matter. Through these stories, through helping other people understand how the particular animals matter, we produce a wider and wider web of connection and identification. Slowly, a new kind of movement builds in which our thinking is shifted, incrementally, almost beyond the realm of our perception, but concretely, person by person. I tell you a story about my dog, you tell me a story about your cow. Tomorrow, I pass on the hamburger because I love my dog and understand what it means for you to love your cow. Again, this is not a strategy that will necessarily lead to objective policy changes to benefit animals. While lawyers and philosophers are busy trying to accomplish those shifts, this book calls the rest of us to take up the affective work of social transformation. This book recognizes that it's a long, hard, and uneven road to change the hearts and minds of people on the subject of animals. But it is possible.

Animal Studies

Over the past twenty years, many academic disciplines have engaged in rigorous interrogations of heretofore "natural" sites of difference. Formations such as gender, race, sexual preference, ethnicity once thought to be hardwired in the body are now being theorized as culturally constructed. The most recent addition to this scholarship questions the distinction between human and nonhuman and has come to be known as "animal studies." What, exactly, these scholars ask, separates human beings from other animals? While earlier ideas located that difference between human and nonhuman animals in conventions such as language, tool use, or emotion, new evidence from a number of fields challenges the certainty of these boundaries and hints at the possibility that humans and other animals may not be as different as we once believed. As pioneering theorist Donna Haraway expresses it, "leaky boundaries" exist between the two entities.[13]

Indeed, Haraway's foundational work in the field, *Primate Visions*, traces the various ways humans have used real and figurative primates to actually produce themselves as different, to shore up the category of human as natural and self-evident. Two hundred years ago, for example, the category of "human" described a very different group of people than it does today; slaves weren't considered human then (they were "savages"), nor were women, according to certain definitions. Our sense of humanness developed, and it did so, she argues, on the figure of the primate. During the apex of civil rights activism, for example, when American racial categories were very troubled, both the space program and modern medicine united us in a common quest to explore the world of outer space and to advance scientific knowledge of biology; we did so by putting chimps in rockets and cutting them open in laboratories. They are not human, the message resounded, but the rest of us are. We all—black and white—belong in the same category, and they are outside this boundary. Thus, a unified sense of humanity emerged as nonhumans were subjected to a lesser code of treatment. As theorist Cary Wolfe articulates, much of our scholarship rests on "what looks more and more like a fundamental repression that underlies most ethical and political discourse; repressing the question of nonhuman subjectivity, taking it for granted that the subject is always already human."[14] Animal studies points out that the animal is the thing we cannot think about or care about if we're going to preserve the primacy of human rights, human culture, human interest, human diversity, human welfare, human being, and so on. At their most provocative moments, these kinds of theories help us understand how and why the suffering of many animals is invisible to many humans.

Much of the work in animal studies suggests that in doing cultural criticism, greater attention should be paid to the construction of the "animal" and "human." In the same way that we believe we "are" black or white, male or female, gay or straight only because those are the only categories available to us for self-expression, human and animal are identities that similarly carve up the world into binary structures. Through many generations of cultural production, we learn to put everything we now identify as human on one side of a line, and all other beings on the other side, and we perform the identity we associate with ourselves. The identity "human" captures us, then, because language and culture have carved up the world on this axis rather than another. These works help us see how the world could be different.

Animal studies, however, exhibits several problems that have made it difficult for many animal advocates to use these works in their own scholarship and activism. First, following much work in cultural studies, there is a propensity in some of these projects toward opaque writing. In the tradition of folks like Jacques Derrida and Michel Foucault, some of this jargon and difficulty of prose is necessary; these theorists are trying to use (old) language to build a new reality, and that's a really hard thing to do. New words, new connections of words, the word as an art form, all these things come into play in this new worldmaking project.

However, there is a lot of valuable work out there that is not being taken up by animal advocates because of the language-jargon problem.

More disturbing than the jargon problem, though, is the reluctance of many animal studies scholars to extend their work to ethics, politics, or activism; many of these works shy away from making prescriptions about real animals or real animal advocacy. This phenomenon is puzzling given that so many projects arising from related fields like cultural studies were and are eager to take on political agendas. Indeed, the field of cultural studies was founded in part on the claim that no scholarship is without politics, that no identity is beyond questioning; the goal of most cultural studies projects, then, is to expose the politics up front—and mostly in support of progressive agendas. Indeed, many patently political projects like queer theory, the intersex movement, transgender politics, critical race studies, postmodern feminism, and other formulations that challenge traditional renderings of identity can be directly traced to cultural studies work in the academy. Providing people outside the academy with new ways to formulate their own desires in relation to identity seems part of the mandate of the field. The libratory politics embedded in cultural studies, to me, makes the field one of the most exciting sites within the university, as it is effectively offering people new models by which to live their lives.

The absence of this commitment when it comes to animals, then, is troubling. The avoidance of normative descriptions in this work renders it somewhat useless to the world of animal activism. The only explanation I have for this refusal is that perhaps these scholars see the step into animal advocacy as too synonymous with a step into existing iterations of animal rights; these scholars see themselves as calling for a new way of orienting liberation around an axis not based on the concept of rights. They are trying to dream their way into a new reality and don't think they can get there if they carry with them commitments to human-centered philosophical formations. In other words, the movement that would naturally align itself with animal studies has yet to be born.

While many of these theories are resistant to drawing moral conclusions from this claim, I think the moment is upon us to move this work toward an examination of our practices toward nonhuman animals. Embedded with many animal studies projects, I believe, are answers that could help us reconfigure our entire worldview with regard to animals. If we follow the animal studies logic that resists unchanging identities into the realm of advocacy, we see new alternatives. From an animal studies perspective, animal advocacy could come not in the form of extending human constructions such as rights or welfare into the realm of animals; rather it could come through new theorizations and reformulations of the shared affective worlds we all already inhabit. Put differently, if animal studies suggests that humanness is not something we "are," but something we perform, with animal advocacy in mind, couldn't it be performed differently?

Work in animal studies gives us glimpses of other ways of configuring "animal advocacy" than rights or welfare. They can help us see that constructing a political theory that will apply to all animals immediately is really an impossible task because we're working in an uneven world. Some people can see and hear and love some animals all of the time, where other people see and hear and love nothing. It's not really that different with people; although we have a public discourse called "human rights," people fall off the map of visibility all the time. Think here about the social isolation of elderly in America, mass unmarked graves of victims of genocide in Rwanda, and the devastating earthquake in Haiti, people whose names are forgotten, lost lives that are never mourned. The map of rights is complicated and all humans are not equal—yet. Indeed, Rwanda is a wonderful example of the jaggedness of love and rights and stories, for not many miles from the lost human graves exists the marked and remembered grave of Dian Fossey's companion Digit, a gorilla mourned the world over when the story of his death at the hands of poachers was told in the book and film *Gorillas in the Mist*. One does not need to be human to be remembered. And one does not need to be nonhuman to be forgotten. The concept of affect gives us ways to discuss these realities.

We must move forward in this imperfect world. Our ethical theories try to straighten things out, to iron out the kinks and wrinkles, but many animal studies scholars sit off to the side reminding us that such straightening is ultimately impossible; they call our attention away to some other, different picture as part and parcel of the problem we think we're trying to work on. In the chapters that follow, I am called into new territories over and over by such thinkers. I think I'm working on the pet overpop-ulation problem, but my eyes roam to the construction of human mas-culinity as intrinsic to the reasons pets are not altered. I think I'm working on the question of whether it's wrong to eat meat, but what appears on my mental screen is whether or not transnational corporations can ever be trusted to care for animals. I think I'm thinking about whether zoos and circuses are morally acceptable but fixate instead on the cages con-structed for humans through the limitations of language and the reality that our worlds are so morally jagged. I think I'm trying to figure out whether it's ever acceptable to perform invasive scientific experiments on nonhuman animals when my thoughts are pulled toward a different kind of violence science performs when it silences animals by making claims of objectivity. Following the work of animal studies into the realm of politics, then, is like inserting ourselves into projects and processes already in motion.

Conclusion

This book clears a path for a new kind of approach to animal advocacy, one that advocates the use of affect in the service of transformation. While I understand that it takes all kinds of approaches to make change hap-pen and do believe that a variety of tactics and theories (including rights, welfare, and utilitarianism) are needed to go about challenging power structures in today's world, I also believe that the kind of approach I call for resonates with many people actually in the movement already. Over the past ten years, I've attended many animal rights conferences and participated in countless meetings, e-mail lists, and websites of the move-ment. In virtually every setting, I've encountered newcomers who ini-tially show up because they love animals. Some have a fondness for a particular cat or dog; others are moved by the plight of abused Premarin horses or zoo elephants. Some rescue pit bull mixes on chains or feed feral cat colonies; others do agility with purebred AKC dogs. Some use horses or dolphins for human therapy; others volunteer at animal shel-ters. They come because they love animals, and they are shocked once they get there to find that the world of animal rights does not reflect this experience of animal love. They are told the only way to be an animal advocate is to buy high-priced vegan products or participate in an action to free animals from confinement. They learn we shouldn't be fighting for bigger cages and better conditions, but rather for "empty cages" and complete liberation of all animals from the human community.[15] They want to join a movement that shares their passion, but instead are disappointed to find that there is little room for loving animals there; indeed, if they share their lives with "purpose bred" or so-called wild animals, they realize they had better keep that fact quiet. I believe that if we can pay closer attention to the ways these real people love real animals, we can build a stronger movement for all animals. In those connections lie the seeds of transformation.

Put a little differently, this book is not a blueprint for a new political platform or philosophical theory around animals. It's not an argument that translates immediately into the law or widespread policy changes. Rather, I begin with the conviction that affective attachments sometimes lead and set the pace for policy change. If that is true (and I believe it is), it simply makes sense to attend to the possibility that cultural shifts in our attitudes toward animals—many of them already under way, as I detail in the chapters of this book—form a foundation for seeing the possibility of change from a different angle. By focusing on affect in our quest for a better world for animals, along with concrete stories of connection, we may be able to offer people a bigger menu of involvement. If we can effectively convey the moments when we get our relationships with animals right, and adequately portray the transformation that accompanies those relationships, we may be able to build a stronger, more viable, more wide-reaching social movement.

This book argues that animal advocacy must become more accepted and more effective, and it can only do so through the process of transformation, by getting more and more people to care about animals. The animal rights movement is now made up of theorists and grassroots activists who have all been persuaded to some degree or another that some, most, or all nonhuman animals matter. While they disagree on how they matter and how justice might be achieved, there exists some general agreement on the value of nonhuman life. I am interested in animal studies because it gives us the tools to see how affect and stories help construct our relationship to animals, and perhaps how some of those relationships could be constructed differently. I believe we've made some wrong turns in our thinking and we need to go back and retrace our steps, figure out where we went wrong, and try again with something different. Animal rights, utilitarianism, and animal welfare are simply not up to that task of changing the world for animals; they take too much of reality for granted. They are very important, yes, but they do not offer a complete picture. Something has to change in the way the questions are framed. Progress does not always mean going forward. If we're on a dead-end road, progress actually entails going backward, finding our mistakes, and correcting them. In the case of animals, I believe, progress will only come by retracing our steps and altering some of the things we take for granted. Animal studies can help us achieve this if we push its insights about affect into the realm of advocacy.

Loving Animals applies the concept of affect to the language of ethics, activism, and advocacy. Throughout the book, I will suggest that because who we love is always a question of politics, the greatest resource we have in the struggle for animal advocacy is the deep connections many of us form with other animals. We need to value animals more because their radical otherness contextualizes our lives. We see our place on earth more clearly, because we see our own limitations and fragilities through them. We are all part of one another. Beginning with processes like identification and love creates space for us to tell stories so that others can see the value of animals more profoundly. Our ability to tell a love story about an animal allows others to see that animal—and other animals—differently. We can only add species to race, class, gender, sexuality as an equivalent identity category if we can make the beings on the other side of the human-animal divide seem more real.

I have briefly summarized these four methods and theories (animal rights, animal welfare, utilitarianism, and animal studies) for a number of reasons. Having a map of where different stakeholders come from can help us if not to overcome then at least to appreciate and understand differing perspectives. In almost all other social movements and the numerous theories that informed each of them, a wider, more legible movement was formed only when people could speak across differences and see something like a common goal of liberation. Certainly this commonality is present in some sense in animal rights today, but we need to expand it. The philosophical elements of the discourse are outlined here, but something bigger needs to draw them together. Understanding animals in various affective frames allows us to see that institutions and practices like capitalism, consumption, religion, scientific objectivity, environmental commitments to categories like "wild" and "domestic," legal theory and practice, language itself, and the rationality associated in Western philosophy all carve up our world to be one way rather than another. I will argue that a discourse on affect can help us dig underneath all these conventions and offer a sustained critique of their limitations. In the end, I will suggest that the concept of affect can also help us imagine better ways of sharing the planet with animals.

In the structure of this book, I will also suggest that affect is best displayed through stories. Although ethical methodologies are critical in setting certain kinds of agendas, moral living can best be displayed through narrative. What stories capture goes far beyond principles in detailing the nature of our relationships with animals. Indeed, narrative can display not simply the value of emotion and connection but the necessity of including affect in the quest for a moral life. In the next four chapters, then, I tell stories that show how things could be different, how living well with animals is contingent upon love and connection. It is not until the final chapter that I offer a theory about the stories I've told. Using the metaphor of clothing, I explicate affect more fully and show there how stories are the best vehicle we have to accomplish social transformation concerning animals. Theory follows stories in this book because stories can display passion, emotion, sacrifice, and love in ways that theories often cannot. We need stories to hold our theories together, to widen the animal advocacy movement, and to help it become more widely accessible and accepted.

Animal advocates need to take up the work of fighting injustice on many different levels. We must work in coalition with lots of different kinds of groups and methods. The chapters that follow expand the frame of the conversation and illustrate how factors such as gender construction, capitalist profit, religious ideology, physical ability, and scientific objectivity all play a part in the ways we think about animals. Many things in the world need to change in order to create a new reality for animals. It's not a question of leaving everything in place and providing more charity, or extending some human rights to the realm of animals. It's a question of asking how we got here, asking what went wrong on that journey, then—slowly and unevenly—remaking the world to reflect a more palpable love for animals.

TWO THE LOVE OF A DOG
Of Pets and Puppy Mills, Mixed Breeds and Shelters

PERHAPS THE MOST HEARTBREAKING ARENA OF ANI-mal exploitation is the way we treat unwanted pets. Puppy mill dogs born and raised in conditions of unspeakable filth, unwanted dogs and cats at a pound killed in makeshift gas chambers and stacked like cordwood, strays on the street used as target practice, captured pets—dead and alive—loaded into dumpsters to be crushed, faithful pets abandoned for poor or no reasons. Most of the millions of pets killed each year are perfectly healthy and don't need to die. We just don't want them. So we kill them and throw them away with the garbage.

At the same time these tragedies are happening, we have never in history been closer to our pets than we are today. In the United States at the turn of the twenty-first century, you would have to be in a coma not to notice major cultural shifts in this area of our lives. Never before in the course of human history have dogs, cats, birds, fish, and even rodents and reptiles been such an integral part of human life for such a wide sector of the population. While the oversentimentalized pampered pet has long been associated with aristocratic classes, over the past half century, pets have become standard in middle- and working-class homes across America.[1] According to some estimates, more than 70 percent of Americans now share their homes with nonhuman animals, and we are spending almost forty billion dollars a year on all kinds of stuff for them.[2] In addition to toys and collars and beds and tanks, pets now have their own magazines, websites, fashion designers, public parks, and beaches. We feed them everything from vegan diets (although there is some controversy over whether vegan diets are appropriate for male cats), to the wildly popular BARF (biologically appropriate raw food, i.e., mostly raw meat and ground-up bones). Whether we take them to the dog park, to grooming appointments, to day care, or to obedience class, we have never been more focused on the comfort and entertainment of our pets.

New trends in animal studies argue that the intimate connections humans have with domesticated pet animals have altered the shape of what it means to be human. Donna Haraway, for example, argues that we humans have become different subjects because of our sustained involvement with dogs.[3] From dog parks to breeding to debates over training and diet, "companion animals" are connecting with another species in a way that forces humans to develop different styles of communication and attachment. For Haraway and others, phenomena such as obedience, agility, flyball, rally, and freestyle competitions mean that humans must learn how to think like dogs, such that the shape of our relationship to the world is actually shifting.[4] Other theorists expand on this work by arguing that as domesticated animals occupy a more significant place in our lives, the very category of what it means to be human has become more porous.[5] For example, the vast amount of news coverage about Katrina victims forced to leave beloved pets behind in the storm and its aftermath (as well as those humans who braved floodwaters to rescue those pets), led to the Pet Evacuation and Transportation Safety Act of 2006 (PETS Act); this federal legislation requires states to incorporate evacuation of service and companion animals during disasters. Pets are now allowed in "pet-friendly shelters" where they have been set up, but communities must make a safe space for them somewhere so that they are not simply left behind. Similarly, advocates pursuing specific rights for animals have developed courses and clinics to address legal issues pertaining to companion animals; law students learn that while pets may not have rights in the strong sense, guardians can legally protect their companions through such mechanisms as veterinary malpractice suits, custody agreements, and pet bequeathments.[6] Pets are emerging as a liminal category in American thinking. Many animal studies scholars argue that because pets are really neither "human" nor "property," we are being forced to develop new ideologies to account for them.

Many of us who live with dogs as central parts of our lives would largely agree that we don't "own" our dogs in any traditional sense. We aren't keeping them penned up against their will; indeed, in my experience, most dogs can get out of most fences and run away if they really want to. We aren't enslaving them, but rather are striking a bargain with them that is unquestionably reciprocal. "Ownership" is a word that never adequately describes how I relate to my dogs, and as more people get involved in dog culture, the idea that we "own" these animals seems more and more absurd. I brought this question up one evening after my dog Jubilee's Canine Good Citizen class; the eleven other women in the class with me all laughed. One woman stated it baldly: "I don't own Hector, Hector owns me." Two women in the class noted that they split with or divorced from their husbands as a result of their relationships with their dogs. Another woman said that she and her husband have decided not to have children as they didn't think their corgi, Amelia, could stand the competition. Several others chimed in their agreement: they didn't feel they owned the dogs; it's more that we are in relationships with these animals, relationships that we all hope to deepen through the process of training.

A new generation of pet owners sees itself not as "owners" at all but as "guardians" of companion animals. This shift in language echoes the sense that in today's culture, humans feel less like owners and more like protectors of the living beings in their care. Indeed, since 2000, fourteen cities, two counties, and the entire state of Rhode Island have adopted "guardian" language to publicly describe the role we humans play in the lives of our animal companions.[7] Although this shift in language does not have bearing in the legal world (where animals are still considered to be property), it does signal a deepened appreciation and respect for the lives of nonhuman animals that share our world and our homes.

In these companion species relationships, new worlds are being born where the boundaries of what it means to be human are being challenged. New "families" are being formed wherein connections with other species may be more powerful than connections with other humans. At precisely the historical moment when our oceans are being emptied of life, when our closest genetic relatives, the great apes, are all on the verge of extinction, when food animals are increasingly treated like flesh machines in factory farms across America, our greatest tool to combat these abuses is the fact that more and more people are treating their pets like family. We can use these attachments as traction to make changes in other arenas around other animals. By connecting pet love to our wider moral sensibilities, the incentive we need to address animal suffering can begin. Indeed, it already has. If we humans can learn to love some animals so intensely, why can't we learn to treat all of them at least a little bit better?

As many pet lovers know, however, the greatest resistance to pet culture comes not from strong animal rights activists but from a segment of the general public that is uncomfortable around animals more generally. Many people believe that indulging animals is wrong when so many human people are sick, hungry, and in need. Why spend money on animals, they ask, when it could be better spent on humans? Some people see our attachment to pets simply as a form of narcissism. For them, animals are not real beings with real needs and desires; rather, we're simply projecting our own emotional interiors onto them, making them into poor substitutes for "real" (i.e., human to human) relationships. Lots of people look on folks who are deeply bonded with their pets as eccentric, or even pathetic. Because, for them, animals aren't real emotional entities that can return love and affection, pet owners are seen as misguided and even a little crazy.[8]

People who don't like animals bewilder me a little, and if they are set on seeing animals as emotionless objects, I'm not really certain it's possible to convert them to the orientation this book calls for. I think of them along the same lines as people who say they don't like music or the outdoors or good food; at some fundamental level animals are, for me, part of the pleasure of being alive, and those who experience them as threats or empty ciphers live in a very different universe from mine. But the human-centered political agenda embedded in antianimal attitudes is ultimately destructive; it shores up the meaning of "human" such that other animals are in effect excluded from the community of value. Devaluing the bonds many of us have with animals by labeling these attachments as sad or oversentimental perpetuates the idea that the only subjects truly worthy of love are other humans, and that everything else in the world (animals, earth, nature) is simply ours to exploit. I suppose the anxiety behind criticisms of pet culture stems from a worry that pets may be displacing children or other humans, both fiscally and emotionally, and that as a result there will be some kind of net loss of respect and support for humans in general. But to those of us who live with animals, this worry is invalid. If we stopped living with and caring for animals, we wouldn't start living with and caring for other humans. We would just be less happy.

My Life as a Dog

When I was in my early twenties, I "came out" to my family and friends as a lesbian. It was an identity that almost fit for a long time; well into my thirties I tried very hard to make that description of myself work for me. For ten years I settled down with one partner, focused on family life, only owned two dogs, one cat (and no fenced yard). I tried very hard to be reasonable about the animals; I would put them in kennels when we traveled and lock them in bedrooms when we entertained. But when I wasn't with them I was miserable. It was as if they carried a piece of my heart, and when they weren't involved in some function or activity, a part of me wasn't present either. When I found myself single again in my late thirties, I decided to pay serious attention to these intense feelings I had toward animals.

So I bought a run-down, ramshackle house in a poorer neighborhood that had a huge fenced yard. Everyone on the block had multiple dogs, so I would fit right in. I took up all the carpets in the house, and moved my purebred golden, Eeyore, and chocolate lab mix, Cameron, in. Within two weeks, a gorgeous black lab had found his way to my doorstep; I brought him in and named him Chester. Then came the cats, Langston, Madonna, and, later, Satine. It seemed to many of my friends that three dogs and three cats were "enough" in a small nine-hundred-square-foot house, but I knew in my heart there was room for many more. When my Eeyore dropped dead of a genetic heart defect, it took two dogs to fill his place in my heart, a tiny old toothless beagle named

Daisy, who slept on my pillow and guarded that spot against dogs five times her size, and my beloved, faithful pit bull Jerome, who deepened my emotional connection with animals in ways that took me beyond my wildest dreams. Jerome is the one who, in many ways, understands everything and holds the whole house together no matter what happens. But I still missed my Eeyore. So when I saw a yellow lab mix who had the same eyes as Eeyore being walked to the kill room at our shelter, I just had to take him home. The staff tried to convince me he was not adoptable: he had developed kennel madness, spun constantly, and didn't like other dogs. But I had to have him. Initially, he fought with Jerome a few times, but we worked very hard to peel away the layers of trauma that surrounded him, and eventually he emerged as my "soft boy," Duncan; he's still very dominant, but because he now knows he's not too bright, he looks to Jerome a lot for guidance. Eventually, the two worked out an understanding. The following spring brought me the truly trying Hattie, a sixty-five-pound bloodhound mix who climbs trees and scales fences, catches and kills birds, and bays so loudly the neighbors call to complain about her. She showed up on my friend Lisa's porch one Christmas Eve and had seven puppies that night. When Lisa found homes for her puppies, Hattie wailed at the front window for days. That's when Hattie landed here; after almost two years together, we are still developing our "understanding" when it comes to whether she can sleep atop my desk or kitchen table, but my other dogs love her and I am sure we will be able to work it out over time. Last fall, when my deaf and blind Cameron finally had to be euthanized, a friend brought me an infant she had just finished bottle-feeding. She became my Jubilee, my joy. Jubilee fits into Cameron's spot perfectly. Well, almost perfectly.

So right now, at this moment, I have six dogs and three cats. Over the past five years, I have fostered almost two hundred dogs into new homes (more about fostering and rescue later), so at any given time in my house there could be two or three fosters in addition to the residents. Currently, I only have one foster, a sixteen-week-old, fifty-pound New-foundland named Tino (short for Valentino because he came to me on Valentine's Day). Several times in the last five years there have been as many as twelve dogs here (six residents and six fosters), and once (after

Hurricane Katrina) I had seventeen dogs here. People think I am crazy. But I have never ever been happier.

There is not an adequate name for the kind of life I lead, the way my desires organize themselves around animals, especially dogs. In the first half of the twentieth century, the heterosexual public either detested or felt sorry for women who were named by the then-emerging category "lesbian." They thought the only women who would ever choose lesbianism were ugly or unfeminine or somehow lacking in the ability to capture a man. Now, on the other side of gay rights and queer theory, such ideas seem silly or quaint, almost forgotten. But can people like me even hope for such liberation, when choosing animals as partners or companions doesn't even have a name? At best, we fall under the radar of identity and are named (wrongly) as gay or straight, single or married, parents or childless. Our most important relationships, though, are never recognized. At worst, we are pitied. Like those early lesbians, people feel sorry for us because we can't seem to sustain real relationships.[9] I came out as a lesbian nearly twenty-five years ago and although that was hard on friends and family who were homophobic, the task of coming out as gay was a piece of cake compared to coming out as—what?

In the interesting and often overlooked work on feminist care theory and animals, Josephine Donovan, Carol Adams, and other feminist scholars argue for what they call a dialogical ethic of care toward animals, where we try to see the world from the standpoint of animals.[10] This ethic of care moves beyond sheer sympathy for the suffering of other creatures into a world where we reorient our moral reactions to take into account the desires they feel and the realities they experience.[11] While this kind of theory always attracts me in the abstract, the problem is that I usually can't figure out how to care like that in such a generalized way. For me, the moment of transformation always comes by falling in love with a particular animal, and when that happens, a part of my own subjectivity shifts and somehow belongs to that animal. When I work with Hattie to try to teach her not to climb on my desk and knock over my computer, when I take Duncan or Jubilee to class where they learn to sit and come and become comfortable in their own skins, it's not just that they are becoming something that is semihuman but also that I am becoming something that is part dog. I am learning their language and world as much as they are learning mine. This is not something that can happen abstractly or universally, but only something that happens particularly.

There is a sense in which care theory flattens the experience of all animals into one "standpoint" or position. (Indeed, standpoint theory is based on the Marxist assertion that all workers share a different perspective on the production process from that of owners.) While this may be true for laborers (and even there I'm not sure), how can it possibly be true for all animals? Surely the cat must have a different standpoint or set of interests from that of the dog. Or the zebra a different standpoint from the lion that is about to eat her. Animals are different from each other, both in terms of species, subspecies (like breed), and even from one individual to another.

As my dogs and I work hard to learn a common language and share a life together, we are all becoming something new, something part human, part dog, a part of one another. Care theory rests on the idea that the way language has divided the world into different "species" is not subject to change. Like the ways we used to think of race or gender "identity," it believes one's species rests on physical markers that are immutable, that belonging to the categories of "dog" or "human" is grounded in a biological essence untouched by culture. Care theory is unable to explore heterogeneity and fragmentation within each of the categories of species, then, because it must legitimate the existence of a particular species-based standpoint by appealing only to similarities within each group. It takes too much of the way things are for granted. It doesn't believe that borders can be crossed.

We used to believe that people had stable identities: my neighbor Anthony is a black, straight, working-class male; I am a gay, white, middle-class female; my student John is a Latino, middle-class, gay male, and so on. But somewhere around 1990, a lot of the certainty about these categories started to deteriorate. Anthony, in fact, discovered that his grandmother was Cherokee; our decadelong friendship initiated me into the culture of our black neighborhood such that, the more involved I become in my neighborhood, the less important skin color seems to both of us. Living here has also made me appreciate my working-class roots; there are no more suits in my closet and mostly these days I live in denim. And of course, I'm no longer really gay, but neither is my student John gay either. She's now Juanita, and her boyfriend is happy to be straight.

Few of us have stable standpoints anymore. We're all changing, shifting, splitting ourselves up this way and that. (Cultural studies labels these affective processes hailing and interpolation.) Where once we saw ourselves affiliated in one way, a new interpretive community emerges to capture our passions and move us differently.[12] I am asking the reader to entertain the possibility that the same kinds of shifts and disruptions happen with categories like "human," "ape," or "dog." As a result of our relationships, interpolations occur; my dogs and I have changed each other such that I am no longer only human and they are no longer only canine. For these particular dogs and this particular person, some rather magical alchemy has happened to alter not only the way we perceive but also the way we live in the world. From certain angles, of course, I will never be a dog: I won't have a tail (but not all dogs do), and I won't grow fur or walk on all fours. The same is true about human interpolations. From certain angles, Juanita will never "really" be a woman; or perhaps it's better to say that the process of gaining social and legal acceptance into the female sex will be a long and arduous task. From many angles, I will never be black; but I can tell you my friendship with Anthony and my integration into the politics of our community has made me much blacker than I ever could have dreamed of being. But from many other angles, Juanita is already living her life as a woman, and my primary community is this block in Durham where black culture seems completely like my world. Anthony is still black, even though his grandmother was Native American. I'm still pretty much gay, but Juanita isn't. Things are mixed up, but even though the boundaries of many of these categories are thick and sometimes impenetrable, given enough time and passion, a persistent desire to belong somewhere else often leads to some kind of acceptance.

Certain kinds of love can undo even the strongest and most trenchant categories. No one would argue that as a result of their physical differences, my dogs experience the world differently than I do (e.g., they hear better and smell better, but can't read or write). But using only those experiences to invoke a unitary and stable world with unbridgeable boundaries for them (what we call species) completely discounts the other experiences they have had as a result of living with me, of our being a family together. They know what my words mean, even if they can't write or speak. I've learned to be much more attuned to smell and sound and other shifts of energy that are hard to put into words. These experiences matter because they change us all. While the feminist ethic of care has as its deepest desire a better world for animals, stabilizing all "dogs" into one solid category—a category that is profoundly and fundamentally different from the category human—denies the possibility that we sometimes overlap and become one. Why appeal to the very system that places humans on top of animals to secure a better world for animals? Why not use the particular love we have for certain animals to challenge the categorization method itself? The particular is critical to this process because it's impossible to identify with or be hailed abstractly. The kind of connection I am talking about happens when a dog looks at you with a certain expression, or does something that just warms your heart. It's that moment when you are captured and brought into her world, where you feel what the universe looks like from her eyes. Stuart Hall, a founding figure in the field of cultural studies, talks about this kind of love and interpolation as a form of "identification," and although he is speaking about humans only, he is worth quoting at length as he describes the difference between identity and identification so well. (I offer animal-centered substitutions in brackets):

> Identifications, not identities [not species]. I speak of the process of identification, of feeling yourself through the contingent, antagonistic, and conflicting sentiments of which human beings [all animals] are made up. Identification means that you are called in a certain way, interpolated in a certain way. And you can't ahead of time either know that or know how to recognize that, or know how to imagine the collectivity that all these folks [animals] might make. For how else would you know them? They weren't there before, or they weren't gathered together in the proper place. You can only come as you were, come together because somehow you can represent yourself and begin to share an imagined community of some kind with others.[13]

You can't know beforehand whether you will identify with a dog. (That's why it's so hard to go out and buy a dog that you then need to fall in love with. The love and identification need to come first. That's also why so many dogs are homeless.) It's about the connection, which is not predictable beforehand. It's about listening to the dog and having the dog listen to you. It's about liking the dog and having her like you. It's about finding this particular dog special, and being able to imagine living with her, building a community with her, loving her. Not just any dog. *This* dog.

For me, that particularity right now almost always revolves around hound dogs with big hearts, lab mixes with big heads, and pit mixes who, as Vicki Hearne once described them, "do grab and hold on; but what pit bulls most often grab and refuse to let go of is your heart, not your arm."[14] Over the past ten years, I have volunteered at several of our local high-kill shelters; it was there in those runs, cleaning up vomit and shit, that the first ideas about this book came into my head. To save them from death, I took many home to foster, and filled my house to the point where I actually once moved my couch into the shed to make room for more crates. I finagled deals with my students to foster them or at least walk them. Week after week I fell in love with certain animals, most of whom were scheduled to be killed very shortly. I had to make many hard choices about whom I thought I could connect with and how they would fit into my home. A few times, I tried bringing herders home, one German shepherd, two Aussies, several border collie mixes; even though they were a little "nervous" at the shelter, I hoped maybe I could connect with them when they got here. But they were all too frenetic, too intent on rounding us all up, too focused on work. Give me a pit mix or a hound dog any day; these guys, like me, don't really want jobs.

Animal Love

Love is a hard thing to negotiate. We live in a media-saturated world that constantly sends us the message that coupledom and marriage are the norm; we blame ourselves when relationships don't work out rather than examining the ideological forces that map us into these structures in the first place. Recent works in queer theory have challenged us to think beyond the structure of sexual identity and coupledom, to help us think about the ways language structures our lives, about the ways heteronormativity colonizes our brain.[15] I can tell you one thing for certain: it is both easier and more fulfilling for me to live with a house full of dogs—probably even, God forbid, a houseful of herders—than it would be for me to live with one other human person. Does that make me queer?

Certainly humanity has been shaped and altered by our relationship with nonhuman animals. Coevolution with horses, oxen, and other farm animals allowed us to develop agriculture, a necessary precursor to civilization. Cats kept rodent populations in check, and dogs helped us hunt for food, herd our livestock, and guard our property.[16] Over time, as we became more industrialized, the dog provided us with entertainment and faithful companionship. We taught it how to sit and stay; it gladly, adoringly, obliged. Isn't *this* queer? Those of us who have primary partnerships and intense bonds with nonhumans know about queerness. We're the people who refused to evacuate a sinking city because the Red Cross shelters wouldn't take our pets. We're the ones who take second mortgages on our house to pay the veterinary bill, or who move our furniture into the garage to make more room for dogs.

Most discussions about the human-animal divide center on the great apes, whether or not they understand language, use tools, or have similar DNA.[17] But these animals are very distant from our daily lives in the United States. What I'm really interested in is how the human-animal divide looks when viewed in relation to pets, that is, how our lives shift and change as a result of the real particular animals in them. For me and my dogs, it's not so much a question of whether we're the same or different, but more about how we emerge together as changed subjects. I think here of the mermaid, a creature who is half human and half fish, and wonder if this isn't a better (albeit mixed) metaphor for what it's like to live with so many dogs. Sometimes I dream I have whiskers and a tail. But the most moving and frightening moments are when I meet the eyes of one of my dogs and forget they aren't human. Or more accurately, when they seem like real people, more real than most of the people with human bodies I meet in the course of an average day. It's as if our love straightens out all our differences. I work all morning while they sleep, waiting for THE WALK, the high point of our collective day. We get to check the neighborhood, what has changed, how the seasons have moved the humans to decorate with Christmas lights or spring flowers, who has passed here before us. I am envious of my dogs' sense of smell on these walks. Anyone can see they are much more "in the world" than I am; with their noses to the ground, joy radiates from their faces. Mostly we stop to smell things I can't even see. What are they smelling? Professional dog trainer and writer Suzanne Clothier suggests we get down on our knees and smell what they smell alongside them, which I do sometimes, but the abilities of my nose limit me.[18] It's as if they are smelling ghosts. But it's not just the walks and smells; everything about me has become doglike. I have become habituated into the pleasures of routine. I am loyal to a fault.

Again, my detractors might call my life sad. I am investing in these creatures, they think, because I cannot "find" a human person to love. But from my shoes, it looks completely different. These majestic, wonderful beings are not empty ciphers; they have needs and desires that they communicate to me in myriad ways, and in listening and responding to them, I am not only changed but fulfilled. They help me carry my burdens and increase my joys. I know I am content when they rest soundly at my feet. It's not so much that I am no longer a lesbian, then, it's that the binary of gay and straight no longer has anything to do with me. My preference these days is canine.

Queer theory teaches us to recognize various forms of intimacy that are often invisible or erased in our culture. It challenges us to resist the dominant institutions of heteronormativity and to celebrate differences of all sorts. Most important, it schools us to recognize that sexuality and intimacy have deep and varied connections. Through the discourse of queer theory, I have come to recognize that I get more affection from my dogs than I ever did from any girlfriend. We all sleep together, sometimes under the blankets when it's cold. When I was gay, was I gay because of a narrowly defined genital act that I performed (increasingly rarely over time) with a person who happened to be another woman? Those words don't make any sense. I was gay then, I believe, because I chose to share my emotional, financial, and daily life with a person of the same gender. Now I choose to share that same life with six dogs. These canines teach me more about life and love than one human ever has or could. And so I ask again, isn't this queer?

If queer theory helps me recognize the intense value of these kinds of intimacies, it also helps me see that this, like any, border-crossing love also mandates ethical responsibilities. Across America today, puppy and kitten mills crank out litter after litter; pet shops sell their cute but genetically flawed wares to spontaneous buyers who rarely can handle a sick and aggressive dog; the public still resists altering their pets; and everyone turns a blind eye to the literal millions of really good animals unnecessarily killed every year. It is my love for these six dogs at my feet that motivates my involvement in the crisis of homeless pets.

What follows in the remainder of this chapter, then, is an analysis of various social forces that conspired to produce one dog as a pet and another as an unwanted shelter animal, as well as concrete recommendations for how we might close that gap. I will confess up front that the rest of this chapter focuses solely on dogs. While I love my cats, they do not have my heart the same way the dogs do; it's dogs that I live for, and dogs that I know best.[19] I call on my readers to produce new stories about the social forces that create other kinds of companion animals and surplus homeless pets, not just cats, but horses, rodents, birds, fish, micropigs, and so on. I suspect the central mechanisms for the production of all these creatures will be similar to that of dogs. Generally speaking, I argue that there are no inherent differences between companion dogs and homeless dogs. Or put more precisely, there may be differences, but they are caused by the experiences of being homeless and hungry, caught or trapped by animal control, confined to a concrete cell block for weeks and months, forced to sleep and stand in your own waste, never able to run. The sorting of dogs into categories of pet and shelter animal is just about the cruelest and most random form of cataloging imaginable. I believe we need to use the love we feel for our own dogs to transform the world for others. We can do this, I think, by softening our hearts to the plight of shelter dogs.

Who Are These Animals and Where Do They Come From?

So, who are these millions upon millions of dogs and cats that end up in high-kill shelters across the country every year, and how did they get there? What kinds of activism would help save them from such miserable fates? To answer these questions adequately, we have to follow a number of different paths in several different directions. Many kinds of social forces and ideologies come together to produce homeless pets, and answers to questions such as who they are, how they got there, and how they can get out are complicated. That shouldn't be surprising: if fixing this problem were easy, the thousands of people across the country working full time or more to help rehome and rehabilitate homeless dogs and cats would have succeeded long ago.[20]

Statistics vary about how many animals are actually euthanized every year. The ASPCA estimates that 60 percent of the eight to ten million shelter animals are killed annually; the Humane Society of the United States counters that only 50 percent of ten million are killed every year.[21] These discrepancies are due to the fact that there is absolutely no local or federal governmental oversight of the animal sheltering system in America. Indeed, as long as zoning laws allow, anyone can open an animal shelter anywhere; in many places there is no licensing or oversight except very general animal cruelty laws that apply to the public. The quality of shelters varies widely from public or private multimillion-dollar facilities, to individual citizens working out of their homes without adequate funding or even access to vet care. No matter how wealthy or poor the shelter is, how quickly the animals are moved out and through what route (i.e., adoption vs. euthanasia) vary greatly as well. Some shelters adopt to almost anyone who wants an animal; others screen applicants so thoroughly that some or most humans are rejected as inadequate pet owners. Some shelters set such high standards for adoption, they actually move very few animals out (and if they don't euthanize them, they are inevitably deemed "hoarders" and are dealt with by animal control). Some shelters are "no kill" and do not accept new animals until existing ones get adopted; most no-kill shelters that take in more animals than they can place quickly find it difficult to care for the ever increasing intake of animals. Although a few well-supported sanctuaries seem able to provide good care for thousands of pets,[22] many no-kill sanctuaries simply warehouse unwanted pets in miserable conditions for long periods of time, sometimes the animal's entire life. Often, these no-kill sanctuaries are eventually shut down by animal control for reasons such as neglect or zoning violations, and many or most of the pets are then euthanized. The alternative to the no-kill shelter is the open-admission shelter. There are reportedly some open-admission shelters in rural counties that have no adoption program in place at all; the kill rate at these shelters is virtually 100 percent. The chemical used for lethal injection is a veterinary-prescribed medicine, but other than that, there is no oversight of who can kill homeless animals, or which animals should be killed. Shelters kill for reasons related to age, illness, injury, size, color, temperament, breed, or simply because they are out of room. Shelters that use carbon monoxide for killing don't even need to be associated with a veterinarian. Some shelters will adopt to anybody who walks in the door and still need to kill a lot of animals; some shelters would rather kill them than see them go to less-than-perfect homes. Some shelters kill all the animals in their care on a given day each week, and are filled up again by the end of the week. Other shelters kill according to their own ideas about which animals are most adoptable; who makes those decisions and how can be fairly arbitrary. Sometimes the dead bodies of homeless pets are cremated; sometimes they just go to a landfill with the trash.

I was shocked at the randomness of the whole sheltering system when I first started working with and researching homeless pets. I have spent much of my life thinking about how life is unfair to humans, how race, class, gender, sexual preference, and ethnicity affect a person's chances of success and happy life, and how random these biases and discriminations are. But the randomness of the system that deals with homeless pets is of a different magnitude. A great dog that enters the system at a bad point has virtually no chance for survival. If she is big or black or mixed breed, even those shelters that try hard probably won't be able to find anything for her and she will die. On the other hand, if a dog lands in a shelter where the whole community has embraced a low-kill or no-kill strategy, even if he's timid or troubled, he'll probably find a home. Dogs that are small or purebred often find good homes, even when they are known to bite other dogs or humans. In the world of homeless pets, there isn't even a veneer of meritocracy. It's like falling through Alice's rabbit hole, where the rules of civilization fall away and you are left with just a bunch of really diverse people making lots of random life-and-death decisions every day. The reasons dogs and cats become homeless differ in urban and rural contexts, but the fact that they become homeless and need shelter seems to be universal.

One way to understand the injustice toward homeless animals is to realize that many animal shelters get started as a by-product of animal control. Whether in urban or rural contexts, homeless dogs—especially when they start to form packs—can pose a threat to humans. Unlike feral cats (and even here there is a debate about whether they can safely coexist with humans), stray dogs (whether feral or not) will organize themselves to hunt in packs and can become aggressive when threatened, sick, or hungry. City and county governments employ animal control officers to remove them from areas occupied by humans, not primarily to help the dogs, but to keep the humans safe from the dog packs. Shelters emerge, then, as a place to put these dogs until the officers (or other volunteers or paid workers) can figure out what to do with them. Many states require animal control to "hold" the animal for a few days to a week before killing him in case an owner comes along to claim him as a lost pet. Sometimes the dog or cat must be held to see if she develops rabies or other contagious diseases. Shelters emerge also, then, as kennels to hold strays and quarantines. Some of these collected dogs may be dangerous and untamable; many of them, however, will come around once they are fed and treated well for a few days. The first task, then, is to figure out which ones can be placed in homes and live happily and peacefully with humans, and which ones pose such a threat that they need to be destroyed.

The majority of shelter animals are strays picked up or trapped by publicly funded animal control officers who work to keep our communities safe from dangerous dog packs (and, debatably, cat colonies). The only other way an animal gets to a shelter is if the owner surrenders him (I will talk more about this later). Either way, at this point, these animals are truly less than valueless; indeed, they are a drain on shelter resources. They don't acquire any value until an adopter or advocate finds them, decides they have potential, and does something about it. So, how did so many animals get produced if nobody wanted them?

Of Shelters and Breeders: Insidious Connections

At the most abstract level, the problem of homeless dogs and cats occurs because pets are treated as commodified objects rather than living beings. They are often produced, sold, and bought in ways that are fundamentally irresponsible. People think a pet might be nice so, with little or no fore-thought, they buy one; and when that dog or cat becomes a problem, they dump it on the street or at the shelter. The story seems simple, and at some level it really is: dogs and cats are feeling creatures and shouldn't be treated as objects. But there are many, many stories underneath this simple one; to lay the blame solely on the irresponsible or ill-informed consumer lets a lot of other people off the hook. There is a long line of people involved in producing homeless pets in America, and that irresponsibility manifests itself in different ways at each point along the way.

So let's start at the beginning by asking who, exactly, produces all these puppies that end up at shelters? Conventional wisdom in the sheltering world suggests that 75 percent of dogs in shelters are mixed breeds or mutts, and 25 percent are purebred. Right off the bat, this vague statistic is problematic because the actual definition of purebred means the dog has documentation from some kennel club (usually the American Kennel Club) tracing his origins and verifying that his genes are indeed "pure." That is, the evidence of his breed rests only in a dog's papers, not his genes. The vast majority of dogs brought into shelters are strays, and few strays wander the streets with their AKC papers on them. Thus, in the shelter setting, "purebred" comes to mean that an adopter or advocate simply identifies a dog as such. The range of play in these identifications is astonishing. As mentioned earlier, if the idea is that language actually creates the shape of the reality we inhabit, nowhere is the role of words and labels more significant than in identification of purebred dogs at a shelter. Let me explain.

The goal for shelter workers is to persuasively identify the dog as a purebred in order to increase his marketability. When I first started working at a local shelter, a young couple came up to me and asked how the purebred basenji in kennel 34 ended up at the shelter. I racked my brains for an explanation: Perhaps his owners had died? Or moved abroad and couldn't keep him? Or maybe he jumped the fence and ran several counties and the owner just couldn't find him? I have friends who have basenjis and I know how expensive and desirable they are. It wasn't until I walked over to kennel 34 and saw that the dog was clearly a mix that sort of resembled a basenji that I caught on to the game. The young couple was thrilled to find such a treasure at the county pound, the dog seemed like he had a great personality, and I bet they all lived happily ever after. In these cases, fudging a little on the identification seems to make everyone happy. The more exotic the breed, the easier it is to suggest that mixes are in fact purebreds. Catahoulas, American dingos, Carolina dogs, smooth-coated fox terriers, water spaniels, flat-coated retrievers, borzois, harriers, Plott hounds, and more have all passed through my house as fosters because some creative person at a shelter had a book with a few photos and put the two together. When I see these breeds in dog shows on TV, I realize the dogs I fostered looked very different in real life. But I have never had a foster returned because it didn't conform to breed standards. Mostly these are good dogs who deserve good lives; assigning them to an exotic breed gives these homeless creatures an ending befitting of Cinderella.

The reverse also happens, however, around the identification of purebreds. The two or three dozen or so most popular dog breeds in America often have local, state, or national rescues associated with their breeds; as a result in part of digital photography and Internet communication, folks involved in such things as Boxer Rescue or Lab Rescue or Beagle Rescue or Yorkie Rescue comb the shelters in their area looking for dogs of that breed to "pull," rehabilitate, and rehome. I have worked with golden, lab, beagle, and boxer breed-specific rescues, and the mission of each of these organizations is to save all the dogs of that particular breed, but not necessarily mixes. Many of these breed-specific rescues are actually founded or maintained by breeders; others are simply motivated by the love of the breed. (Some purebred rescues only take owner surrenders that have AKC papers, and don't take shelter dogs at all.) The goal of these rescuers viewing homeless dogs in shelters, then, is to define the breed as narrowly as possible to save valuable rescue resources for what they see as the most deserving purebred dogs. In some ways, these misidentifications are just as arbitrary and bizarre as those described earlier. My local golden retriever group, for example, will only intake goldens that have feathering and "ears that can cover their eyes." Lab rescue prefers dogs with "square heads." Beagle rescue won't take a dog over fifteen inches at the shoulder. Boxer rescue won't take anyone whose nose points.

In the shelter, the line between mixes and purebreds is extremely

artificial and subjective. What counts as a purebred at the point of rescue or adoption is almost completely arbitrary. The statistic that 75 percent of shelter animals are mixes and 25 percent are pure is an imaginary
number designed only to communicate to the public that the kind of
dog you may be wanting (or some facsimile of it) may be found at your
local shelter. But the broad categories of "mix" and "purebred" do shed
light on another way to think about what kinds of dogs are at a shelter,
and that is the question of whether a dog's birth was accidental or intentional. This distinction doesn't follow perfectly along mix-pure lines
(many people still intentionally breed mixes although most of them have
little value in today's dog market, and many pure breeders, of course,
have accidental litters, often containing genetic flaws that prevent the
dogs from being sold). However, "accidental mixed breed dogs" versus
"intentional but unwanted purebred dogs" may be a useful distinction
for thinking about which humans produce the dogs and puppies that end
up as homeless pets and why. I'll begin with a discussion of the accidental births and then move to the question of intentional ones.

By now, I hope every reader in every community has heard the mantra
"spay/neuter" at least a million times. Many folks on the West Coast
and in the Northeast can have the surgeries done for as little as five dollars, and some communities even periodically offer them for free. There
is a lot of community pressure to alter the reproductive capacities of all
pets. So why are there are still so many unwanted accidental litters?

First and foremost, although there are cheaper ways to get your pet
spayed or neutered, it's still not exactly cheap, nor is it easy. Of the two
hundred or so dogs I've fostered to adoption, about half have been unaffiliated with a formal rescue. (Breed-specific or not-for profit rescue
organizations usually have arrangements with local vets for lower-cost
spay/neuter; their adoption fees cover part of the cost of vetting and they
fund-raise or receive grants for the remainder.) My vet charges about
three hundred dollars for a spay or neuter, which is usually cost prohibitive for my freelance fosters, so I use one of the two low-cost spay/neuter
vans that service my area for these dogs. Low-cost spay/neuter vans are
usually nonprofit enterprises and often function as a training experience
for veterinary students. They are designed to help folks who can't pay the
cost of a regular vet visit, and they are popping up as vital community

resources across the country. The cost for a full vetting at one of these vans (including surgery and rabies and DHLPP vaccines) is between ninety and a hundred dollars per animal. Ninety dollars is certainly better than three hundred dollars, but that's still not cheap. And it's not easy. To take advantage of these services, you must have reservations three to four weeks in advance (the vans service my area only once or twice a month). Once you are able to secure a reservation, you must meet the van in an assigned parking lot at 7:00 a.m., with cash only and your animals, for drop-off. This means, for example, on a winter morning with a litter of, say, five puppies or kittens, you are waiting in an abandoned parking lot, in the dark, with around five hundred dollars cash. When the van arrives, you are given a pickup window of time, which could be anywhere from noon to 5:00 p.m. (All surgery is done on the van itself, and vets and techs want to drive away soon after the last surgery is complete.) You must arrange your schedule (or find a friend) to be there for pickup exactly when they tell you or you are charged an extra fee for lateness. When you do pick up your pets, they are very often still unconscious and unable to walk. The few times I've used the vans for large dogs, I've often had to transport them home in the trunk because there was no physical way to get them into the backseat of the car (I have since bought a van, in part, to address this problem). When you bring home an animal that is partly or fully still under generally anesthesia, you just hope and pray and watch her until she comes around. But it's a little scary.

Drawbacks notwithstanding, these vans are a step in the right direction. Without them, people would not be able to vet large numbers of animals. But for the new pet owner who is feeling her way through the web of responsibility associated with pet ownership, these vans may not be convenient or cheap or safe enough. We need better solutions.

Underneath this obstacle to spay/neuter lies the even bigger impediment of ideology. For her final project in a class, one of my students recently conducted a short survey of people relinquishing litters of puppies or kittens at an open admission shelter in Raleigh. The sample was small (only thirty-seven participants), and more scholarship needs to be done in this area, but her findings were salient. All thirty-seven respondents knew that spay/neuter was available for their pets but chose not to sterilize for the following reasons: 8 percent didn't have the money; 19

percent didn't realize the animal would get pregnant so quickly; 38 percent felt they wanted to experience "the miracle of birth"; and 35 percent believed that having a litter would calm their female dogs down. During the same semester, a different student in the same class conducted a similar survey in a rural shelter, but this time targeted the research toward unneutered male dogs. She found that of the twenty-two people relinquishing intact adult males (all dogs), 5 percent stated that they did not have the money for a neuter, 8 percent stated that they thought they would be able to keep the dog from roaming and therefore didn't need a neuter, and 87 percent stated that neutering would have made him less fierce or "less of a watchdog." (Ironically, many of these people were relinquishing the dog because he was "too much to handle.")

This is a really small study, and self-reporting is often a problem as folks are likely to tell the interviewer what they think the interviewer wants to hear. Nevertheless, these data are interesting because they make it clear that barriers besides cost and convenience exist when it comes to widespread sterilization. The correlation between inappropriate and incorrect perceptions about gender and reproduction in pets and the number of unwanted animals in shelters seems certain; convictions such as "procreation calms a dog down" or "testosterone makes a better guard dog" may account for up to 75 percent of the animals killed in shelters. So why isn't the message about spay/neuter overriding these incorrect assumptions about gender-based behavior?

Many Americans still have distorted notions about gender in general. For a lot of people, notions about masculinity and femininity rest in anatomical function; to be a "real" man means "having balls"—both literally and figuratively, and a "real" woman is only one who has "her own" children. I'm not saying these ideas are widespread any longer; a lot has changed, and feminism has challenged these configurations deeply. But biological determinism and old-fashioned ideas about gender still exist and are, sadly, projected onto pets. This is heartbreaking because, when it comes to domesticated animals, these outdated ideas about gender are simply wrong. Leaving male dogs intact usually makes their lives in urban and suburban settings miserable, and exponentially increases the likelihood they will be dumped at a shelter. And forcing a female to have a litter and taking those infants away from her to be killed doesn't make her calmer or more feminine, it only makes her sad. Slippage occurs between the male dog's testicles and his owner's ego, between the female dog's uterus and her owner's sense of self. Even though study after study demonstrates that altered animals are healthier and temperamentally much sounder, the human public's ideas about human gender prompt them to refuse the surgery for their pets. For this reason alone, animal activists and feminists could find common cause to help educate the general public on the need for more expansive ideologies about gender, sexuality, and reproduction. Instead, I see almost no crossover between the two movements.

But let's go back to the shelters and see who else awaits a dark fate there besides the unintentionally bred dogs. The topic of intentional dog breeding is a difficult one, perhaps the most complex ethical dilemma in the topic of homeless pets. Quite frankly, neither side of the current debate seems right to me, so in what follows, I will first describe the conflict and then nod to a few ways that might help us forge a new middle ground. I recognize that it may look like I am trying to wiggle out of taking a stand here, but—as is so often the case with entrenched moral conflicts—when neither side gets it right, sometimes the only solution is to establish a new way of thinking.

As it stands right now, most animal rights activists—and even many who would call themselves animal welfarists—argue that there is no need for any breeding whatsoever. With so many dogs being killed for lack of a home, they suggest, "Don't breed or buy while millions die." Having worked in shelters and in rescue, and witnessing for myself the needless deaths of so many good dogs, I have to say that part of me is sympathetic to this position. It's very hard to watch hundreds of really good dogs die because people think they prefer a dog that looks a little different. I have a good friend, for example, who is politically far left on every single social issue imaginable, yet she continues to buy Yorkie terriers, one after the other, from the same (irresponsible) breeder (I say irresponsible because every dog Tracy buys has had serious and expensive medical and behavioral problems). But Tracy says she is attached to the breed (although she's never had any other), and has a relationship with this breeder, and so she shells out thousands of dollars for dogs that have all kinds of issues. Both animal rightists and welfarists find this dynamic

unacceptable; indeed, many on this side argue that the intentional creation of any "purpose bred" dog—whether for conformation (show dogs)
or work (such as guarding, hunting, or herding)—is immoral. They argue
that the sport of dog shows should be shut down entirely, and that existing homeless dogs can be trained to do all kinds of jobs. Shelters and
rescue organizations most closely aligned with animal rights hold this
position so strongly, some will not even adopt their dogs to homes that
already have any unaltered animals.[23]

The other side of the debate, taken up by both breeders and fanciers,
argues that dogs are simply property and owners should be allowed to
do whatever they want with their own property. Moreover, they suggest
that for hundreds of years dogs have been bred to do specific jobs to help
humans; the world of dog shows that arose from these specific breedings
is now an international sport that boasts hundreds of thousands of participants. These fanciers enjoy the game of producing the best dogs in
their breed and group, and Americans enjoy buying dogs that look like
the ones they see on TV. The vast majority of dogs destroyed in shelters,
they argue, are mixed breeds; the only purebreds that are killed are sick,
old, or have behavioral problems. There isn't really a pet overpopulation
problem, they insist, as the dogs in shelters are not "the right kind." The
small part of me that is sympathetic toward this position, as I will elab-
orate further, rests with the idea that the world is a better place for having
many different kinds of dogs in it. If we stopped all intentional breeding, we would lose all specificity within several generations; there would
be no more labs or boxers or Aussies or beagles. Although this seems
wrong to me, I do believe that changes need to be made in the way our
country breeds and disposes of animals.

Breeding genetically sound show dogs is a complex and weighty
task, and when done poorly, it leads to many health and temperament
problems that are generally absent in the mixed-breed dog. Journalist
and dog advocate Mark Derr has done a wonderful job documenting the
crisis produced by the stringent conformation criteria used by the American Kennel Club; when dogs are bred only for a certain "championship"
look, the gene pool of that "look" becomes smaller and smaller and generally less healthy.[24] As more and more people participate in "the fancy"
(dog breeding), the genetic health of many breeds has virtually been

destroyed. From Dalmatians to cocker spaniels, from boxers to goldens, a much too narrow pool of genes increasingly constitutes the most popular breeds, resulting in dogs with much shorter lives, expensive health problems such as hip dysplasia (which is at epidemic proportions among many breeds today), and, most problematically, aggression. These are the true purebreds that end up at the shelters, the dogs who are inbred and have little to no bite inhibition and lack the kind of sociability that makes them good pets. I can't count the number of purebreds I've met that can't get along with other dogs, that have no tolerance for anything that displeases them, that can't make eye contact with humans, that let you know (or worse—don't let you know) they will bite at the least provocation. These traits occur much more rarely in mixes (unless they have been severely abused). Bad breeding practices, I believe, account for the majority of purebred dogs in shelters.

Most of these dogs come from puppy mills, breeding facilities where sometimes hundreds of dogs are kept in small cages; these dogs literally live in their own waste their entire lives and are forced to produce litter after litter of puppies to be sold in stores or over the Internet. Puppy mills pay little attention to the health or temperament of their dogs.[25] As long as they have the proper papers demonstrating their breed lineage, the AKC will register them as purebred dogs. The unwitting consumer thinks these papers mean something about their health or temperament. They don't. No one should ever buy a puppy from a pet store or online without seeing the parents in person and visiting the kennel. You won't get a champion dog from a pet store or online. But chances are very high you will get an aggressive or disturbed dog with many health problems. Producing dogs in such settings is unacceptable both because the dogs themselves suffer tremendously and because their would-be human owners are not really getting good companions.

But there is another side to this story of breeding and that side rests with those "responsible breeders" who have fallen in love with a specific breed of dog and spend their time training, rescuing, and occasionally breeding their dogs to improve the line. As I said, most animal rights activists feel it is wrong to breed show dogs because they believe that purpose-bred dogs are almost always both genetically compromised and treated poorly. To verify this assumption, I spent about a year participating in events at my local kennel club, watching these purebred dogs compete in conformation, obedience, and agility trials, and getting to know their owners and handlers. I understand that Durham Kennel Club is not Westminster, but over the course of the year I visited the homes and kennels of six different fanciers and found, with one exception, well-maintained conditions that were not only acceptable but superior. For the most part, these folks produce a litter once every two or three years (and have a home for every puppy before it is even conceived); they never, ever inbreed (mate brother to sister) and rarely line-breed (mate granddaughter with grandfather, or aunts with nephews); they worry about the function and temperament of a dog and not just the way he looks. These dogs sleep on the bed with their owners, get top-quality vet care and food, have coats that shine and eyes that twinkle. You would only have to watch Michelle with her rotties or Eva with her goldens or Karen with her dachshunds or Barbara with her whippets to know beyond a shadow of a doubt that these relationships are not about profits or even about blue ribbons; they are about love. When you see dog breeding done morally, you begin to realize how wonderful it is that we do have different kinds of dog breeds to share our lives with. Although I adore my mixes and wouldn't trade them for anything, I also think the breeding programs of these women are not at all objectionable.

The problem, of course, is that there are no clearly delineated lines between puppy mills and responsible breeders. Dog breeding is a spectrum: on one side lies the despicable puppy miller who indiscriminately breeds thousands of inbred purebreds every year and ships them anywhere in the nation to pet stores or to people who buy them on the Internet. On the other side rests the responsible breeder who follows her championship dog's history back seven or eight generations, always breeds dogs who are completely unrelated, tests her dogs for known genetic flaws in the breed, delivers her dogs in person to prescreened families with mandatory spay/neuter clauses in the contract (if the dog is to be a pet). If we knew which was which, it might be easy to outlaw the former while supporting the latter. But there's a huge gray area in the middle consisting of folks who maybe are not heartless but who also aren't the most stringent in their mate selection, rearing, and adoption practices.

This gray area, what many call "backyard breeders" or "hobby breeders," is filled with all kinds of people, in my experience. Some of them are responsible and just enjoy breeding dogs; others are folks who are trying to make a little money on the side and are breeding quickly and less responsibly. I used to think the difference between responsible breeders and irresponsible (backyard or hobby) breeders could be measured by whether the studs and bitches had championships, but my research taught me differently. Through my research, I visited several noncompetition kennels that I thought would verge on puppy mills; when I got there, though, the dogs would be inside the house and clean, and there would be fewer of them than I expected. On the other hand, over the year I visited one championship kennel that housed a large number of dogs in very small crates in a hot garage. This family was really into the fancy at one point in their lives, but now have kind of lost interest in that end but are still breeding to make a little extra money. This breeder was a nice woman who had won several national titles with her dogs, and the demand for her puppies pushed her to the point of mass production. Her heart started in the right place, but things just got out of hand.

The one thing I am certain about in this moral quagmire of breeding is that we need to establish some form of oversight for the breeding of dogs. The American Kennel Club seems to be the natural place to turn for such a service. Founded in 1884, AKC was established "generally to do everything to advance the study, breeding, exhibiting, running, and maintenance of the purity of thoroughbred dogs." But now, more than one hundred years later, the tenet of maintaining breed purity is severely at odds with maintaining the health and the well-being of both breeds and specific dogs. Because the AKC stud book registry is now closed (i.e., no new dogs can be registered unless they come from registered parents), most breeds can trace their ancestry back to somewhere between ten and thirty dogs, creating a world of purebred dogs rampant with inbreeding and genetic defects. More important, the AKC feels it's not in its mission to oversee the raising and handling of dogs in its registry; the club's job, as its members see it, is to guarantee that a dog's parents are certified as purebred. They do not have the resources, they say, to inspect kennels to determine which are puppy mills and which are responsible breeders. Perhaps one project for future animal activists will be to create an alternate kennel club authority that will rate kennels according to cleanliness, placement practices, soundness of breeding philosophy. Imagine an organization that examined the breeding situation for every puppy produced in America and extended a "seal of approval" to every home that provided sound parentage, adequate space, nutritious food, regular socialization, and love to the dogs it bred. Such a resource could help change the world for dogs.

Beyond that, we need to recognize that what is fueling this problematic industry is the public's lack of understanding about what makes a good pet. Many people think that a good pet is one that simply looks like a dog they saw on TV or at the movies; indeed, breeds like collies and Dalmatians became very popular after movies like *Lassie* and *101 Dalmatians*. People don't realize, however, that dog breeds are not natural genetic entities but products of selective breeding, eugenics really, and that breeding for good looks (also known as "conformation") is not the same as breeding for good companions. That's worth repeating: dog breeds are not natural entities. We've made dog breeds by selecting for a trait or look, and intentionally matching, over and over and over, two dogs that have that characteristic. We keep the puppies that have that trait and kill or sterilize the ones that don't. We've mated brother to sister, father to daughter, mother to son, and so on to try to get that trait to appear in every puppy in every litter. Generation after generation, litter after litter, if we keep doing this long enough and enough people get interested in the game, a breed begins to emerge. By most standards, there are roughly about 400 existing dog breeds on record worldwide; however, the AKC only recognizes 150 of them to be "pure" and official. It's tough work to make a dog breed, and even tougher to get it recognized officially.[26]

But if we stop and think for a moment about what we've just done, it's a little appalling. We humans have overridden natural selection by breeding dogs for a certain look. We couldn't breed mother to son and brother to sister in humans very often and still expect good outcomes. Early human communities and animals in the wild developed practices that helped them avoid inbreeding; young women were traded as goods or given as gifts, for example, or adolescent males are rejected from a pack and forced to seek mates elsewhere. So what we're doing with dogs flies in the face of both natural selection and common sense. Responsible breeders know there are ways of avoiding many of the pitfalls of inbreeding through introducing mates from different lineages. But when a breeder doesn't pay attention to the science, dogs suffer. Indeed, the fast, irresponsible breeding of both collies and Dalmatians after *Lassie* and *101 Dalmatians* created dogs that couldn't breathe, couldn't hear, had heart and hip problems, and were intensely aggressive. As I say, you can't breed brother to sister long and expect a good outcome, in humans or dogs.

Good pets are created when attention is paid to traits such as aptitude, intelligence, lack of aggression, soft-mouthedness, even temperaments, ability to be trained (biddability). Puppies who don't have a good balance of these characteristics become many of the dogs that end up at the shelters. There are other aspects of a dog's character that go into making good pets that are hardly even discussed: willingness to cuddle, honesty, ability to make eye contact, general sweetness, sense of humor, a good sense of self-control. The tragedy of the current situation is that when we do find a great pet that manifests all these attributes, chances are high that—whether he comes from a shelter or a rescue or a breeder—he has already been altered and we cannot "pass down" the genetic material that helps constitute his excellent pet qualities. Consumers today are not well educated about what to even ask for when it comes to pets. They want a dog that looks just like one they saw on film and don't know how to ask for the rest. Despite the fact that dogs are more important than ever in the American family, few dogs—if any—are intentionally bred solely because their parents are excellent pets. That is, most dogs today are either unintentionally bred mixes, poor-quality dogs from puppy mills or backyard breeders, or bred with the intention to show but were found lacking and thus deemed "pet quality." If, as I suggest, the key to a change rests on our experience of individual animals, animal advocates ought to be paying much more attention to the character of future generations, as they are some of creatures who, I believe, can help people soften their hearts toward all other animals.

Right now, my dog Duncan, a yellow lab mix, is enrolled an introductory obedience class at a new facility that serves primarily purebred dogs. Despite the fact that Duncan was locked in a kennel at the shelter for almost eight months and—to my thinking—is a little "off," he is a very popular guy in the class. The other dogs, almost all purebred labs, are generally more obedient than Duncan is; they perform their sits and stays with greater ease. I know we're never supposed to compare our dogs with others, but it's pretty clear to everyone that Duncan has something that makes him a little different from the other dogs there. It's hard to put your finger on it exactly; I would say he is more anxious—but also more knowing, more aware of everything around him. The head trainer recognizes how hard he is working to overcome his traumas; she calls him sweet. The assistant trainer really loves Duncan and brings him chicken (needless to say he adores her too). An (irresponsible) lab breeder herself, she told me recently that she had to cull (kill) a whole litter the previous week; despite her better judgment, she said, her breeding mentor had encouraged her to inbreed two great dogs and the results had been disastrous. She told me she wished she could take some genes from Duncan's "character" and insert them into her own dogs. It's that sweetness and kindness, she said, that are often bred out when we're looking for good conformation. I'm not arguing that Duncan understood her words, but maybe the thing that makes him a great pet is that he wasn't produced like a quality-controlled commodity to be approved or rejected. His creation was random, unplanned, but the spirit he inherited was able to sustain him through many desolate, homeless months. Despite his past, he is generous of heart. That's that kind of quality we should be breeding for, I think, if we are going to breed at all.

This sounds like my argument is heading back toward the idea that mixed-breed dogs are the best pets for everyone (and I do think most owners can find a mix that will fit their energy level and lifestyle). I do have sympathy, however, toward those future owners who really want the experience of a small puppy but also want to retain some control over qualities such as size and coat. Adopting puppy mixes of unknown origin is a bit of a crapshoot in terms of size. Additionally, some folks are allergic to certain kinds of fur and do better with shorthaired or wirehaired dogs.

In the most ironic twist of fate, a new kind of mixed-breed dog has appeared to fill their needs—the designer puggles, labradoodles, Maltipoos, bagles, and cockapoos. These dogs are the most expensive pets on the market today, sometimes selling for four or five times the amount of their closest purebred cousins. These designer dogs have what's called "hybrid vigor," which exempts them (along with every other mixed-breed dog) from the genetically determined health and temperament problems associated with purebreds. But their size and coat texture are mostly predictable. Advocates and breeders of designer dogs believe they can intentionally select the best of two breeds and join them together—the smartness of a poodle with the sweetness of a golden retriever, for example; often, they are looking for great temperaments to combine with intelligence and a certain kind of coat or size. Although old-fashioned fanciers are appalled by these hybrids, their success with the public is beyond question. A quick Google search for labradoodles, for example, reveals more than a thousand breeders selling their dogs at costs ranging from eight hundred to twenty thousand dollars. No titles, no champs, no pedigrees. Just expensively engineered mutts.

Housing the Homeless

Anxious to acquire a new dog for my then-small pack, in 2000 I inadvertently stumbled onto the world of dog rescue. Although I'm sure individuals have always rescued dogs independently, the birth of high-speed Internet in the late 1990s spawned a new form of rescue through nonprofit organizations. At that time, I wanted a beagle and decided to try my luck on the computer to find one. I did find one, my Daisy, through Triangle Beagle Rescue, but I also found a lot more: the fascinating and complex social formation of animal rescue. In the ensuing years, I have volunteered with many different rescue organizations (both breed specific and mixed breed), made lifelong friends who feel like family, learned more about dogs than I could have previously imagined, and fostered about two hundred dogs into new adoptive homes. The dog rescue network is composed of thousands of people who devote much of their free time to transporting, vetting, fostering, caring for, and placing homeless dogs into permanent homes. For many of these people, rescue is not just a hobby or even a "good cause," it is a lifestyle.

In some ways, dog rescue is pretty uneven and disorganized. In my experience, these organizations, groups, and clubs often depend on one or two people to coordinate and motivate dozens of others; when those leaders leave or burn out, sometimes the organizations falter or fail. Other times, someone new steps up to the position and often gives the organization a different mission or character. Some leaders push the organization to save shelter dogs and strays; others push for accepting more owner surrenders to keep those dogs out of shelters. Some want to save as many dogs as possible and will take in biters or dogs with other aggression issues; others only want to rescue the dogs with the best temperaments. Some leaders are also successful fund-raisers and raise money for expensive surgeries like hip replacements; other leaders hate raising money, or are unable to, and consequently have to turn away dogs that need even minor medical care.

One might assume that this world of rescue is closely aligned with animal rights ideology in general. In my experience, however, this is rarely the case. If, as I have argued, there's a big and unnecessary gap between animal rights and other social movements, an even bigger gap exists between animal rights and animal rescue. Animal lovers may have founded rescue organizations, but there is rarely any visible association with a larger animal rights agenda. For example, at most functions of these groups, there is a significant amount of meat served, with no attention to where the meat came from or whether it was humanely raised and slaughtered. Folks who rescue animals wear leather, and indeed several of the women involved in one organization wore fur coats to a winter fund-raiser. I've even met a handful of rescue people who work in the pharmaceutical industry, some even conducting experiments on other dogs (never their own breed).

I've tried to think about the reasons for this gap from both sides. Most rescuers really love their dogs. Taking unknown animals into your house is not always an easy proposition, and many of these women love their dogs so much they are willing to make all kinds of sacrifices—including money, carpets, furniture, and even a couple of husbands—to take in and foster the dogs that need help. Because of the chasm that exists between dog rescue and animal advocacy on a larger scale, however, they are unable or unwilling to extend that love to other animals. I've talked to a lot of people about this issue over the years, and the general sentiment is that animal rights agendas are extremist and not really focused on saving specific animals. A few women told me that they thought "animal rights" was only about two goals: veganism and stopping all scientific progress. Some breeders felt that "animal rights" was about limiting private ownership of animals, and that laws introduced to address issues like tethering were the first steps on the slippery slope to a world without any animals. For the rescuers, nothing compares to helping real, specific dogs.

But rescuers need to think more broadly about the many ways we can help a wider spectrum of animals. Not long ago, for example, I was on the phone with the director of a local purebred rescue about planning a fund-raiser barbecue. I had requested that we buy humane hamburgers and hot dogs from local, free-range farms to sell at the event, and she scoffed. This organization had just spent over ten thousand dollars for Ranger's medical bills, she told me (Ranger, it turns out, has chronic health problems but is also a biter and is therefore taking a long time finding a home). Free-range meat costs about three times what Costco's cost, she went on, and we simply couldn't afford it. When I weigh all the pain and suffering the Costco cows and pigs endured to become cheap meat against replacing two hips on a biter, I become something that looks pretty close to a utilitarian. Although I want to avoid the pitfalls associated with a stringent utilitarianism mentioned in the preceding chapter, even the most modest interpretation of "the greatest good for the greatest number" would place the happy lives of, say, a dozen cows and pigs over Ranger's hips. Rescuers, I believe, need a shift that introduces some other animals into the equation.

But that's only half the story. Part of what keeps rescuers from embracing a broader advocacy agenda is their perception that animal rights people are extremists interested only in pushing vegan, antiscience, and pet-owning agendas. I know this extremist characterization is complicated and media hype concerning certain actions misrepresents what a lot of activists are fighting for, but suffice it to say that people involved in animal rescue are prime candidates for caring about all kinds of animals, and if animal activists can't convert them to broader agendas, something is drastically wrong. Perhaps the best place to start would be for more animal rights people to get involved in rescue themselves. While some activists may be involved in rescue, in my experience that is not the norm. To bridge the gap between animal rescuers and animal rights,

I think more folks in the latter category need to step up and take in a homeless dog or cat for rehabilitation and rehoming.

Which brings us back to the question of shelter animals. Rescuers in breed-specific and mixed-breed organizations are usually one step removed from the horror of most shelters. Shelter work is probably the toughest job on the planet when it comes to companion animals. While some people approach it as simply a job, or others are there to satisfy some sort of community service requirement, in my experience most people are called to shelter work through their love of animals. But the relentless stream of unwanted pets causes compassion fatigue; although they start their work with their hearts in the right place, they often burn out quickly. A lot of people who work in the shelters I have volunteered in have really lost the kind of empathy I would want them to have. I don't blame them; it's the job that often turns their hearts cold. You almost have to have a hardened heart to survive working in many shelters for long periods of time.

Workers in high-kill shelters cope with burnout by seeing themselves as performing the necessary evil of euthanizing the throwaway pets in their communities. They insist that the problem of pet overpopulation is one the community created; they are simply performing the required task of killing the unwanted. They are convinced that an open admissions policy whereby all animals are accepted with few questions asked is the only way to guard against a slow and painful death on the streets. Most of the shelter workers I have talked with defend their work as being an important form of animal advocacy; they are very proud of the fact that they provide a dog with a little bit of love, a clean towel, or a good meal at the end of the dog's life. This may be the only love that dog has ever known, they tell me. Shelter workers in the open-admission, high-kill facilities I've worked at insist that "no-kill" shelters and the no-kill movement is simply displacing the problem of unwanted animals onto them. This is a problem created by a larger community, they argue, and no-kill shelters that only accept highly adoptable pets are not the solution. In my experience, an "us against the community" ideology is fairly widespread among shelter workers; that is, shelter workers share the worldview that the general public is largely heartless toward pets, and they are their sole protectors, even though that protection often entails killing them.[27]

In other words, shelter workers who kill many or most of the animals in their care think of themselves as benevolent but necessary triage workers, sorting the good dogs from the bad, the healthy, sound ones from the sick and aggressive and old ones. They believe they are forced to kill the unadoptable dogs almost immediately, saving space for the adoptable ones, which they will hold as long as they can. Sometimes it's only a week, sometimes in slow seasons it can be months.[28] The way decisions are made about which dogs should die is very uneven. One of the shelters I worked in immediately euthanized all pit bulls and chows, believing that, by virtue of their breed, these dogs would never become good pets. Another killed all bully breeds—including pit bulls, rotties, bulldogs, and sometimes German shepherds—believing that most of the potential adopters only wanted them for fighting. One shelter dealt with animals on a case-by-case basis, but employed a very strict temperament test that most dogs could not pass. The dogs that failed were then euthanized; the rest remained available for adoption unless they developed illness or kennel madness. The final shelter I worked at did not discriminate based on breed or temperament. Its policy, instead, was to make every dog that did not have serious health issues available for adoption, regardless of age, size, or breed. Any dogs that did not get adopted were then killed to make space for new intakes; this place killed the whole kennel every Tuesday. All shelters (except this last one) employed some sort of temperament test in which a certified trainer or tester pushed and pinched the dog, took his food away, stared him in the eye (the test varied according to location; some included testing dogs to see how they responded to other dogs, some did not). Usually, if a dog growled or showed any signs of aggression at all he was euthanized. The test is intended to weed out dogs that have a poor bite inhibition, but often dogs "failed" even if they didn't actually bite but just appeared aggressive.

There has been a great deal of controversy in the past decade surrounding the efficacy and morality of these temperament tests. Part of this criticism is directly marshaled by no-kill activists who claim that killing a dog based on a ten-minute test in an extremely stressful environment, sometimes after the dog has been hungry and on the streets for extended periods of time, is wrong. These folks claim that such a test is not at all a good indicator of the kind of pet a dog could become and that most of the dogs currently living as pets would not pass these tests. According to the no-kill community, these tests are simply justifications for killing; that is, they function to help alleviate the shelter workers' guilt. The temp test also creates a great deal of controversy because it is so subjective; dogs that fail with one trainer often pass with another.

Because the kill rates for open-admission public shelters in most areas of the South are so much higher than in the Northeast, programs have been developed where dogs from various southern states are transferred to northeastern shelters for adoption. The chosen dogs are temp-tested at both ends. However, because the test is so subjective, dogs that pass in the South often fail once they get up north (and quite likely the stress of the transport—where dogs are often passed from car to car sometimes over the course of several days—adds to the state of panic the dog feels upon arrival). I witnessed such an exchange as one of the shelters I worked at here in North Carolina was partnered with Sue Sternberg's Roundout Valley Kennels in upstate New York. Sternberg found several of our most temperamentally sound dogs unadoptable and killed them; the partnership was disbanded.[29]

As heartbreaking and heartless as the temperament tests seem, they are not the primary source of my criticism of high-kill shelters. After all, given the huge volume of dogs such shelters traffic in, it's fairly apparent that some dogs are going to have to die. As blunt as it is, the temperament test does offer some means of determining which dogs might become better pets. My main criticism of high-kill shelters—based on my experiences volunteering in them—is directed at the other end of the process, that is, with excessively stringent adoption criteria. Again, these varied greatly from shelter to shelter, but I found the adoption criteria for most of the shelters and even many of the rescues I worked with to be completely unreasonable and unacceptable. In many of these organizations, would-be adopters had to have a spotless pet history (no previous dogs who ever ran off, or got hit by a car, or had any suspicious accidents). Would-be adopters had to agree not to leave their new dogs outside while at work or at night (even if the dog preferred to be outside). If the would-be adopter owned another dog that was kept primarily outside, he or she was turned down. Adopters had to have a fenced yard or agree always to leash-walk and never to tether the dog with a chain or a rope. They could not use electric or invisible fences, or shock collars to keep their dogs contained. And, of course, they could not let their dogs roam free. Adopters could not have other intact animals in their home, even if they were show dogs (which must be unaltered according to AKC rules). They couldn't own more than two, or in one case three, other dogs at the time of adoption. If the potential adopter owned cats, the cats must be kept indoors only and not declawed (unless they had been rescued already declawed); if their cats were indoor/outdoor, they could not adopt a dog. Potential adopters could not own other animals that had been cosmetically altered (tails docked or ears cropped—unless the animals received those alterations before being adopted), even if the AKC required that alteration for showing. In most shelters, vet checks were mandatory, so persons who were first-time pet owners and had no relationship with a vet could not adopt. If the potential adopter's other animals were or ever had been behind on their shots, the adopter was declined. In some cases, the adopter had to be employed or show proof of income. No college students could ever adopt, no matter how old they were. No transients could ever adopt pets; if the would-be adopter rented, he or she needed written permission from the landlord approving the adoption of a pet. Adopters could not use dogs for hunting. You could never adopt a dog for someone else, even if that person was homebound, requested the adoption, and fulfilled all other criteria. Puppies were not adopted to homes with children under six or eight years old, or to homes where children under eight visited. All members of a household must visit the dog before adoption (so surprise pets for children, say, were not possible). In most cases, you could not adopt a dog if you had ever relinquished a pet to a shelter or a rescue, or if you had ever given a pet away to another person (losing pets to divorce was dealt with on a case-by-case basis). In many cases, you could not adopt a dog if you lived outside a thirty-mile radius of the area. There was always at least a three-day waiting period before you could get your dog. If you wanted to foster a dog rather than adopt, you had to be part of a nonprofit 501(c)(3) organization. Even then, only one person from each organization (an intake coordinator) was authorized to pull the dog from the shelter. (And all the shelters I worked in discouraged volunteers from contacting purebred rescues about a pure-bred dog that had come into the shelter; if the rescue organization wanted dogs badly enough, someone from it needed to check the shelter or its website.) And if you lied about the answers to any of these questions on your application or in your interview, the dog would be taken from you.

Although it's true that not all these criteria were mandated at every shelter, it is not an exaggeration to say that it is extremely difficult to adopt a rescued, homeless dog from a shelter (or from some rescue orga-nizations). In environments where the vast majority of animals are killed because they lack homes, I find these strict criteria ridiculous. I myself could not adopt a dog from some of the shelters I volunteered at because they think I already own too many pets; over the years, the applications of countless friends, family, and coworkers have been declined because they did not meet one or more of these conditions. When I talked to shelter workers about why their standards were so stringent, they elab-orately explained why they believed them to be important; they had seen so many dogs go out and come back, and these rules, they believed, pre-vented such bad placements. But in my opinion, harsh as it sounds, I think it mostly revolved around the fact that they had gotten used to killing, and many would rather see the dogs die than let them go to what they believed to be less-than-perfect homes. I would like to call on animal activists of all types to get more involved in the transformation of shel-ter culture, but with the "us against the world" ideology shared by most shelter workers, I recognize this can be very difficult.

Perhaps my volunteer experiences are unique and the rest of the world is full of kindhearted shelter workers who have only dogs' best interests in mind. I hope so. Or maybe I just have a really hard time killing dogs needlessly and therefore can't see the benefit of such severity. But my experiences tell me that the shelter situation today is in crisis. With so many dogs dying daily, I think anyone who sincerely wants to adopt ought to be given the chance. Accidents happen, people's lives are complex; the world of sheltering and rescuing needs to be more flexible than it cur-rently is in order to save the lives of as many dogs as possible. These are the same beings—species, identities; they have the same shape, form, communication skills, and ways of being in the world as the creatures I call my family. Yet, most people in shelter culture treat their murder as routine. I lose sleep at night over their deaths and feel terrible when I can't take them all home. Hard as it may seem, everyone involved in animal advocacy in every form has to wake up to this crisis and start to take control of the situation. And in the meantime, we all need to work hard to keep every dog we know out of the high-kill shelters.

Keeping Dogs Out of Shelters

Animals end up in shelters for myriad reasons: owners die; people need to move and can't find a place that will take their pets; they run into financial trouble and can't afford to feed themselves let alone their pets. Much of the time, people simply get tired of, bored with, or annoyed by their pets and throw them away like disposable commodities. In almost every circumstance, a dog's chances of being adopted out of the shelter, or indeed avoiding the shelter in the first place, would be greatly increased if that dog had better manners.

I would bet that the creators of the Disney animated children's film *Lilo and Stitch*—in which a young girl adopts a dog from an animal shelter and the dog turns out to be an evil alien from outer space—based their story line on a firsthand shelter adoption experience. Having adopted or rescued many dogs from shelters, I can vouch for the fact that many (maybe even most?) of them seem like aliens, at least at first. They come into our homes and pee and shit anywhere they want, chew on anything they can find, scale six-foot fences and run into busy streets, sometimes start fights with bigger and more dominant residents, and generally are usually very poorly behaved. It often takes a long period of negotiation to get them under control. Even though I am convinced that most of the dogs in shelters started their lives as someone's pet, you wouldn't know it from the way they come into a new home. Indeed, many of them are relinquished to the shelter or to the streets because their owners simply can't control them. Most dogs are not born knowing how to live with us. And unfortunately, their time at local shelters or on the streets makes many of them even less adapted to living with humans.

It's worth repeating that the central problem is that many pets today are treated like commodities—cars, clothes, books, DVDs, and other collectibles. When we're done with them, when they've served their purposes in our lives, when they become too much of a burden, out they go. The underlying problem when it comes to homeless pets is that we live in a disposable society that encourages us to buy new things rather than repair the old. Our shelters are full because pets are treated like objects. Now, more than ever, we need a mind shift to occur with regard to these animals. As Temple Grandin so eloquently states, "Animals are not things."[30] They, like us, have nervous systems that allow them to experience all kinds of feelings, such as pain, fear, and hunger, along with joy, love, and security. Like us, they have memories and a psychic universe that needs tending. For dogs, that tending is best accomplished, I believe, in the form of training. On the surface, training is important simply because it helps to teach the dog how to behave. Having a dog that knows the meaning of "sit," "down," "stay," and "come"—and is willing to offer these behaviors when asked—is often the difference between a good pet one can live with, and a bad pet that ends up (dead) at a shelter. But the most important work accomplished in training is not learning "sit," "down," and "stay"; what is most important is the affective connection that happens when we work with our dogs.

The idea behind the shift that this book calls for rests on the conviction that the emotional bonds humans have with specific animals can become a strong foundation to enhance our moral orientation toward animals. More robust and passion filled than philosophical tools like rights or welfare, a politicized concept of love for particular animals can be manipulated and abstracted to address the well-being of many animals. If everyone who ever cared about a specific dog or cat or bird could be persuaded to re-create and reexperience that love toward lots of different kinds of animals, the earth would experience an unprecedented change. We could begin to see ourselves as one type among many living things, and take up less destructive practices toward our fellow travelers. And all this can start, I am convinced, with the love of a dog.

The most objective and practical way to express and measure this powerful emotional bond is through stories. I can tell you I love my dogs in general, but what I really mean is that I love the way Duncan crosses his paws when he sleeps, or Daisy runs straight to the park three blocks away whenever she gets loose, or Jerome waits for permission from me to eat his dinner. It's the particular things about these creatures that we love, the small things that are unique to them, that make them who they are, that animates our love for them. The best thing training gives us is not perfect sits or stays, but the time and attention to notice who our dogs are. It gives us the space to fall in love with them.[31]

Moreover, training draws into sharp relief how much most dogs really want to please us. Once they get the idea that we are asking them for something that they actually can do, like a good sit, they learn—maybe for the first time—that they have the power to make someone else happy. And realizing the power to make someone else happy is, after all, the foundation of all relationships. Dogs who were so severely neglected or abused by humans that they refuse to make eye contact often look at you for the first time once they understand that they've made you happy. Something magical happens in those moments; it's as if the dog turns her face into the light and you see her differently. Training gives both the dog and the human the space to bond; in training, we humans produce the stories and memories that will carry us through the difficult, trying times. I'm not talking about championship obedience work here either; one short six- to eight-week session with a good teacher can change the outcome of the relationship. It's enough to get dog and owner started on the road to a lifelong connection.

One September during my research for this book, I adopted Jubilee. The vet thought she would be a small dog, but she turned out to be a large pit bull mix. I certainly didn't need another dog, but a friend of mine found six infants taped inside a box in the woods; I couldn't resist. Jubilee was exuberant and grew very fast; it was kind of like watching a hydraulic lift in slow motion. I was pretty busy that semester and didn't give her much attention. By the time she was about five months old, however, I realized that if we were going to live together for the long haul, she needed better manners. So I took her to obedience school. She was at the bottom of the class. Really. She didn't have a reliable sit, and concepts like "down" and "stay" completely escaped her. She was big and ungainly, and I could barely even walk her on a leash. Then one night in about the third class, she won first place in a "watch me" contest. The watch me command basically consists of my holding a piece of hotdog up between my eyes and forcing her to look at me without breaking eye contact. Jubilee saw me—probably for the first time—that night. Her watch went on and on for over three minutes (an eternity for this dog), and when she won the prize, the whole class applauded. I fell in love that night, and although I didn't know it then, that love would later transform my life.

But that's only half the story. Affective connection, as any good trainer knows, is not a one-way street. It's not just about getting them to recognize us, but about us recognizing them right back. Training is a metaphor for how to live together, and the alterations of affect don't take place only on their end. A simple example: During the early stages of writing this book, I fell down some stairs and sustained a minor knee injury. It meant changing my exercise routine from mainly walking to swimming; that was fine with me, as I love the water, but it wasn't fine for my dogs. Although they have a huge backyard to run in, someone (still not sure who) felt they deserved their daily walk, even if it was only ten minutes. In the first few weeks, they were compassionate; they could see I was hurt and suffered their lack of daily walk in silence. But after a few weeks, "things" went awry. By "things," I mean, someone got into the garbage. I had loads of foster dogs in the house during this period, but all of them were crated when I left the house. That meant one of my own people was tipping the garbage over on occasion when I left.

I was beside myself because my dogs "know" (read: are trained) not to get into the garbage. I have a huge expensive metal can that is very hard to get into, and in all my years living with dogs, this had never happened. The really beguiling thing is that it didn't happen every day, only occasionally. So at first I thought it must be that there was something in there that smelled so good, they couldn't resist (that is, I didn't connect it to their lack of walk at all). I emptied the garbage daily. Still, almost every day, the garbage can was tipped over and whatever was in it, even if it was only paper, was strewn about the house. I tried duct-taping the can shut, but that didn't work; they just ripped the tape off and chewed it up. What was so puzzling (this was during an autumn when the weather was unusually rainy) was that the garbage wasn't raided every day—some days were skipped. That's why it took me so long to figure things out. It started a few weeks after the knee injury and was inconsistent. It felt like a bad habit someone had picked up, but why were they skipping some days? And what prompted the behavior in the first place? Finally, after almost a month, I realized the garbage was compromised only on sunny days! I have several dogs who hate the rain and walk reluctantly even when it is only drizzling. On rainy days, they didn't mind missing their walk. But on sunny days, the garbage was a message. Once I understood that, I hired a dog walker until my knee healed, and the garbage was never touched again. Now they get a walk even if I don't feel like it or don't have time for it (unless it's raining). In a very real way, they were training me.[32]

The point is, they are real beings who have needs and desires and affects of their own, and communicate with us in the best ways they can. Affective connection demands that we do our best to listen to them and respond to them with open hearts and minds.

As you can see by now, I am pretty obsessed with dogs. Whether on TV or at the shelter or on the street or in my own home, I think dogs are just about the best thing on earth. There isn't much I wouldn't do to help a dog in need, and I think I give those dogs that cross my path a good enough life; I know they make my life worth living in every possible sense. The theory behind this book rests on the idea that almost every human can make this kind of connection with other animals. It may not be dogs for everybody, but there are, thankfully plenty of other options. The connection doesn't even have to be with a pet; it can be with wildlife or even more abstract, with other kinds of animals in many forms of representation. One of my best friends is obsessed with tigers; she would never own one, she admits, but as a result of early zoo encounters, she thinks and dreams about them frequently. She is identified with tigers in the same way I am identified with dogs. We understand ourselves to be part of someone other. I believe animal advocacy should be about the business of fostering those identifications and connections, of turning people's hearts toward the interconnectedness we humans can have with other species. Arguments based on rights, welfare and utilitarianism will all be enhanced in the transformation that this kind of love can offer. Once we help people feel that love, perhaps we can help them open their minds, awaken their spirits, and soften their hearts to the plight of all tortured animals today.

The idea that this love can travel toward many different kinds of animals is fairly new to me. I am almost ashamed to admit that it was less than a decade ago that I really only cared about dogs. The pigs and chickens and cows suffering in factory farms to become our meat, the myriad animals held captive in zoos and circuses and labs, all seemed to escape my attention. They were nameless entities that didn't possess anything close to personalities. All that changed when I ventured out and met two pigs named Mary and Joseph who were more like my dogs than I could have ever imagined. I'll tell you their story in the next chapter.

THREE THE ANIMAL
ON YOUR PLATE
Farmers, Vegans, and Locavores

IF THE WORLD OF PETS IS PERHAPS THE MOST HEART-
breaking aspect of the way we treat animals, the world of meat, eggs,
and dairy products is without question the largest and most horrifying.
The vast majority of our animal products come from "factory farms" or
CAFOs (confined or concentrated animal feeding operations): these industrial operations house our food animals in automated cages, tin sheds,
and feedlots where animals are packed in at astounding rates. They never
once get to walk in the sunshine and smell the clean air and kiss and
cuddle their mates or children. As a result of disease, many of these animals have open sores and tumors the size of footballs. Most of them live
their whole lives standing in their own waste. They are fed unnatural diets
of corn and soy full of pesticides, hormones, antibiotics, and even other
animals. Unless you know where your meat, eggs, and dairy products are
produced, they are, most certainly, coming from one of these factory
farms.[1]

Fortunately, there's a revolution happening in the United States today
and part of it affects animals. It's about food, and Americans are slowly
waking up to the fact that we've been sold a bill of goods that is killing us,
destroying our land, and torturing our animals. Virtually every community

across the country holds meetings about this revolution every week and millions upon millions of people attend. They're called farmers' markets. Not everybody who frequents a farmers' market understands it as a political gesture, but it unquestionably is. The local food movement stands as one of the most potent social movements in America today. Armed with the powerful tools of forks and dollars, these consumer soldiers are turning the tide of American health, working to save our land from devastation and improving conditions for millions of animals every day.

However, many strong animal rights advocates in America today reject this return to meat grown on pasture. In their continued insistence on veganism as the only true litmus test of animal compassion, many in the most orthodox wings of the animal rights movement set a narrow national agenda that many Americans cannot and will not sign on to. While some vegans are attentive to the problems associated with industrial agriculture, many animal rights adherents accept and endorse any food that contains no animal products—no matter how processed that food is, how much corn or soy it contains, how far it has traveled, how little nutritious value it has. Instead of embracing the millions of Americans now seeking a better relationship with both earth and animals, some animal rights advocates take up the position that veganism is the only necessary or adequate response. But this position ignores too many of the problems brought on by industrial agriculture, from the degradation of the land to the devastation of human health. A different approach is necessary, one that allows for the possibility that eating reduced amounts of food animals raised in free-range conditions with relatively long lives on small local farms is not wrong. The true enemies of animals and their well-being are the monsters capitalism has produced, namely, CAFOs and factory farms.

Motivated by its unquenchable thirst for greater profits, American agribusiness has virtually destroyed the small farm and replaced it with biological monoculture. Where the older model of farming produced both animals and plants (the animals ate the parts of the plants not consumed by humans, and produced manure that fed the plants), today farms are modeled on the Fordist factory assembly line and produce one product in very high volume.[2] If that product is animals, the foods for those animals are imported; if that product is plants, the food and often the water the plants need are imported. And because these monocultures are so unnatural, all kinds of drugs, from hormones to pesticides to antibiotics to herbicides, must be brought in as well. Virtually all these imported products are government subsidized. The cost of buying the products of monoculture may be lower, but the hidden costs to our health, our land, and our food animals are beyond tally.

I am not arguing that existing vegans need to start eating meat, of course, but rather that animals who have a happy, drug-free, and relatively long life can be ethically consumed, along with their products like eggs and milk, as long as those are harvested morally as well. Mine is an argument that claims that the bigger picture of farming in America warrants our attention and that being vegan may not necessarily encompass the kind of critique animals and environment need most today.[3]

My Vegan Year

Like many others, the first time I encountered descriptions and images of animals raised in CAFOs or "factory farms," I immediately stopped eating animal products. By the time I found this information in the early part of the twenty-first century, the food industry had already seen the profit potential in developing specialized vegan/vegetarian products that looked and sort of tasted like real food. I started buying these products in the frozen food section of my grocery store; I thought they tasted pretty good, almost just like real hamburgers and bacon, and I tried not to let the list of unpronounceable ingredients bother me. As long as they didn't have any meat in them, I ate them. I wrote letters to Morningstar Farms, a subsidiary of Kellogg's, thanking them for their products and for helping me become a real vegan. More and more of my food came in boxes or brightly colored bags; sometimes things came in cellophane bags packed inside boxes, or vice versa. Nothing looked like what it really was. My burgers and chicken nuggets were made of corn and soy. My eggs were made of soy. My white bread was processed, then enriched. I started drinking soy milk and eating soy ice cream, both of which were made with high fructose corn syrup and soy. That year for Thanksgiving, I cooked a "tofurkey," also made of corn and soy. Sometimes I ate fruits and vegetables, but the logic of the frozen food aisles made the fresh ones seem much less palatable (some of them actually still had dirt on them!), so I bought and ate highly colored boxes and bags of washed, processed, and frozen peas, potatoes, corn, strawberries, and peach slices. Maybe they didn't taste as good as their fresh counterparts, but my taste buds were being retrained by my new food regime and I believed I had to put my own pleasure behind my politics. Even my pets got on the program: I fed my dogs expensive vegetarian food made from fish, corn, potatoes, soy, and "stabilizers," and got into fights with my vet about whether such a diet was healthy for my cats. Granted, it felt like I was often paying more for packaging than for the product itself. (More and more, I felt like I was living in a sci-fi movie where I was really only eating two things—corn and soy—that had been altered and reconstituted to appear more palatable.) But at least I was vegan.

My food ethic consisted of the simple dictum that no piece of flesh or any other animal products would ever pass my lips. I couldn't really see exactly how my practices were making a difference to real animals, but the growing animal rights movement told me veganism was the only answer, and so I persisted. My new friends and I were quite satisfied with ourselves. We thought of ourselves as morally pure and were even a bit smug about it. The rest of the world was unenlightened, we thought. We shored up our superiority over vegan potlucks by eating mounds of corn chips and canned salsa and reconstituted corn and soy products of all types. At animal rights conferences, we paid ten dollars for ice-cream bars that were made of soy and corn syrup. When we did eat out with "flesh eaters," we made a big deal about grilling the waitperson about ingredients. If animal products appeared in our food, we painstakingly picked them out and shoved them aside. We had the conviction of converts to a religion we thought could save our immortal souls. We became what I now call "vegangelicals." We would go to fast-food restaurants, order burgers with all the toppings, take the beef out, and throw it away. I always felt bad for the cow who had given her life to become a hamburger that I was simply throwing away. But our newfound religion told us that as long as no animal products touched our lips, we were saved.

There's a reason why the vast majority of vegans are twenty-somethings or younger. A steady diet of mostly corn and soy mixed with a lot of sugar ravages most middle-aged bodies. I gained thirty pounds that year, developed insulin-dependent diabetes and chronic headaches. (But how could this be? I asked. Animal rights materials claim that diabetes and health problems came from eating meat, not from vegan products!) My doctor told me to exercise more, sent me home with bags of medicines, and implored me to change my diet. I simply could not understand what was wrong with my diet; after all, I wasn't eating any meat. I kept a food journal and tested my blood after every meal; I noticed that almost every time I ate one of my vegan processed foods, my blood sugar spiked higher than if I had eaten a candy bar. My doctor pointed out that all those ingredients whose names I could not pronounce were actually forms of sugar, and both corn and soy were essentially sugars as well. You need more animal protein, she said. I felt lost. How could I save my body without betraying the animals and my own eternal soul?

That's when I met Mary and Joseph, a pair of pigs kept by local farmers who helped change my life for the better. A friend who was not a vegan suggested that maybe there was a way to eat meat morally and recommended I check out this relatively new local farm. She told me that Audrey and Henry had started the farm only a few years earlier; both had grown tired of fast-paced corporate life and wanted a simpler life on an old-fashioned farm. Like me, they had once been vegans and were still animal lovers, but they wanted to eat meat again and felt the only way to do so was to raise the animals themselves. When Audrey got pregnant, my friend said, she was really hungry and craved meat. That's when they decided to start the farm. It turns out, my friend elaborated, having food animals around was also really good for the vegetable garden. The pigs ate the plants and roots and garbage, so Henry didn't need to plow that much, and they pooped out this great compost manure, for free. My friend said they killed eight to ten pigs every year—more than enough meat for them with plenty left over to sell privately to friends. They had other animals as well. I would like it, she said. I was skeptical; after all, these were food animals, exploited for their flesh, kept caged or tethered, and made to produce things for human consumption. How moral could it be? But I called and made an appointment to visit.

Some of my skepticism dissipated when I drove up to the old farmhouse to find two huge pigs just lying on the front porch. I expected to find them in sheds like the ones in the animal rights film clips, or at least in crowded pens. But these pigs were napping under the swing along-side a dog. "Come on in," Audrey shouted from just inside the door. "That's Mary and Joseph. They won't hurt you. They're tame." As I approached, the pigs and the dogs got up to greet me. Audrey came out with a handful of Milk-Bone dog biscuits and made the dog and the two three-hundred-pound pigs all sit for a treat. It was a little surreal.

Through the house and around the back was just as trippy. There was a small goat on the couch next to a young child; both seemed to be watching a game show on TV. "That's Marvin," Audrey said. "I was just about to give him his bottle, but he can wait." I wasn't sure if she was talking about the goat or the boy. (I soon learned Marvin was the goat; I didn't get the child's name until my second visit.) It seemed like there were about a half-dozen cats. The screen door to the back was propped open with a chair and the door led out into what now feels like an extremely untidy Garden of Eden. Animals pretty much everywhere. More goats chewing on grass. A big pig, bigger than Mary or Joseph, chasing one particular chicken around the yard at full speed. Other pigs. Lots of chickens walking around with lots more cats. A mama cat and her kittens. A donkey over by the fence, more pigs walking around. Straw, lots of straw, almost everywhere. A dog came out from the only small barn and rushed up for a Milk-Bone. Once some of the pigs realized Milk-Bones were being distributed, they rushed up, too. Audrey handed them out in small pieces, apologizing for the fact that not many of them "know their sits." A baby pig ran by, squealing for his mama. None of these animals, including the ones on the porch, were penned up in any way. They could have run off if they wanted to. But they didn't. Off in the distance, there were fenced-in areas with pigs in them, but the pens were huge. I was expecting pens sort of like the ones on Auntie Em's farm in *The Wizard of Oz*, but these pigs had acres. It would have taken me the better part of an afternoon to walk the perimeter of their area.

I could have stayed there forever, I think, playing with the animals, watching them, learning their ways. But this was a business transaction for Audrey. I was there to maybe buy pork chops and whatever else I found to be moral. She was a busy farmer and, of course, Marvin was waiting for his bottle. I told her about my situation and asked if I could ask a few questions before I bought anything. Sure, she said. We headed back to the front porch.

There I sat for over an hour (while she bottle-fed Marvin and I scratched Mary's back with its stiff hair) and learned about the lives of these animals. Audrey and Henry made most of their money off vegetables and pork. It was barely a living, but they had saved enough money to buy the land and the foundation stock outright, so they didn't need much to live on. The pigs were an heirloom breed, abandoned by what she called "the industry" because they couldn't be raised in confinement; they were too ornery when kept close. Their meat was very tender and had been featured in Alice Waters's cookbooks. (I didn't even know who Alice Waters was back then, but I nodded enthusiastically.) It was the end of tomato season; Henry was off delivering the last bushels to local restaurants and the pigs in the pen had just been let loose to root in the plants. They were very happy. She had already canned seventeen bushels for their use in the winter, saving the seeds, of course, for next year. The sows gave birth in the small barn in the spring, and most of the piglets were allowed to roam free during suckling. They loved to make nests with straw, so there was lots of it around. No pig was killed for meat before it was four years old. Audrey explained that she knew it was an arbitrary number, four years, but she felt if she gave them four years of a good life, that that was a good enough deal. (Factory-farmed pigs are killed at six months; wild pigs can live up to sixteen years.) If a pig showed itself to be particularly tame and sweet (like Mary and Joseph, who sat at my feet), they didn't slaughter it until much later, or maybe not at all. Her mother had rejected Mary a few years earlier; she was a runt, and Audrey considered her more of a pet than meat. She had bottle-fed her in the house in her infancy and doubted she would ever be able to kill her or eat her. "But we'll see," she said. Joseph was just a terribly sweet boy who sought human affection over everything, and Audrey thought there was no way he was going down either. All of the pigs outside the pen had names and access to shelter if they wanted it. They ranged from infancy to five years. They were, as Audrey put it, her babies.

The goats were Henry's project. They had started with four three years earlier, and Henry loved to milk them. The mothers lined up to get milked after their babies lost interest; Henry fed them Quaker oatmeal while they were being milked. They made two kinds of cheeses from the goat's milk and sold them to visitors. Goats are like dogs, Audrey said. You could train them to do anything. They had sold two infant goats to a local farmer to raise for meat last year, but Henry had felt so bad about it she didn't think they would do it again. Through that experience, she said they had figured out that in the future they would only sell their animals with a contract that stated they would not be slaughtered until a certain age. More and more humane farmers were using these kinds of contracts, she said. It was a way to make sure we gave animals a lot before we took from them. She also added, "This farm thing is a work in progress. You live and learn."

Audrey and Henry didn't sell their chickens for or as meat, but they did sell their eggs. Audrey didn't really like chickens, but they were great at keeping the bugs down, she said. They had about fifty hens, and she got about four dozen eggs from them each day. Most of the chickens went in the hog barn at night, and you just had to go through each morning and collect "piles of eggs." The rest of the time they were free to roam the property as they wished. Audrey didn't understand why chickens were kept in confinement, as they preferred to lay all their eggs in the same place anyway. "Maybe it's the fact that their poop is so slimy," she offered. Henry had killed and cleaned three chickens himself last winter for their own use. The chickens did not have names. They did not keep a rooster as she said they would be overtaken with baby chicks if they did. Almost all her chickens were donations from local grade school classes that wanted to experience egg hatching. She only accepted females from such donations. Because they were different breeds, the eggs came out in different sizes and colors, which sometimes made them hard to sell. "You'll never get a fertilized egg from us, though," she insisted.

While they only had two dogs, both altered, they had a lot of cats. Maybe too many, she thought. Even though both dogs helped keep the cats and chickens from being preyed upon, twice now she had seen hawks fly away with kittens, and once a young chicken. She worried about that. They had wanted a lot of cats because they milled their own grain for both hogs and chickens, and the rodent population was bad the first year. Twice, though, in recent years she had had kittens that grew up to chase chickens. She couldn't allow that, she said, and moved those cats to a feral cat colony. "If you can't get along with others here," Audrey said, "you've gotta go."

Audrey was very articulate about the slaughter process. While the FDA rules permitted them to slaughter chickens themselves (even if they sold them to the public), pigs and all other mammals had to be slaughtered at an approved facility. She used two different slaughterhouses, one about thirty miles away and the other about forty-five. It was difficult to get reservations for small numbers like she took in, so sometimes she had to wait a week or more. She always felt bad about taking a pig in, and always took in the one or two that were the least social, the least tame. "Some of these pigs are pretty mean," she said, a little defensively. "You really don't feel bad about killing them, especially when they're tough to have around, when they're mean to others." No matter how mean a pig is, she or Henry walked it to the slaughter ramp (she kissed it good-bye although she didn't think Henry does), thanked it for its life, and waited there with it while it is killed quickly with a captive bolt gun. She did not leave until she was sure it was dead. When I asked her about undercover video footage of living pigs and cows allowed to bleed out or being scalded alive, she answered that that only happened in places that were too busy, or with slaughterhouse workers who didn't know what they were doing. "Those kind of places wouldn't even take reservations for two or three pigs," she said. That was "the industry." That was what she had built this farm to avoid. Both of her slaughterhouses were owner run by one man; in one case, the owner's son also helped out. She assured me that she had witnessed a swift death for all her animals. It was still hard, she said. Which is why she couldn't ever imagine driving Mary or Joseph in. Maybe if they were so old they could no longer stand up, it would feel different. "Then," she said, she knew they "would want to pay us back for all the love we had given them in their lives." Mary, she revealed at the end of our conversation, slept in bed with them until she was about fifty pounds. "She'd want to become a part of us forever." The only downside to using local slaughterhouses, Audrey maintained, was that neither of hers were licensed to cure bacon. She missed bacon, hadn't had it in five years. I mentioned how much Morningstar Farms Breakfast Strips tasted like bacon and she laughed. "That's exactly what I built this farm to avoid," she replied.

I left that day with two pounds of sausage, two pounds of pork chops, one pound of a very tart goat cheese, one dozen very weird-looking eggs in all different colors and sizes, six heirloom tomatoes, and a new perspective on life. I will admit that while I was grilling the sausage I felt very guilty. An animal had died for this—was it really going to be worth it? Even though I was pretty certain it had had a very happy and relatively long life, I worried that its death was too big of a moral burden, given that it had become, after all, "only" food. I sprinkled the crumbled goat cheese on top of the sliced tomatoes while the sausages sizzled. Even the cheese bothered me a little. Some poor goat had given her milk for this—was it really worth her sacrifice when tofu probably would have tasted just as good? I reminded myself that the doctor had said all the corn and soy was killing me, and so I sat down to the meal ready to bear my guilt in order to regain my health.

Imagine my surprise when my first bites proved to be some of the most pleasurable moments of my life. This food was fantastic. It tasted completely different from Morningstar Farms and the frozen, canned, processed fare I had been living on for the last year. The tomato was like nothing I had tasted before in my life, ever. The cheese burst with flavor. It felt as if my taste buds had been asleep for years and were suddenly coming alive. I joined Audrey in thanking that pig and that goat for their great gifts to my life. I understood myself to be in their debt. I vowed to myself right then that I would find ways in my life to pay back all animals for the gift of this great food.

Over the next year, I found other local farmers willing to sell me their food if I drove out to their places. Adam and Steve were raising mostly broiler hens along with rotation crops; their heirloom chickens produced smaller breasts and less meat, but I was learning in this world of local meat that a little really goes a long way. Steve, also a former vegan, told me that no one should eat more than four ounces of meat a day—about the size of the palm of your hand. The meat industry was so screwed up, he said; it produced all this factory-farmed meat and then had to get the public to buy it so they sold chicken breasts and steaks in ridiculous sizes. The portions are all messed up, he went on. Meat should be treated like a side dish, or maybe even a flavoring. Both Mark Bittman and Michael Pollan make this point in their writings, he said (and I knew my next stop had to be the library). It becomes bad for us when it's the main thing on the plate. I remembered back to a dinner I had with my brother a few years ago at Outback Steakhouse; Frank ordered some kind of steak that was literally hanging off the plate. It must have been two pounds. He ate it all, and then didn't have room for his baked potato or salad. I could see what Steve was driving at.

Speaking of steaks, I visited the farm of Mike and Nancy, who had a small herd of pasture-raised cows, about fifty at any given time. Although they had never been vegan, they did love animals, they said. Nancy in particular said she'd always wanted to be a rancher because of her love for animals. Their cows were all named and most were very tame. I spent an hour one afternoon listening to her talk about their stories. Hans just loved to be near Norma, but Norma really ignored him. Justin was scheduled to go to slaughter next and that was going to be very hard because he was a really good boy. Mike and Nancy only slaughtered another cow when all cuts of the last animal had been eaten or sold. The price of their meat was high and the steaks were cut small, so they didn't kill more than twenty cows a year, and that brought in enough money for them to make a decent living. They also sold composted manure. No cow died before it was four years old, and most lived much longer. (Justin was almost eight.) Mike and Nancy both took the cow in together, and they drove it to a very small slaughterhouse in Virginia because they really felt like the animals are treated better there than anywhere else. The slaughterhouse was three hours away, and it was a hard trip for them, she said, both going and coming home. They also had to make the trip again two weeks later to pick up the meat. But it was worth it. The man who owned it was very clean and very spiritual, she claimed. Back on the farm, their cows were never confined; they lived on about fifteen acres of grassland and were moved from pasture to pasture as they ate the grasses low. The cows on their farm stayed on their pasture from birth to death and never went to a feedlot to be "finished off" (i.e., fattened up quickly before slaughter). Their calves were weaned naturally; mothers were never "hooded" in order to take the babies away, and the babies stayed with the mothers as long as they wanted. No cow was ever fed corn or grain. Nancy claimed that feeding cattle corn all the time (an industry standard) would be like a human living on candy bars; you couldn't do it for long. "We want healthy, happy cows that don't need drugs," she said. "That only seems fair. We give them a good life out here in return for their meat. That's the right way to farm." She went on to say that keeping those creatures confined to a feedlot wasn't natural and would come back to haunt us. When I asked her if she ever felt bad about eating them, she answered, "If we didn't eat them, they wouldn't be here. Nobody's going to keep a cow for a pet; they're just too big. Eating them means they get to live here in this good life for at least a little while. Everything has to die sometime. It's better to have this life than no life at all."

Two women had recently quit their jobs and started their own cheese farm, so I headed there next. They had eleven cows pastured on about ten acres. They milked them by hand, twice a day, and made artisanal cheeses from that milk. The cows all had names and distinct personalities, and Patty and Fiona seemed to love them about the same way I loved my dogs. They had pictures of the cows in frames in their living room, and kitschy cow art that was kind of the counterpart to my kitschy dog art. If I knew myself to be a dog person, these were cow people. They'd only been in business one year and only had one female calf so far (whom they kept; she was their eleventh); their plan if they had a male was to sell him with a contract that stated he could not be slaughtered until he was at least five years old. Two counties over I found another herd of thirty dairy cows that were kept for milk and ice cream. This was a family-run business with three generations working on it today; they had a small store and ice-cream parlor attached to the barn that sold milk in returnable glass containers. These cows had about one hundred acres to roam but were milked twice a day by machine. They were lured into the milking barn with handfuls of corn.

Although my vegan readers must be appalled by these discoveries, I have to confess that as a result of eating these products, I started feeling better almost immediately. My headaches stopped, my need for insulin decreased steadily, and I lost weight. I started thinking about food less as an objective set of political rules and more as a highly subjective set of needs. As a result of our different histories, genetics, and overall orientation in the world, perhaps our different bodies need different kinds of nutrients to keep us healthy. My body just couldn't make do with highly processed fake food; I needed the kind of protein that came from animals.

An important caveat is necessary here. I recognize that I was the wrong kind of vegan, the kind who didn't do her homework about nutrition. I now know there are lots of ways of being a vegan and eating all that processed crap is a stupid way to do it. It's just another way American capitalism gets to sell us high-priced, poor-quality food to make lots of profit. However, in my researching of the issue at the turn of this century, I found very little information in animal-rights-based vegan literature that directly discussed nutrition or the need to avoid processed corn- and soy-based foods. Instead, many of those early vegan recipes called for specific processed soy-based meat replacements. I now know there are many vegans totally tuned in to nutrition and the revival of the small farm. But in the early part of the decade, I didn't encounter any vegans invested in sustainability; indeed, the animal rights folks I was friends with bought and endorsed the high-priced, low nutrition industrial agribusiness substitutes as wonderful alternatives to meat eating. Their goal was to remove all animal products from our diet, but nothing else.

I have come to believe we need a different and wider agenda, one that addresses human health right alongside animal welfare and conservation of the earth's resources. Simply being a vegan doesn't guarantee any of these other things. This journey into local farming convinced me that the question of meat is only one of many when it comes to ethical eating: nutrition, carbon footprint, environment, quality of life for animals, the distance food travels, portion size, care of the soil itself, and many other issues all need to be juggled as we sort through how to share this planet with other beings. I have become persuaded that it is acceptable to eat small quantities of meat and animal products, as long as I am absolutely certain the animals have been given good and relatively long lives. Indeed, the world is richer for the joy and pleasure of the farm animals I encountered here in North Carolina; they taught me that their lives are valuable and that being a part of their food chain is a good way to live.

To be fair, I'm sure that a large part of my physical transformation came from the fact that whatever farm I visited, I bought not only their meat, eggs, and dairy, but whatever in-season vegetables they were selling as well. Most of these farms weren't certified organic farms; the farmers said, apologetically, that certification was expensive and they just couldn't afford it or didn't see that it would be worth it in sales. Their customers trusted them, they said. Most of them didn't spray pesticides or herbicides, and none of them fed their animals any hormones or antibiotics; people could visit anytime and verify that for themselves. Organic certification, they said, was affordable only for really big operations, most of whom were monocultural. Nonetheless, the fruits and vegetables were very fresh and seasonal and tasted absolutely fabulous. When I did buy produce from the grocery store—even from our local Whole Foods—it didn't even compare in terms of flavor. The stuff available in the grocery store was usually picked before it ripened and was shipped sometimes halfway around the world. When it finally got to me, it had lost much of its flavor and nutritional value. The produce available in grocery stores was as different from the local seasonal fruits and vegetables as the factory-farmed meat was from the local free-range version. Why would anybody buy a flavorless tomato shipped in from Chile when the local one was exploding with sweetness? Why would anybody eat the meat of tortured animals pumped full of drugs when the real, local kind tasted so much better? Good questions.

How we went from eating fresh, seasonal, local food to eating unripe things frozen in cellophane and shot full of chemicals is an interesting and frightening story. When faced with the choice of a plate of local, seasonal, free-range food, or a plate of unripe, factory-farmed hormone- and pesticide-ridden food shipped in from all corners of the earth, almost all of us would choose the former; so why is it that we can't find the ingredients of the former meal in most of our grocery stores? As recently as the 1950s, almost everything we ate was produced locally, as long-distance shipping for most items was both impractical and expensive. But a series of related shifts changed all that: refrigeration and shipping, centralized sourcing, transformation to monoculture, use of chemicals and additives, and aggressive advertising have changed the way we eat. I recognize that my readers are more interested in animals than they are in plants, so I'll summarize these horticultural shifts quickly. They're important, though, because, as you'll see, virtually everything that happened to plants eventually and inevitably happened to animals. And the consequences for the animals themselves—both human and otherwise—have been cataclysmic.

Big Business, Monocultures, and the Demise of the Small Farm

It took awhile for the industrialized, mechanized, "Fordist" approach to the production of goods to reach the domain of food because most food does something that other commodities like cars and clothes do not: it spoils. Before deep freeze was invented, most meat and vegetables had to be purchased within five to ten days of harvest, which seriously prohibited inter- and transcontinental shipping. Canned and dry goods had been shipped across the country and even around the world for some time, but the cost of shipping fresh vegetables in ice trucks was, until relatively recently, too dear. Even as late as the 1960s, most things green either came from a can or a nearby county.

The changing demographics of postwar America and the invention of refrigerated trucks changed all that. Because families moved to larger houses in the suburbs and Dad drove into the city to work every day, more and more roads were built, gas prices dropped, and the infrastructure for a new trucking economy emerged. Over the second half of the twentieth century, the economy boomed and Americans began to drive farther and shop more. But buying bread from the baker, meat from the butcher, and fruits and vegetables from the greengrocer seemed terribly inefficient. Thus, the supermarket was born. Instead of a few, local, seasonal products, supermarket shoppers were gradually given a wider range of seasonless goods from which to choose. As freezing and shipping foods across the country became possible, and stabilizers and fillers were added to products to extend their shelf life, consumers had the luxury of buying more and more "fresh" products with shelf lives of weeks and even months. Vegetables and fruits were harvested long before they were actually ripe and shipped across the country to round out the supermarket's plentiful selection. By the end of the twentieth century, the small, locally owned grocery stores that sourced seasonal food from local farms had given way to the supermarket, which stocked virtually everything, whether it was in season or not.

To lure new customers away from their established relationships with the butcher, baker, and greengrocer, supermarkets had to offer a reliable inventory at cheaper prices. And to maximize their own profits, these food companies needed to buy the cheapest products they could find, from suppliers who could guarantee delivery in every season. Thus huge, mechanized farms that grew only one or two types of plant crops—but vast amounts of them—emerged. These new industrial monocultural farmers started buying up land to grow corn, soybeans, lettuce, tomatoes, wheat, and other products that fit well with mechanization. They brought in chemicals and machines to transform the soil. The small family farm that grew all kinds of foods went bankrupt because it could no longer compete. To give you some idea of the scale: most of the small farms I frequent locally are between 10 and 50 acres; the monocultural farms producing most of our food today are between 10,000 and 150,000 acres. These big farms grow only one or two crops, and everything from plowing, planting, watering, spraying, and harvesting is done by machine. One of my local farmers once called farming an art; she was talking about the fact that she had learned not to plant tomatoes too soon after strawberries in the same field, and that a lot of farming was about "understanding how crops related" and "imagining what the soil needs." For the folks who work 100,000 acres of only one product, farming isn't an art. It's more like running a factory.

In this new world of agribusiness, it doesn't matter how far away these big farms are from supermarkets; it's always cheaper to ship products across the country than to look for local alternatives. This makes sense if you think about it: Imagine how much quicker it is to place one order for corn from the guy who plants 100,000 acres of it than to contact the one hundred local farmers who may plant small cornfields as one of many different crops. The big guy is more reliable, he's probably going to give a much better price, and the uniformity and mechanized nature of his farm allows him to pretty much guarantee the delivery of his product—even if that delivery is half a world away. Thanks to the "locavore" movement, lots of people are becoming interested in how far food travels to get to our plates.[4] A flyer I picked up at our local farmers' market illustrated things perfectly. A local conservation group had drawn up a chart of how far the food at the market had traveled compared with the same produce in our local Whole Foods store: local strawberries, 25 miles; Whole Foods strawberries, 1,700; local asparagus, 17 miles; Whole Foods asparagus, 4,800 miles; local lettuce, 3 miles; Whole Foods lettuce, 2,700 miles. The group's point was to show that local food was leaving an infinitely lighter "carbon footprint" than the food imported from the West Coast and other continents.[5] I also couldn't help thinking about how much better the local stuff tasted.

Monoculture agribusiness is bad for the land, and not only because we have to use fossil fuels to ship it. Growing only one thing depletes the soil. Rotational farming that combines different mixtures of plants and animals and returns all necessary nutrients to the soil is impossible for the mechanized farmer: his tractor can pick either corn or tomatoes; it can't do both, especially not at the same time. But without diversity, chemicals need to be added to substitute for what other plants and animals would have contributed to the soil. Beginning in the 1950s, with the leftover chemicals from wartime, engineers started crafting pesticides, herbicides, and synthetic fertilizers from petroleum and other chemicals, and farmers started spraying their crops like maniacs. At first it seemed like a miracle. The bugs were gone, and plants absorbed the artificial nutrients as if they'd come from rich soil. But then people noticed that wildlife was disappearing. Rachel Carson published *Silent Spring* in 1962; in the book she documented the devastating impact of DDT on the environment, especially on birds. Farmers who used these chemicals started falling ill and dying.[6] And the land itself suffered even more.

By the end of the twentieth century, scientists started trying to solve the pesticide problem by genetically modifying the plants themselves to produce their own insect repellants. While they were in there tampering with the genes, the scientists who worked for the chemical companies also found ways to make the plants resistant to herbicides such as Monsanto's Roundup; fields can now be sprayed with herbicides that kill the weeds but leave the plants (the plants are resistant to the effects of Roundup).[7] Those scientists also rendered the plants sterile so that time-tested methods of saving the seeds from only the best plants for next year's planting are no longer possible. With the rise of these new genetically modified organisms (GMOs), one company produces the seed and all the chemicals needed to raise that seed into a crop. The farmer simply supplies the land and the labor. This is the state of agriculture the twenty-first century inherited.[8]

Consumers today buy these inferior-tasting, pesticide-enhanced, Roundup-ridden, genetically modified, unripe foods because we have been tampered with ourselves. While our grandparents knew you could only have fresh tomatoes in the summer, the industry tells us we need not settle for such old-fashioned limitations. We are told that we deserve whatever we want, whenever we want it. With the new monocultural agribusiness, we now can have fresh fruits and vegetables in the dead of winter. Nature itself has been overcome. Aggressive advertising campaigns reeducate us about food and teach us to crave not only variety and availability but also ease of preparation. Enter the era of processed foods. Easier than fresh food, which needs to be cooked, you can just pop processed food in the microwave; these products emerged on the shelves and in the refrigerated cases of our supermarkets just as our televisions told us these products were healthier, easier, better tasting, and consistently available.[9] We are so lucky, they tell us, because we now have choices about what we eat. And we don't even have to prepare it ourselves! Little by little, we relinquished flavor, freshness, quality, and nutrition in favor of more choices of faster food.[10]

But the amount of choice involved is often quite illusory. Think about the breakfast cereal aisle of the grocery store today compared to the half-dozen brands that were available in the 1960s. Are we really better off? Or think about strawberries to put on that cereal; we now can buy them in the supermarket every day of the year, but none of them tastes even remotely like the strawberries we get for eight weeks in the spring from the farmers market. Is this really progress?[11] And what about the fact that when in season, so many fruits and vegetables at my local farmers' market come in many different varieties. Last Saturday I bought seven different kinds of lettuce (they were all great). At the supermarkets, almost all variation within a certain type of fruit or vegetable has been lost; we get one type of tomato, one type of strawberry, one type of plum, one type of broccoli, and if we're at an upscale supermarket, maybe three or four kinds of greens. We are taught to believe that the supermarket offers us variety and choice, but does it really?

While some of these shifts are a result of lazy and uneducated consumers, the vast majority of the blame needs to be placed on transnational corporations and the U.S. government subsidies that support them. That's right. Our tax dollars keep these big guys thriving. While historically farm bills functioned to safeguard the local family farm (and our food supply) from natural disasters such as droughts, floods, outbreaks, and infestations, today agricultural subsidies go only to big corporations raising big crops of mostly corn and soy. Why? Not only are corn and soy the basic building blocks of most processed and fast foods, they also constitute the basic ingredient of another product Americans feel very passionate about: cheap meat. (More on meat in the next paragraph. Really, I'm almost finished with plants.) The farm bill today funnels millions of tax dollars into the pockets of corporations, and while Farm Aid and other groups try to raise awareness of the current crises, as a nation, we've lost interest in where our food comes from, which is exactly how the industry wants us to be. Under the guise of making sure that food is cheap enough for all Americans to afford, U.S. government and transnational corporations underwrite the future of monocultural agribusiness and processed food, and virtually ensure the demise of both our land and our health. All in the name of profit.[12]

Just because America's monocultural farms no longer use animals to fertilize the soil doesn't mean Americans have stopped wanting meat. Indeed, the reverse has actually happened. Since we started farming industrially, Americans want meat, we want more of it than ever, and we want it to be cheap. Historians tell us that in the 1960s, Americans on average ate five ounces of meat per day, usually all at one meal. Today, the general sentiment of many folks is that, whether breakfast, lunch, or dinner, it's not a meal without meat. By some estimates, we eat not three times the amount of meat we ate fifty years ago, but five times. And while the price of every single commodity in America has risen in the last fifty years, the price of hamburger and chicken has remained low in comparison to other goods. How can this be?

Meat is more plentiful and cheaper than ever because we've moved the animals off the farm and into sheds and feedlots called CAFOs or factory farms. These are the mechanized equivalent for animals of the Ford assembly line. Uniformity, automated care, and cheap ingredients are the norm. Animals are stacked and crowded and jammed and packed, tortured to the point of insanity; think of a thousand chickens in your bathroom and you begin to get the picture. These places are not natural for the animals, of course. Chickens packed in cages so tightly they can't even open their wings peck at each other, so we cut off their beaks without anesthesia. Hogs in close quarters chew on each other's tails and ears, so we cut those off without anesthesia as well. Even the most docile breeds cannibalize their infants in these conditions, so we take the babies away as soon as they're born. We pick the fastest-growing breeds and over-feed them so that they get fat faster; with no opportunity to exercise, the legs of pigs, chickens, turkeys, and even cows can't support their weight and break. They get no veterinary care at all, but because they will inevi-tably get sick from being packed so tightly, we feed them a constant and steady supply of prophylactic antibiotics to ward off disease. Still, the animals don't grow big enough fast enough to turn a quick profit, so we inject them with steroids and other growth hormones to make them hungry all the time. For protein, we feed them ground-up animal parts and blood from animals just like them. And though they are meant to eat grass or roots or bugs or seeds, what do we feed them to make them grow so fat so fast? You guessed it—corn and soy.[13]

The parallels between shifts in plant farming and those in animal farming are striking. Refrigeration and shipping allow meat that used to be available only locally to come from centrally sourced factory farms. The centralization encourages monocultural environments to emerge; im-porting (from outside the farm) cheap subsidized corn and soy is much more efficient than growing grass, roots, seeds, or grain. While agribusi-ness farms feed pesticides and herbicides to plants, CAFOs feed antibi-otics to animals to compensate for the loss of clean air and pasture space. While plants receive chemical fertilizers such as Miracle-Gro to supply nutrients, animal growth is enhanced by hormones and steroids. And once again, aggressive advertising manipulates us—the consumers—to believe not only that meat is the central part of any meal but that this CAFOed meat is no different from the free-range variety that comes from the old-fashioned farm. It's good for us, they tell us, and it's so cheap. Never mind that it's full of drugs and unmentionable waste products. We can even get bags of piping hot, prepared, tasty, meaty meals without getting out of our cars. But the animals that become this meat are not sitting on anybody's porch, they're not playing in the sun, they're not doing anything that could be counted as fulfilling or natural. They are miserable beasts who suffer unimaginably every minute of their short lives.

Enter the Locavore

People who resist these new models of both plant and animal agriculture—most of whom identify as locavores—are motivated by many different concerns. Let me say right off the bat that most local eaters and people who write about local eating don't see themselves as revolutionaries: Wendell Berry, Michael Pollan, Barbara Kingsolver, Brian Halweil. These are pretty mainstream folks who looked around and decided something was really wrong with the way we're eating in America today.[14] Their transformation was organic, not in the sense of no pesticides, but in the sense of arising naturally from oppressive social conditions. Like the millions upon millions of women who went out of the home to work in the 1970s and 1980s because they needed a better income for their families and only later became feminists, local eating emerges because everyday people are worried about their land, their communities, their health, and the lives of animals. The political impact of local eating is often noticed after the fact, or sometimes not at all. Invested in local eating for many different reasons, locavores are challenging the corporate powers regarding food in America today.

Some locavores are simply motivated by taste. While the rest of America has been duped into thinking the strawberries in the supermarket taste good, or the pale yellow yolk color of uniform white eggs is natural, those who eat locally know different. Distance and uniformity do not a good meal make. Even when it comes to meat, the color, texture, and taste of local products are very different from factory-farmed products. Some locavores are motivated by food safety. Remember the *E. coli* outbreak in spinach in 2006, or the salmonella scare of 2008? Those of us who eat locally didn't bat an eye. With most of the country's food coming from centralized sources far away, industrial growing has put consumers in a vulnerable position when it comes to food; locavores bypass this vulnerability. Many people eat locally to improve their own health. Knowing the farmer who produces your food is the best way to measure how much pesticide, herbicide, nitrogen fertilizer, antibiotics, hormones, genetic modifications, and other toxins you are actually ingesting (in most cases, none). Local food is food with a farmer's face on it. In terms of animals, eating local free-range meat also avoids the long-range, large-scale illnesses associated with factory-farmed meat (e.g., bird flu and mad cow disease). More and more research shows that these new contagions emerge from confining animals and feeding them an unnatural diet. Moreover, the contaminants in factory-farmed waste are health hazards. Local farming of both meat and plants can help us avoid food-based illnesses of all sorts.

Many locavores are concerned with the environmental sustainability in a number of different ways. First, shipping food across the country or the globe uses too much energy. In the face of global warming and climate change, we need to reduce our carbon footprint as much as possible. Second, when it comes to plant agriculture, monoculture is simply not sustainable because it causes too much erosion. Soil does not get what it needs from growing only a few plants supplemented with chemicals. Diversity is what makes soil rich. Third, in relation to animals, CAFO waste is causing unprecedented pollution. Annually, CAFOs in the United States produce six times as much urine and feces as all humans in the entire world. In eastern North Carolina, the hog waste lagoons are so toxic, residents within thirty miles are often forced to abandon their homes: local wildlife dies off, the smell is unbearable, the water undrinkable, their land becomes worthless, and the humans become refugees. As Wendell Berry aptly expressed it, "Once plants and animals were raised together on the same farm—which therefore neither produced unmanageable surpluses of manure, to be wasted and to pollute the water supply, nor depended on such quantities of commercial fertilizer. The genius of America farm experts is very well demonstrated here: they can take a solution and divide it neatly into two problems."[15] Locavores believe that eating locally can turn this mess around. We believe small farms enhance the look, feel, and sustainability of our communities.

Some locavores are interested in supporting our own community's economy. We think keeping most of our money in the community means keeping it out of the hands of the worst kinds of capitalists, those so removed from the process of production that they no longer have any connection to conscience. Many commentators claim that as few as ten corporations produce more than half the food consumed in America today, with about 140 people in those corporations deciding what will be served for dinner everywhere.[16] We believe our dollars shouldn't go to conglomerates but to folks in our counties and communities. Keeping our resources in our own area means we all benefit. Moreover, the best way to know what's in your food is to know the farmer who made it; give her a good living and she will give you a good product.

And last but not least, many locavores are committed to improving the world for animals. This gets articulated in many different ways. Some locavores—like the folks involved in the Slow Food movement—believe that the local farm is the best way to save heritage breed animals from extinction. The meat and dairy industry uses and refines farm animal breeds that are docile, easy to contain, and gain weight quickly and easily. In general, then, almost all industrial meat comes from three or four breeds of each chicken, cow, turkey, pig, and so on. The Food and Agriculture Organization of the United Nations estimates that fifty years ago, there were more than 7,600 different breeds of farm animals used for meat and dairy; today that number stands at fewer than 20. In fact, almost 2,000 breeds are now officially endangered, with an additional 350 fully extinct. Local farms are turning this around. By giving animals more room and a healthier lifestyle, they are bringing back many different breeds from the brink of extinction.[17]

It is here that we crash directly into one of the hardest questions concerning animals and morality: is it okay to kill animals for their meat? The local farmers from whom I buy my meat assure me their slaughterhouses are not those of corporate industries. There are no downer piles, no live animals left to bleed out or to be scalded to death. There is no suffering, they tell me. They stay with their beloved animals through this process, and death, although always sad, is swift. I choose to believe them. But even still, the question of whether it's ethical to kill animals for meat haunts me.

Killing Animals: Three Perspectives

Soon after the publication of Michael Pollan's *The Omnivore's Dilemma,* the alternative magazine *Satya* ran two full issues of articles commenting on the new phenomenon they called "Happy Meat"—meat from free-range, organic animals.[18] The essays are instructive because they address the question of "humane" meat from all existing ethical frameworks (the three positions I outlined in the introduction: rights, welfare, and utilitarianism) and offer different solutions depending on the methodology employed. Although the vast majority of animal rights literature that condemns the eating of factory-farmed meat simply overlooks local free-range alternatives, this is one of the few resources I could find that dealt with the question, "Is it ethical to eat meat from animals who are given good, healthy, and long lives?" To answer this question as fully as possible, I review the arguments presented by the rightists, welfarists, and utilitarians in *Satya.* I will then show how the stance I take expands on these existing methodologies. I believe a different understanding of animals—built on insights harvested from affective connection and a politicized concept of love—can supply us with a different kind of answer to the question of whether it can ever be ethical to kill animals for consumption.[19]

The critique of all meat, whether CAFOed or free-range, from the animal rights (in the strong sense) perspective is swift, strong, and totalizing. Articles by James LaVeck (one of the producers of the documentary *Peaceable Kingdom* and founding member of Tribe of Heart, an animal rights group), Eddie Lama and Gene Bauston (both affiliated with Farm Sanctuary), and about a dozen other animal rights activists work hard to discredit and disavow the idea that any meat can be obtained morally.[20] For them, animals have an inherent value, and the primary consequence of that value is the right not to be owned or killed by humans. From this perspective, it doesn't matter how well animals are treated or how long they live. Killing them is wrong. Period. Recall, here, that the model most animal rightists use when thinking about animal oppression is slavery. Reform is not enough, they say; only complete abolition is acceptable. Thus, the fact that local farm animals have better lives is certainly not justification for killing them. As Lama writes, "Animal rights' raison d'etre is not to put a seal of approval on better living conditions for the doomed or better methods of killing animals, but to advocate against killing them at all!"[21]

A central aspect of rightist criticisms revolves around the conviction that farmers cannot be trusted to act morally when profits are involved. These writers believe that "compassionate meat" is an oxymoron, that the killing of any healthy animal is in itself an act of such violence that it must always be wrong. In much the same way the corporate food industry duped us into thinking the processed food in our supermarkets is actually better than seasonal products, local animal farmers, in this view, are now duping the public into believing that killing and eating animals are actually in the best interest of the animal. For these theorists, the idea of killing an animal for its own good is ridiculous. From this perspective, farmers may mislead the public about living conditions in order to increase profits, they argue; moreover, the very act of killing fundamentally renders all meat immoral. As discussed in the introduction, the most radical animal rights activists would rather see endangered species and breeds become extinct than keep them alive by enslaving, killing, and eating them. The idea of compassionate or humane meat, for them, is simply a marketing ploy.

In these animal rights essays, there also seems to be a general mistrust of the consumer that manifests itself in a number of different ways. Some authors feel that advocating small-farm meat might trick people into thinking the meat they buy from a grocery store "might" be humane, or that all meat was really produced in such a pastoral setting. Others worried that vegans and vegetarians will start eating meat if, as one rightist put it, "the line is not vigilantly held."[22] That is, if animals are treated humanely, vegans and vegetarians might feel comfortable eating them. Wrapped up in this criticism of the consumer is the identity of the animal rights movement itself. Animal rights sees veganism as the litmus test for animal advocacy; it signifies the uncompromising moral high ground of the movement. How will rightists be able to tell who the true animal activists are if some of them start eating meat?

A second way of looking at killing animals for consumption can be found in the welfarist orientation, and perhaps the best example of animal welfare on this issue is Michael Pollan. Commensurate with animal welfare as I described it in the introduction, Pollan thinks that many benefits follow from treating food animals better. In *Satya* as well as his writings elsewhere, Pollan is critical of both factory-farmed meat and meat that meets legal standards of organic but still is raised in fairly industrial conditions. For his research for *The Omnivore's Dilemma*, Pollan visited the farm that produced an allegedly free-range chicken he had bought at his local Whole Foods store. The chickens on that farm, he discovered, were "free-range" only in the most legalistic sense. They were kept in sheds twenty-three and a half hours a day, and a small door was opened to give them access to a small yard each afternoon for about half an hour. Most of those chickens didn't even bother to go outside. Pollan concludes, much as I have here, that the only way to guarantee the animal's conditions is to see them for yourself. But Pollan's investment revolves not only or even primarily around animal welfare; he also worries about the environment, human health, and perhaps most important, flavor. As he told *Satya*, "There's a good business reason to treat animals better, it makes their meat a better quality."[23] The point is that welfarism here (and I argue in many cases) looks like a win-win situation for all; Pollan gets to have his steak and eat it, too.

Finally, the third perspective, utilitarianism, is also present in the *Satya* issues in an essay penned by Peter Singer (coauthored with Bruce Friedrich), and also later in an interview with Singer. According to Singer's calculations, the greatest good for the greatest number requires him to pronounce humane meat a step in the right direction. "Not only is it possible to work for liberation while supporting incremental change, such change is inevitable as we move toward this goal."[24] Unlike Pollan, Singer would never say that eating free-range meat was morally right, but rather that it is a better option than eating factory-farmed meat (because less suffering is involved). Also, he disagrees with Pollan on the question of corporations. For Singer, any movement away from suffering is to be supported, even incremental change at the corporate level. While Pollan distances himself from corporate compassionate meat based largely on flavor, Singer believes even corporations can take measures to assist the well-being of animals. His focus, in other words, is totally on the animals themselves. For him, change happens slowly.[25]

A More Nuanced Approach

I agree and disagree with segments of each of these frameworks. Right off the bat, I diverge from the rightists on many levels. While they want to assign to animals something they call "inherent value," humans are the ones assigning value, and this is then highly subjective. In the realm of the human, for example, we have a public rhetoric of "human rights," but as it's played out today there are lots of people in the world who don't really benefit from those rights.[26] Most humans also believe that we earn our so-called station in life and are assigned value based on our merit and contributions. In other words, to exist in the world today, most beings need to make some kind of contribution to justify their place in the world. Farm animals contribute their flesh and milk and eggs. An affectively based interpretation of farm animals, then, might look something like this: farm animals pay their dues in life with their products and flesh, but they would rather have lived and loved and played in the sun and the dirt and the rain, than not be born at all.

Eating the flesh of animals you've known and loved, or paying farmers higher prices to provide those animals with a good life, can be seen as a good deal for those animals. They would not have the joy of living if they didn't also make that sacrifice. The horror of factory farming moves farm animals indoors to intolerable lives, lives not worth living; but the movement toward veganism banishes them from the earth altogether. I believe farm animals need to live so that they and we can know the joys of pigs rutting in the mud on a hot summer day, cows chewing timothy grass on a hillside, and chickens pecking and clucking and enjoying earth's bounty and each other's company. Can't we see the possibility that some animals would rather have been alive for a while enjoying the grace of creation than not be born at all? Farm Sanctuary's Gene Bauston states in one of the *Satya* essays, "If we can promote a plant-based lifestyle, we will, at the end of the day, prevent enormous amounts of animal suffering."[27] We will also prevent enormous amounts of animal—and human—joy. Very few farms—if any—are going to keep these large animals as pets. The world will be a much sadder place without farm animals, just as sad as it would be if we have no dogs or cats or other kinds of companions. The animal rights activists who insist on veganism as the only moral strategy are only telling half the story. They're missing the joy, grace, and goodness farm animals bring to our communities. They're ignoring the fact that some farmers get it right by treating animals with love, care, and respect.

Animal rights literature often promotes veganism or vegetarianism as a major solution to the problems of pollution and climate change. A recent story in *VegNews*, for example, claimed, "Choosing vegetarianism lightens our environmental footprint because the less meat we eat, the less we contribute to worldwide air and water pollution, and water and land misuse."[28] Such sentiment appears frequently in animal rights literature, but it also often overlooks other crucial factors. First, the vegetarianism that *VegNews* promotes here says nothing about dairy and egg CAFOs, which pollute the environment right alongside meat-producing operations. Intensive farming of any animal degrades the soil, even if the animals are not killed for meat; diary and egg industries are patently harmful. Moreover, there is absolutely no evidence that a small number of animals used in rotational farming with crops on small farms produces any pollution at all; indeed allowing plants and animals to share land, soil, and water has been an established, sound farming practice for centuries. It is the CAFOs that are polluting our country, period; animals kept in small numbers on small farms are not the problem. Animal rights literature must be willing to concede this point and grant the validity of established farming methods. Indeed, by sanctioning a plant-only lifestyle, it seems to me that animal rightists are not only endorsing a world without animals, they are forcing farmers to use chemical fertilizers to replace manure for soil nutrition. This stands in direct opposition to what we need, namely, small self-sufficient farms. If small farms need to import nitrogen fertilizer and other forms of plant food, we essentially handicap the local farmer by forcing him to become dependent on chemicals. Such an approach is not sustainable.

The problem with the stance Pollan takes, and the welfarists' perspective in general, is not so much their outcome as their method. What they miss is that our individual love for certain animals makes the well-being of all animals paramount. We can't just care about animals when it's convenient or when it dovetails nicely with our own immediate interests. Having compassion toward animals is sometimes going to entail sacrifice on the part of humans. Put in concrete terms, I think those of us who eat meat ought to eat free-range meat even if the industry finds a way to make factory-farmed meat taste better. The shift I call for in this book asks that sacrifice go both ways: that humans make sacrifices to nurture the joy and well-being of other animals because it's wonderful to share the earth with them and not just because they taste better.

Finally, although I am drawn to the logic of Peter Singer's utilitarianism, I disagree with his position on corporations' ability to be truly humane. Utilitarianism can be cold, clinical, and sterile. In other words, it lacks heart. I think that's the case with Singer's evaluation of corporate ethics, both in the *Satya* issues as well as his recent book with Jim Mason, *The Way We Eat: Why Our Food Choices Matter.*[29] The question at hand is whether large corporations and "earth-friendly" grocery store chains like Whole Foods, Trader Joe's, and Wild Oats can source meat from free-range farmers, or whether their interest in the profit margin will inevitably force them to source from large agribusiness operations that cut corners to make money. Singer thinks any steps in the right direction, even steps taken by large corporations, are good. I have to disagree. In his *Moral Man and Immoral Society,* the ethicist Reinhold Niebuhr argued that most good, moral people act differently when confronted with large institutional structures that demand compromise. Niebuhr's insights hold relevance for today's world. It's not that I believe the farmers, transporters, buyers, boards, and CEOs of these new companies are evil people trying to trick us into buying falsely advertised products; it's more that the structure of corporate profit requires more conscience than any individual character in the corporation can demonstrate. The food that has moved through this corporate system has lost the image of the farmer's face. And I think, when it comes to something as important as animals, that loss is not tolerable.

The owners of these conglomerates know how to say the right things to keep us hoping, even going so far sometimes as putting actors made to look like family farmers into their ad campaigns. In a public exchange with Michael Pollan about whether Whole Foods could rise to the challenge of local eating, Whole Foods president John Mackey pledged ten million dollars to a national endeavor to get more local products into Whole Foods stores in 2007.[30] I've been watching my local Whole Foods pretty carefully and see very little change in where food comes from. Even when produce is in season in our area, we're still offered only strawberries and asparagus from Florida, the West Coast, or beyond. A quick check with some of my local farmers verified that it's still impossible for them to get their goods into Whole Foods markets, that the minimum amount Whole Foods will order is twenty, fifty, sometimes a hundred times higher than what my friends can supply. As it was with the new gleaming supermarkets twenty and thirty years ago, it's cheaper for Whole Foods and other new chains to work with a single supplier of one product—even when it's far away—than to deal with many and varied small farmers. And because Whole Foods is a for-profit corporation, it always comes down to the bottom line.

Not too long ago, my local Whole Foods had a huge banner outside the store announcing, "Local Organic Chicken Now Available." The banner showed a large photo of an older white man in a plaid shirt surrounded by blue sky and free-range white fluffy chickens. It also gave the farmer's name and small town, a place about ninety minutes from here. I drove over to the small town, and after asking directions at the gas station, was sent to the town's outskirts. I was hoping to find something that looked like Adam and Steve's place where I buy my local chicken now, chickens running all over, roosting on the porch, chasing bugs around. I felt sick to my stomach to drive up and see aluminum shed after aluminum shed, twenty-eight of them in all, each the size of a small gymnasium. There were no chickens outdoors. Maybe these chickens were let out half an hour each day, and maybe they weren't shot full of drugs and hormones. Maybe their advertising was, technically, true. But something about the place verified my belief that a corporation can't appropriately manage the kind of politics I am calling for in this book. Unless you can see the farmer's face, words like "free-range," "humane," "organic," and "pastured" seem to mean very little, at least the way things are now.[31]

I will leave it to you to decide whether a local co-op or even a small co-op chain can be trusted to source its food from the right kinds of farmers. Two counties over from Durham, they have a great co-op that gets virtually everything local, or if they do import things like coffee and wine, they do their homework and buy the best products for earth, human workers, human health, and animals. It's kind of like a farmer's market that's open six days a week! I hear from other friends about other co-ops and even restaurants across the country that serve only local food. Slowly but surely, we are all realizing that there's too much at stake to let these corporations control our food any longer.

It's not only that I trust the farmer over the corporation to give animals good lives, although that is definitely a part of it. I want to buy meat from farmers who understand the weightiness of their decision to grow animals for meat, farmers who name their animals and love them and feel bad taking their lives. When I talk to my farmers about slaughter, most of them do feel worried and unhappy about killing. Some of them kind of frown and nod their head, maybe shuffle their feet a little. Others take a stiff-upper-lip position and say things like, "Now I know they had a good life," or "Everybody's gotta eat and they understand that." There's nobody I buy meat from who is happy about the killing. They don't think it's wrong, exactly, just sometimes very sad. I think that's great, and it makes me feel good to buy from them. We should be confused about killing for meat; we should examine ourselves and our motives and eat meat for only good reasons—health and nutrition—and not because it's cheap or convenient or the industry tells us to. I really want to raise my own animals for meat one day, hopefully soon. I want to be able to look them in the eye and understand their life and death as a sacrifice. I want to understand my life as a sacrifice to them as well. My mother thinks I will not be able to eat anything I raise. We'll see, I tell her. If I can't do it, then I will stop eating meat. Until I can afford my own farm, I'm trusting Steve, Adam, Eliza, Henry, and all the other farmers I buy from to hold the severity of their decisions close to their hearts.

Strategies, Coalitions, and Common Denominators

A huge part of my own heart lies—or wants to, at least—with the animal rights people who want to speak uncompromisingly about animals. I really don't think it's a coincidence that the contemporary animal rights movement has grown up and flourished in the general environment of factory farming. Although it's true that animal rights is related to other contemporary social movements, such as civil rights, feminism, and gay and lesbian rights, I think it's unquestionably the case that a critical number of us would have emerged even if these other liberation movements hadn't happened simply because we just cannot abide what happens on factory farms.

But I believe that by staking its identity in veganism, the animal rights movement does a disservice to itself. There are millions of people who reject the hell on earth of the factory farming (and industrial agriculture in general), and animal rights needs to embrace all these fellow travelers. Our common enemy is the way capitalism invades every aspect of the integrity of contemporary life. In relation to food, I say let's shut it down. Through legislation and consumer movements and farmers' markets, let's send a message that we will not support a world where animals are treated badly, or where the food we eat poisons our bodies. Let's tell the world that we believe we owe animals a good life in return for their sacrifice, and we will gladly pay whatever the price to have meat that comes from animals that, while alive, knew joy, happiness, love, and peace. Additionally, we will no longer accept the processed soy and corn products that are advertised in our glossy vegetarian magazines. We, like our animals, need good food and happy lives, and capitalism cannot and will not colonize this aspect of our being. As consumers and citizens, we have the power to change this situation.

If animal advocacy is going to become a mass movement that creates a change of heart in the general population, it has to find a way to be more tolerant of difference. And I think the locavore movement is a good place to start. Whether you justify it by the terms of utilitarianism—as Peter Singer does—or by the cultural terms that I lay out here, the eating of certain kinds of meat (in much smaller quantities) should be seen as acceptable. Monocultural farming is the story seekers of change should be attending to, I believe; rather than focusing attention on whether a diet contains any animal products, those hoping to build a better world for animals would do better to think about where their food comes from more generally. Veganism is a radical lifestyle change that most of society will never embrace. It's too much like the kind of lesbian separatism that circulated in the 1970s, a radical ideology that felt the world would be a better place without any men in it at all. Animal rights advocates feel the world will be a better place without any farm animals, and that's just wrong, I think. Lesbian separatism had to learn to have conversations with others in order to stay alive. And in those conversations we changed. Black feminists, black lesbians in particular, told us they weren't living in a world without men, that their sons and fathers and brothers mattered, and that black men occupied a different social position than white men did. Then AIDS came along and the gay men who once seemed to be part of the enemy became our brothers. Gay and lesbian centers popped up all over the country, sometimes in the very same location where "women only" spaces existed only a few years earlier. Things changed. We moved forward in the world, but only when we were open to change. The same is true for animal advocacy, I believe. The animal advocacy movement is stuck, or at least it's lagging far behind where it could be. Locavores and others fighting corporate farming know that it's going to take a huge effort on the part of consumers to break the highly consolidated market of industrial food. If animal rights joined this effort and embraced this movement, we stand the chance of shutting down industrial farming and factory farms, and returning the country to a healthier world for both humans and animals.

We need a strategy that allows us to continue living good, healthy lives with animals. Think about the fact that there are no sustainable ecosystems on the planet that do not contain animals as part of the food chain. Animals are absolutely essential for agricultural sustainability; if you don't have animals on farms, you must import synthetic fertilizers (and possible herbicides and pesticides as well). This is not to argue that everyone has to eat eggs or milk, or that we need meat and dairy in the quantities that we're used to eating in the United States. It is to say that making membership in a social movement solely contingent on a plant-based diet is shortsighted; some people need some amount of animal protein to thrive, and if they are very careful about where that comes from—careful to ensure the animals have a long and happy and healthy life—in my book they can be counted as animal advocates.

The other problem with mandatory veganism is that it lets people off the hook for all the other ways we oppress animals. Many vegans act as if they are guilt-free of any animal abuse. They are not. None of us are. All of us are responsible for every animal suffering in a shelter or zoo or lab. There are many vegans, granted, who care about all animal issues, and I honor them. But the vast majority of the literature coming out of organizations like PETA and Vegan Outreach claims that all you need to do is stop consuming animal products and everything will be fine. It won't. Veganism is at once too much and not enough; what we need is something much deeper and broader. We need a shift in our affect that reorients us to honor and connect with all animal life. I think a lot of animal lovers can and would get on board with this ideology if animal rights orthodoxy would accept the fact that people might want to eat eggs from free-range chickens, milk from pastured cows, and if they want to occasionally, meat from animals that have had a really good life.

In his book *Meat Market*, Erik Marcus suggests that animal advocates would do well to reduce attention to both health and environmental concerns. I understand that he is so passionate about farm animal reform that he doesn't want anything to water down the animal agenda. But drawing connections between these issues and building coalitions is absolutely essential to every social movement. Denouncing people who are doing the right thing for what Marcus perceives are the wrong reasons is self-defeating. Animal advocacy has to widen its scope to see the bigger picture, especially in relation to farming. In a sense, I am asking the animal rights movement to practice a different kind of compassion when it comes to food: compassion for those of us who love animals but still need some animal products in our diets to sustain our own health; compassion for those of us who drive the extra fifty miles a week and pay the higher prices to eat the milk and eggs and meat of animals that have had a good life; compassion for the farm animals themselves, whose joy has all but vanished from our countrysides. I am not asking vegan animal advocates to start eating meat or drinking milk, but rather simply to recognize that some of us are consuming these products with a sense of ethics.

In keeping with convictions that language and stories can change the shape of the world, the first place to start, I think, is with our words. The signifiers "vegan," "vegetarian," and "meat eater" do not function to capture and proliferate the shift that is already happening. Our language needs to catch up with this reality. We need words that make distinctions between the kind of flesh we eat, and the kind of eggs and dairy we eat. Such a signifier could function to educate people that there are ways of eating dairy and meat morally. The word locavore is the first step in this direction.

Eating Animals

Currently, the debate about meat eating among animal advocates takes place as if all meat eating were similar. I believe that whether your sausage came from factory-farmed pigs or free-range pigs matters. It matters a lot. There has to be a linguistic way of distinguishing these practices. We need more refined language that captures and creates a world of compassion. We need language to do the work of reflecting these complexities. As long as animal rights activists insist that veganism is the only moral choice, the limelight is kept off the possibility that there is a third option of eating locally sourced meat. That's good for the corporations because they don't want people to start buying locally; that would take away from their market share and eat into their profit margin. Folks who are vegetarian but consume commercially produced eggs and dairy don't get the whole story, don't understand the right story. They think all dairy and eggs are the same. And because animal rights tells them all meat is murder, they think all meat is the same. They then consume dairy and eggs from CAFOed sources while passing up free-range meat from small farms. This makes no sense to me.

A lot of readers will view the idea of getting most of our food and all of our meat, dairy, and eggs from local family farms as quaint and interesting, but ultimately not doable. One major criticism is that meat from local farms costs more than factory-farmed meat available at the grocery store. Sometimes the cost can even be triple or even higher. Americans aren't going to spend that kind of money on something as insignificant as food. After all, you're thinking, we're only going to eat it, it's not like it has any lasting value. There's no reason to invest extra money in something that's just going to disappear.

Right here is where we need the biggest change in affect of all. The concept of affect roots our emotions and desires in our corporeal bodies; affect tells us that our sense of self, our feelings, sensations, and sentiments, the way we inhabit and perform in the world, are all based very loosely in our fleshly existence. From this perspective, food doesn't just "disappear." It becomes who we are. The idea that what we eat is not important and shouldn't cost too much money is fantastically absurd; it demonstrates just how much we've all been brainwashed when it comes to food.

What we eat matters, once again, for three reasons: environment, health, and animal advocacy. The cheap meat and vegetables we eat are a large part of the force that is destroying our earth. If we destroy the earth's capability to produce food, people in the future will not be able to eat; that is what "sustainability" means. The way we're farming now, there will not be any topsoil or fertile ground left for our children or grandchildren. This has to change. In terms of our own human health, think of it like this for a minute: Scientists tell us that every cell in our body is fully replaced every seven years. Those new cells are made with something and that something is the food we eat. Talk about not disappearing; food becomes us. We truly are what we eat. And a healthy seasonal diet not full of corn or soy or antibiotics or hormones or unpronounceable ingredients pays off. In seven years you could have a whole new body built with the wholesome goodness of local food!

Most important, we need a shift in our affect concerning the worth of farm animals. Here I turn to a woman I know named Carol. Carol works full-time as a secretary; she is raising two children and three grandchildren on her income. She cleans houses at night for extra money. With six mouths to feed, every dollar counts—a lot. But nearly every week I see her at the market buying pricey meat. She once told me that she used to get her meat at Costco or Walmart; she would buy it in bulk and her family ate it a lot. Then, she said, she started thinking about the millions of chickens and cows and pigs in these big stores; in a sense, she simply didn't want to be responsible for them not having a good life. "I don't know," she said with a fairly thick Southern accent. "When I saw meat in the regular small grocery store, it didn't bother me. But one day at Costco I was about to buy a bag of something like forty chicken breasts for some ridiculously low price, like twenty-five dollars. These birds have to be worth more than seventy-five cents each. Something is really wrong here. If it only costs seventy-five cents to make this bird—and some of that is profit—that bird must have had a rotten, miserable life. That's when I decided I wanted to eat less meat but without the guilt." Carol had the kind of softening of heart we all need to have with regard to meat and money. We share this world with many other creatures, and if we're going to eat them, we better make sure they had a good life first. No matter how much that costs.

Many people wonder if local farmers can really produce enough local, free-range, pastured meat to serve our nation's current rates of consumption. These folks argue that we can't all start eating local meat, even if we could all afford it; there simply wouldn't be enough to go around. These critics are absolutely correct in their thinking. We cannot sustain current rates of consumption, and that is why reducing our meat intake is a critical aspect of the locavore movement, and of animal advocacy in general. Even many farmers will try to convince you to do more with less. Different people have different ways of thinking about reducing meat consumption. Michael Pollan encourages us to think of meat as a flavoring, or at most, an occasional side dish. Mark Bittman's strategy is to be vegan before 6:00 p.m. and also to cook several dinner dishes per week that are vegetarian. I used to be one of those people who thought it wasn't a meal without meat; once I found local meat and shifted away from veganism, I couldn't get enough of it, and for several months had meat at almost every meal. But after a while, I found it easy to eliminate the sausage and bacon from breakfast, and a few months after that found it just too time-consuming to cook meat for lunch. For several years, though, I still had meat or dairy at almost every dinner. But as I became exposed to more and more vegetables and grains, and to great vegetarian recipes, things inside me began to shift. I remember one day specifically when I made a new casserole recipe that was really complicated with quinoa and butter beans and lots of grilled yellow peppers and garlic; I said to myself, "Man, that smells good. Now, what meat should I add?" Right then, the phone rang, I got involved in some discussion, and the casserole was done. It wasn't even a decision not to add meat, I just didn't have the time. But as I sat down to eat that wonderful dish, I realized I didn't even need or want the meat that I might have otherwise cooked mindlessly. It all clicked; my idea that it wasn't dinner without meat shifted dramatically at that moment. I still eat local meat, but now once or at most twice a week. I enjoy it more than I did before, but it's no longer something that has to be there to constitute a meal. Now, I find it easy to prepare a fabulous dinner without it.

I have cut my meat consumption by about 75 percent in the past five years. Local eating requires most of us to do something fairly similar, but we can do it at our own pace. There's no pressure to achieve a certain reduction by a certain date, but rather a process of being more connected to food, a process that enables all of us to enjoy the bounties of the earth more mindfully. Reducing meat consumption is critical if we want the supply to be available for everyone in our communities, but we can do it in lots of different ways. Vegetarian meals, smaller cuts of meat, stretching ground meat into several dishes, experimenting with unpopular cuts of meat—these practices are part of what it means to enter the world of local food. We cannot sustain current rates of consumption, but we don't have to give it up entirely. Eating less allows us to eat it with greater awareness.

I also imagine a kind of skepticism about the question of convenience. Vegans, vegetarians, and omnivores alike, we live in a fast-paced world in which we can't always spend time on food. Who in his right mind is going to drive fifty miles to get ground beef when he can get an already cooked hamburger without getting out of the car? Or a fully processed soy burger from the freezer without leaving the house? Getting food from a small farm is like going backward in time, you're thinking. It's not going to happen, you're saying; we've made too much progress to go back. One of the central convictions of this book is that our culture today has made a lot of mistakes, and many of them have been made around food. As I said in the introduction, progress does not always mean going forward. If we're on a dead-end road, progress actually entails going backward, finding our mistakes, and correcting them. I believe that we are at such a dead end with our food, and that we need to go back and find out where we made our mistakes and start over. This necessarily means going back to the small local farm. I believe we can resist the heartlessness of late capitalism by renewing our commitment to good food and to our food animals. It's not that hard. Change is possible. Look into the eyes of a cow, or a sweet pig like Mary or Joseph, and there I believe you will find the message that it's not *that* we eat them but *how* we treat them that makes all the difference in the world.

FOUR WHERE THE WILD THINGS OUGHT TO BE

Sanctuaries, Zoos, and Exotic Pets

THROUGHOUT THIS BOOK, I HAVE ARGUED THAT ANI-mal advocacy can and should be expanded to embrace affective realms. In some ways, as I've suggested, practices are already emerging today that can be seen as examples or illustrations of this new orientation. These include the recent rise in money and time spent with companion animals, as well as the movement to return animals to free-range living on small farms. I have argued that the intense power of love for other animals, whether dog or pig or cat or cow, can be used to expand our ethical thinking about animals. Using the way we feel about certain animals, the way we care for them, identify with them, and love them, will not only enhance our principled deliberation, it can also function to pull more people into the animal advocacy movement. Understanding ourselves as subjects constructed by affect and stories gives us new tools to make a better world for animals.

But so far, the only animals I've discussed have been domesticated. What would it mean to move this thesis beyond pets and farm animals into the domain of so-called wildlife? What could it mean to love wild animals? While our passions may be shaped by the stories and films that teach us about them, what kinds of attitudes, policies, and treatments best serve real, existing wild animals? While many animal rights advocates believe that wild animals are happy only when they are free, many professional animal behaviorists argue that certain animals can flourish in the captivity of established and accredited zoos. (And increasingly, some species may only be able to live in captivity because of the destruction of their habitats.) Can animals really be happy in captivity? And if so, are there any other places in addition to zoos that can provide these animals with a good enough life?

To better answer these questions, I spent six months exploring the lives of captive wild animals in North Carolina. By visiting accredited zoos, private owners who keep wild animals as pets, and many different kinds of animal sanctuaries, I was able to get a better sense of what it means to keep a wild animal in captivity. Over those six months, I met wolves and wolf hybrids, tigers, lions, servals, caracals, bobcats, bears, small primates, and a variety of other wild animals in settings such as public zoos, urban people's living rooms, huge well-funded rural animal compounds, and private menageries in suburban backyards. As a result of my travels, I also started volunteering at one local big-cat sanctuary, and, at the time of this writing, have spent about thirty hours with specific big cats in that facility.

While I am not an ethologist or animal behaviorist, I want to put forth a controversial thesis that extends the argument of this book into the realm of wild animals: that some animals are generally better off when they are enmeshed with and connected to humans who work with them, advocate for their well-being, and love them. By this I do not mean that every species on earth can or should be domesticated or brought into human care. Nor do I think animals that live in cages are happy just because they are alive. Rather, what I do mean by this proposal is this: given the shrinking space of the undeveloped "wild" world, those animals that can learn to live in connection with humans may have the best chance for survival. In other words, I will suggest that in contradistinction to both the animal rightists' claim that wild animals should exist only in the wild, and the professional zookeepers' claim that captive wild animals should only be kept in zoos, many so-called wild animals can flourish, be happy, and be safe in a wide variety of settings. The human species is overtaking the earth at an astounding rate. Pragmatically speaking, then, those animals that stand the best chance for long-term survival are those that can develop some rudimentary bonds of relationship with us. My hope is that all animals, including wild ones, can become their own advocates through the personal experiences humans share with them.

My experiences of one particular weekend helped me crystallize this thesis regarding wild animals more clearly. I spent most of the day Saturday at our state's zoo, a 535-acre facility in the heart of North Carolina; it is the largest walk-through natural habitat zoo in the nation and also one of the top-ten progressive zoos (i.e., zoos that use a great deal of natural habitat in their enclosures). That day I watched and filmed three lions (one male and two females) for about four hours. Despite the fact that they had a lot of room—probably around five acres—and what seemed like a fairly natural habitat, they barely moved all afternoon; they simply slept in the sun the entire time I watched them. In looking at the video afterward, I saw that roughly once an hour they would get up, stretch, and switch positions. About three dozen people came by to observe them before quickly moving on; the animals did not have names and very few people stopped to read the informational board describing their natural habitat and location in the wild. While the lions were clearly not miserably tortured or starving, they seemed rather lethargic and unengaged.

The next day, Sunday, I went to my volunteer job at a local big-cat sanctuary, a privately funded ten-acre facility that houses about forty lions, tigers, and other big cats. My newbie volunteer status did not allow me direct contact with the animals, so I spent my time emptying trash and shoveling gravel. That afternoon, six young lions caged together in about a half-acre pen were throwing donated pumpkins around like volleyballs. They were clearly playing; it didn't look that different from the way dogs at a dog park play. Right in the middle of what appeared to be a game something like "keep away," an older human man and woman walked over a hill and started calling out: "Henry!" "Mathilda!" "Where are you?" In response to these human voices, two of the lions in the pen started to spin, jump, and roar. The noise was deafening. The humans went right up to the fence and started feeding those two lions raw chicken legs on a stick; the lions munched them like popcorn. When the chicken was all gone, the woman pulled two very large pillows—they looked like dog beds—out of a garbage bag she was carrying and hurled them over the fence. The lions each took one and paraded around with it in its mouth. The couple spent about an hour talking to them and taking pictures of them while I shoveled gravel. I caught up to them as they were leaving.

Their names were Martha and Bob, and they were retirees who had been volunteering at the facility for three years. They loved animals and had each "adopted" one of the lions. No, they were not hoping to ever take the lions home, but they came to the sanctuary as often as possible to spend time with, as they call them, "their kids." They made them toys and bought them presents. They had pictures of them all over their house. Bob adopted Henry three years before, when he and Martha first started volunteering, because "the bond was immediate."[1] He found his relationship with Henry so fulfilling that he "gave" Martha Mathilda last year for their fiftieth wedding anniversary. His hope was that Henry and Mathilda would bond for life like he and Martha had. The annual donation of two thousand dollars was going toward building them a new pen, which was actually what I was shoveling gravel for. Where they were now, Bob said, was just too crowded. They were working toward building the kind of relationship with the lions that would allow them to actually go inside the enclosure with them once they were moved. Staff would always have to accompany them, but everyone felt hopeful that Henry and Mathilda had the kind of temperaments that would allow human interaction and contact. Bob came out to visit Henry almost every day. Martha came less frequently but sewed toys and blankets for them almost every week. She often used old clothes because they contained the human smell the animals liked, she said. They had no children but couldn't love these lions any more than they did. They were their family, they said. They had planned their estate so that these two would have a secure life here forever. And they planned to bring each lion a turkey for Christmas, and if they could find one, a deer carcass as well.

Although this account is clearly anecdotal, the difference in behavior between the animals in these two settings was striking. In a world where undeveloped lands are rapidly disappearing and species are becoming endangered at alarming rates, is our only or even our best option really zoos, with their long histories steeped in conquest and colonialism? Could a new model of wildlife captivity be emerging in the privately run sanctuary, a model founded not primarily on putting animals on display but on developing relationships with them? What would it take to ensure the well-being of these animals in such settings? Clearly, private ownership guarantees neither bonded connection nor adequate care. But I do believe such settings can provide good lives for these animals. This is not an abstract question. Here in North Carolina, for instance, legislation has been introduced that if passed, will close down all of the private owners and sanctuaries (perhaps except one) in which I conducted my research. Companion bills S.B. 1477 and H.B. 1614 (Inherently Dangerous Animals) will outlaw the ownership of wolves, lions, tigers, cougars, bears, monkeys, apes, elephants, crocodiles, alligators, rhinoceroses, hippopotamuses, hyenas, and many other exotic animals.[2] The legislation is aimed at private owners only and excludes circuses, university research labs, some sanctuaries (if they don't breed, sell, adopt, or make any money off the animals), production companies that use them for movie or television work, and zoos accredited by the American Zoo and Aquarium Association. North Carolina is one of only nine states that don't ban or regulate the use of nonnative exotic pets, although some towns and counties have their own ordinances. While it may come as a shock to some readers that people would choose these kinds of animals as pets, the keeping of exotics is a widespread practice. No one knows exactly how many exotics there are in the state, but several people I spoke with suggested, for example, that there are more wolves and tigers kept as pets in North Carolina than exist in the wild worldwide. The proposed ban will restrict individuals from purchasing, breeding, or trading for any new exotics; it allows current owners to grandfather in their existing animals only if they procure two million dollars' liability insurance on their animals (a cost that would be prohibitive to every owner I interviewed in every setting). The insurance would be mandatory even if the owners didn't show their animals to the public.[3]

Proponents claim that the proposed legislation comes about as a result of the mauling in 2003 of a young boy by his aunt's pet tiger in eastern North Carolina. The keeping of such animals in private settings, they claim, is unnatural because they are wild animals. But there's a bitter dispute over how much of a public safety threat exotic animals truly pose. Opponents of the bill come to the statewide meetings with fact sheets stating that more people are killed by horses, cattle, bees, deer, and dogs each year in our state than tigers or any other exotic pets. They also claim that animals contained in zoos are more likely to harm the public than those in private settings because private owners are held to a stricter set of regulations, and that animals in the wild are more likely than any to harm humans, livestock, and pets. Defenders of the bill scoff at these claims and appeal to what seems to them to be the self-evident truth that wild animals do not belong in people's homes or backyards. These meetings are often tense sessions in which the danger of these animals to the public is only one point of contention, and both sides believe they are doing the right thing for the animals. Each believes the other puts profits and politics ahead of the well-being of animals. Fights break out in parking lots after the meetings, with animal rights activists in Patagonia jackets, slogan T-shirts, and vegan shoes on one side, and exotic pet owners in fur-trimmed jackets and leather boots on the other.

It has been said that politics makes strange bedfellows and nowhere is that more apparent than Senate Bill 1477 and House Bill 1614, which are cosponsored by the Animal Protection Institute (API) and the Association of Zoos and Aquariums. The two organizations back the bill for very different reasons. The API, a strong animal rights abolitionist group based in California, actively campaigns to end all livestock farming and use of animals in scientific research.[4] A strong national animal rights lobbyist group, it strives toward complete abolition of human use of animals in every setting. For API members, all animals should be set free, and this bill shuts down at least part of the so-called enslavement. I spoke with a representative of API at a recent animal rights convention and asked her why API sanctioned keeping animals in professional zoos but not in smaller facilities. She answered that API didn't sanction keeping animals enslaved in any setting, and that this bill was just a first step. She also stated that she thought animals under private care probably had worse lives than those in zoos.

The other backer of this legislation, the Association of Zoos and Aquariums (AZA), is the national zookeepers guild.[5] Membership in this organization entails a large annual fee, and member facilities are inspected at least once every five years. At state meetings, AZA spokespeople claim that their training in animal behavior and conservation efforts makes them uniquely able to care for captive wildlife. One can't help but notice, however, that the passage of this legislation effectively eliminates most of their competition. In terms of mammals, for example, only two facilities in North Carolina are AZA members.[6] These two AZA members will be the only facilities in the state that can continue to breed, hold, and exhibit mammalian wildlife if this bill passes.

The bill also includes an exemption for a very narrowly defined "sanctuary." The legislation's definition of sanctuary would not include most or perhaps any of the sanctuaries I visited; in terms of this bill, a sanctuary must have 501(c)(3) (nonprofit) status; it may not sell, trade, give away, or adopt out animals, offspring, or body parts; it may not breed or propagate animals (that is, all animals must be sterilized, even if they are threatened or endangered in the wild); it does not allow direct contact between the public and animals. Facilities cannot make money from exhibiting the animals and must belong to either the Global Federation of Animal Sanctuaries (formerly The Association of Sanctuaries, or TAOS) or the American Sanctuary Association (ASA). Not one of the sanctuaries I visited meets these criteria; indeed, according to the ASA website, there is not one approved sanctuary in the state of North Carolina. One big-cat facility I visited did say that it had ceased all breeding and applied for membership in TAOS in anticipation of the passage of this bill; my tour guide privately told me she thought the facility would be denied because of the ten-dollar admission fee it charged the public to visit the tigers.

While this bill is specific to North Carolina, similar bills have been proposed in many other states, and the questions such legislation raises are relevant to people in all states and jurisdictions. While similar concrete conflicts over who gets to keep wild animals in captivity and in what conditions have emerged in Texas, Florida, Nevada, and California in recent years (a few of which I will address later), the larger question of how we live with wild animals plays out virtually everywhere. I use this bill as an example, then, to study the range of spaces wild animals currently occupy and to imagine the kinds of spaces we might be able to share with them in the future.

Wildlife today exists in four different zones or spaces: the wild, zoos, private homes, and (variously defined) sanctuaries. Each of these locations is organized, constituted, and authorized by a competing ideology about what kind of being a wild animal is and where he or she belongs. What follows more thoroughly examines the ideologies, principles, and beliefs embedded in each of these spaces. There are two questions that loom large: first, are the animals themselves happy; do they seem to lead fulfilled lives (and, if so, how do we measure that)? Also, because so much of the argument against owning wild animals rests on the idea that it is dangerous to hold them captive, I also ask questions about human safety. Thus, I set out to ask for each venue, "Are they happy?" and "Are we safe?"

Zone One: The Wild

Americans are in love with the idea of the wild. From Thoreau to the Western cowboy movies, from Teddy Roosevelt to the Sierra Club, from Christopher McCandless to Timothy Treadwell, we love the sense of danger and adventure going "into the wild" gives us. The wild is simultaneously hard and rough and unspeakably beautiful, and learning to live by nature's laws appeals to our romantic notions about human character. Nowhere is this romance more apparent than in our love for the wilderness and wild animals. Professional zookeepers call those wild animals that everyone wants to see "charismatic megafauna"; lions, wolves, bears, elephants, tigers, eagles, and great apes have taken central roles in the stories we've told for millennia. We love watching them in the wild, both in real life and on film, because they seem to represent all that is good about the earth.[7] In certain ways, these animals symbolize the beauty of the landscape itself. The untamed ways of the wild call us, and the animals that live in harmony with nature become examples for us of how we might achieve such harmony as well. When we think about animals as symbols and metaphors of the wild landscape, it feels wrong to capture, imprison, or forcibly breed them; they are tortured in confinement and their offspring often become pale imitations of the majesty of their ancestors.[8] In this light, we can only love them properly if they remain in the wild.

The problem is, of course, that undeveloped wild lands are shrinking rapidly. While our stories may teach us to love the wild, our development is destroying it. We should fight this destruction, of course, and work to protect native habitat for all animals all over the planet. But it is becoming increasingly clear that we cannot win this battle in time to save many species, especially ones that need a lot of room. Conservation efforts for large and particularly for dangerous animals are failing; many wild spaces are located in impoverished and underdeveloped countries, exactly the places human population is exploding. Asking poor people to live next to dangerous animals so that wealthier Westerners can observe the animals on ecotourist vacations is ethically troubling.[9] It's also not working. Poaching is on the rise everywhere. The answer to our guiding questions "are they happy?" and "are we safe?" may both be answered negatively in the frame of current rates of habitat loss. The coyotes who are wandering into suburban neighborhoods here in the United States aren't happy; they've lost their homes and food sources and are seeking shelter too close to humans. Our pets and children aren't safe when these animals enter our territory looking for food. The same is true on a bigger scale for tigers in India or lions in Africa. The ways that humans are currently expanding our control of the earth virtually ensures the suffering of specific animals, the eventual doom of many species, and the great possibility of harm to ourselves as we force them out of their habitats.

The best way to help wild animals is by protecting their habitats, of course.[10] But despite conservationists pouring millions of dollars into protecting animals in their natural dwelling spaces, the number of species on the planet is in rapid decline. In addition to human encroachment on habitat, pollution and climate change also are exacting a steep toll. Our relationship to wild animals has changed in the last generation; while we always ate them, skinned them, studied them, and displaced them, we now also surround them. Conservation strategies are becoming more difficult as scientists must now take into account the effects of climate change, especially flooding, temperature fluctuations, and drought—in other words, animals may not want to stay in the land we protect for them. These problems are not going to be solved in time to save many species from extinction. Conservationists respond to statements such as mine with the claim that if all the money that were spent on keeping animals in captivity went to preservation of wildlife refuges, the situation may not be so hopeless. While I am sympathetic to this position, it's hard to raise funds for protecting land in faraway places; humans long to at least be able to see the animals their money supports and perhaps even interact with them. That's why zoos and sanctuaries are so popular; it's not just that we want to know the animals are alive somewhere, we want to see them and possibly connect with them as well.

So much of our thinking about wild animals is rooted in the belief that wild animals are better off without human contact or management. But the time when animals can inhabit the earth free of the involvement of humanity is rapidly ending. At the beginning of the twenty-first century, this planet belongs to humanity; there is no turning back from that reality. We have inherited the earth and its animals and must now figure out how to manage both better. Dreams of setting the animals free are impractical. Suggesting that some animals should exist in this romanticized notion of the wild forces those animals into the increasingly shrinking space that is not occupied by human culture. Especially as the human population increases, demanding that wild animals stay only in the wild is shortsighted and unrealistic. Animal advocacy demands that we find ways of sharing the planet with them, and part of that mandate means figuring out how to provide them with what they need to lead full lives in captivity.

Put differently, I believe we must challenge our thinking about the essential differences between "domesticated" and "wild." What happens if we question the perceived reality that domesticated animals differ in kind from wild ones? If language shapes and constructs reality, then perhaps it is not the genes or ontology of animals themselves that makes them "wild," but the way human language organizes the world for them. We have erected these categories of "wild" and "domestic" to better manage our world, but perhaps they do not point to a hardwired reality. Perhaps these are broad categories with many exceptions. Perhaps nature is much more complex than our ability to organize it.[11]

What would happen for animals if the human distinction between "domesticated" and "wild" could be remapped? There are already many spaces where these categories break down: house cats left on their own for three years almost always become "feral" (i.e., wild); their offspring are almost always wild. Most of these feral cats cannot be tamed or reintroduced back into homes. Dogs running in packs for long periods of time are said to revert to the wild; while some of them can be redomesticated once they're brought into training, not all can. Conversely, some of the animals we keep in our homes might actually be something closer to wild: some birds, rats, snakes, and mice, for instance. In these examples, it's the cage or the size of the animal that allows us to contain them without harm to ourselves, not the fact that they are truly tamed or domesticated.

I believe the time has come for us to rethink these classifications for the sake of the animals themselves. I am not suggesting that animals currently living successfully in the wild should be captured and brought into captivity. Rather I am suggesting the possibility that some of our most charismatic megafauna can lead happy lives in captivity. I believe that domestication is not hardwired by species (dogs and wolves, after all, are exactly the same species), but rather is something like a contract we make or can make with individual animals. Relationships with animals—even so-called wild animals—are about reciprocal care. Am I, the human, getting enough out of this relationship to keep you and live with you in the way that you want to be kept and kept happy? Are you, the animal, getting enough out of this life I provide for you here not to run away when given the chance or to bite, attack, or maul me to get that chance? If animals can actually think, feel and relate, I believe they can also do something that is very close to making deals with humans. We often call such deals "training," and although we recognize that almost any animal can be trained, we continue to argue that the wild ones cannot be tamed or domesticated.[12] This is not to say that ten thousand years of selecting for tameness and submission haven't influenced the disposition and temperament of a given species: it's a lot easier to live with a beagle than a wolf. It is to say, however, that these histories do not guarantee the genetic outcome, character, or disposition of all animals; put most simply, that is, not all beagles are "domesticated" and not all wolves are "wild." My underlying argument here is that wildness and tameness are slippery, nebulous categories that overlap and tell us only the broadest genetic history of a given animal.

For a long time we thought humans did all the work in changing wild wolves into domesticated dogs. Early humans, the story went, robbed dens of wolf pups and raised those infants to live with humans. Little by little, we selected for traits like submission, bite inhibition, size, and color, and eventually ended up with dogs. New research in the fossil record has caused Raymond Coppinger and Lorna Coppinger to develop a competing thesis: it was in the character and best interest of some wolves to allow themselves to be tamed.[13] As scavengers, wolves lived on the margins of human society, and the bravest wolves that would come closest to humans got the best food; those wolves who eventually moved in with humans virtually decided to sacrifice their wild nature for the food and protection offered by the human pack. The domestication of the dog was really a two-way street; it wasn't just that humans claimed a specific animal for their own. It was also the animal that claimed the human right back. Why isn't such a two-way street of taming possible with other kinds of animals, especially if and when they do have the character it takes to live well with humans?

In Judy Irving and Mark Bittner's excellent 2005 documentary film *The Wild Parrots of Telegraph Hill*, we were introduced to Mingus, a wild parrot who truly wants to be tamed. Even when given freedom, he wants to come inside and live with humans. I am suggesting that given the current rate of wild land degradation, it may come to pass that the only animals that will survive will be the ones that *want* to be tamed, the ones who *want* to live with humans.[14] The predominant view that the wild is always better needs to be reconsidered. What if there are animals of every species and breed that would prefer living with humans to a harsh life in the wild, fighting humans for water, clean air, and territory? How would this change our thinking about the necessity of the wild?

Zone Two: Zoos

Almost everyone agrees that the history of zoos is a troubled one. Zoos are products of colonialism; as far back as the ancient world, people in positions of power maintained menageries of animals brought back to them from conquest of foreign lands. Thus, zoos have a long history as symbols of power; zoo animals for centuries were like jewels for the wealthy.[15] Public zoos emerged first in 1828 in London, and most were located in the middle of growing cities, so urban dwellers could get to them easily. Exotic animals from faraway continents were put on display for the viewing pleasure of the middle classes; they were entertaining and signified the conquest of new lands and empires. But most urban public zoos were horrible places for animals. These concrete prisons remained the dominant form of animal keeping for 150 years.[16]

In the past thirty years, however, new ideologies have emerged addressing concerns of animal welfare. As a result of various forms of animal advocacy, new "progressive zoo" ideology emerged claiming that zoos should be less interested in representing colonization and more concerned with benevolent themes such as education and conservation. The debate about zoos now centers on whether these progressive zoos are in fact a new and acceptable form of wild animal keeping, or whether they are simply a dressed-up version of the colonizing, concrete prison model.[17]

Promoters of progressive zoos argue that viewing live animals on display fosters a greater sense of compassion toward those animals. Indeed, many zookeepers enter their profession prompted by their love for animals and concern for their welfare. They argue that being kept in captivity does not harm all animals and that many of them live longer and healthier lives in a zoo than they would in the wild.[18] Put simply, in their view, for most animals, captivity is not equivalent to slavery and it can be better than life in the wild. These theorists note that the wild is not an unrestricted zone of freedom; all sorts of factors—limited food, predators, human encroachment, illness, and disease—hamper animals in the wild. If given the choice, most humans would choose to live in the safety of a home with adequate food, shelter from inclement weather, access to health care, and other benefits; why wouldn't animals make those same choices? Whereas zoos of the past may have been concrete prisons, they no longer need to be, these zookeepers claim. They suggest that zoos provide animals with decent lives, and in return the animals provide humans with close encounters with wild animals. Especially in a utilitarian framework, the deal is one that many animal advocates think animals would readily agree to if they could.[19]

Most animal rights advocates in the strong sense argue that even progressive zoos are unsatisfactory because the primary point of zoos is to satisfy zoogoers' curiosity about exotic animals; that is, zoos are not designed for animals but for humans to view animals. Indeed, they point out that because so many zoos are still located in cities, managing the animals in natural habitat, especially during off-hours, is difficult. Thus, they note that in many locations, much of the habitat shift is cosmetic only or animals only occupy natural areas when humans view them; when the zoo is closed, they are confined to cages. Often they are separated from plants, trees, and other landscape architecture by wires; thus this natural habitat is there for us, not them.[20]

Zoo advocates believe zoo animals provide the public with education and an understanding of the need for conservation. Wild animals inspire people, especially children, to care about other creatures and their environment; zoos raise awareness about conservation and the plight of endangered species, they suggest. Some zoos actually do breed endangered animals for reintroduction to the wild (although that's a really hard thing to do and most reintroduction of captive-bred animals fails).[21] Many zoos breed endangered wildlife for maintenance of captive stock, and for purposes of general biodiversity. Zookeepers believe the public wants to view wild animals in real life, and providing people with the opportunity to do so enhances human appreciation of animals. The Association of Zoos and Aquariums (AZA) is quick to point out that more people visit zoos and aquariums each year than attend all professional sporting events combined;[22] providing that much pleasure to that many people, these advocates claim, is certainly a good thing.

Critics of zoos disagree. Many animal rights advocates and even some conservationists argue that what zoos teach is not a love of animals but rather the acceptance of the human domination of nature. There is no question that zoos do raise some money for conservation, but the amount of money is minuscule compared to private grants, nongovernmental organization fund-raising, and corporate donations. Conservationists note that keeping endangered wildlife alive in zoos is not really addressing the needs of wild ecosystems. When zoos breed endangered species, the plan is rarely to reintroduce the offspring back into the wild, they suggest. Breeding captive animals to be released is very difficult; most animals born in captivity are not sufficiently afraid of humans to be reintroduced. The kind of space needed to teach them how to hunt and live on their own is rarely available in a zoo setting. Moreover, the kind of individuals that live and breed best in a zoo are usually the most docile or even the laziest members of the species; the kind of individual that will fare best in the wild is the most independent and ferocious. Finally, the conditions that prompted the initial endangerment or extinction usually persist (such as habitat loss, pollution, human encroachment). Releasing new animals to the same grim fate is not the answer. Zoos are fond of seeing themselves as modern-day arks—but many critics note that for most zoos, there is no plan to get the animals off, no end point where they are restored to fullness. They are born to remain in this liminal space where they enjoy neither the freedom of the wild nor the pleasure of companionship. Even the most progressive zoos breed primarily to preserve their collections.

Zoos, moreover, are increasingly functioning like corporations.[23] That is, in the United States, more and more public institutions (like public zoos) are being privatized; with public money being withdrawn from health care, social services, emergency services, education, and even the military, zoos rank low in allocation of taxpayer dollars. During the eight years of the George W. Bush presidency, our government ceased funding what we think of as basic American infrastructure and started outsourcing these enterprises to private companies. Academics call this trend late capitalism or disaster capitalism and argue that such practices are increasing the gap between rich and poor. I don't suggest here that privatizing every aspect of our lives is a good or acceptable thing at all. It's not and we need to resist it. But if state and federal governments aren't going to fund social services or emergency management, they are not going to fund zoos. In zoos today, many exhibits are closed; gift shops and fast-food vendors are everywhere, and many nonanimal "pay as you go" exhibits (such as carnival rides or short movies) now occupy spaces where animals once were.

I suggest it might be the case that even the most progressive zoos may be inheriting a corporate model that places profit above animal welfare. Even when professional zookeepers want to do right by the animals, they are working in a climate of increased pressure to become self-sufficient. The irony is that while many of the concrete prisons of old were partially or largely funded by public moneys, the increasing privatization of all zoos worldwide has introduced commercial goals that often compromise the well-being of the animals. Many zoos since the 1980s have had some or all public support withdrawn from their budgets and thus are forced to make up the difference themselves. The corporatization of zoos means that a shrinking number of dollars goes to animal care and a growing amount to marketing, development, and communications. Even though most AZA-approved zoos are nonprofit establishments, the bottom line for most is clearly financial. In the world of late capitalism and increasing privatization, financial solvency emerges as the primary measure of success for many zoos. It's hard to keep your eye on animal happiness with increased managerial pressure to make and save money.

Even if most workers have the animals' best interests at heart, zoos turn out to be less than thriving zones for most animals. The AZA is not a government agency; it is a private group accrediting zoos that have met certain standards and have enough money to pay the membership fees. Corruption abounds: the animals that are displayed in most zoos are usually all young and healthy and able-bodied; that's what the public wants to see, that's what sells the most tickets. Sick, weak, old, and disabled animals are often off-loaded to other locations. Some make it to sanctuaries, some are simply euthanized, but many end up in the exotic animal trade, an underground network that moves unwanted animals to a variety of settings. No public records are kept on these transfers.[24] The fear of many animal advocates is that most of these animals end up as prey for canned hunts.[25] The bottom line is that a zoo, like any other corporate structure, can't really sustain those who can't or won't carry their own financial weight.

Moreover, in an environment where profit is a central objective, reintroduction of endangered species into the wild is not only extremely difficult, it is also counterproductive. As both advocates and critics suggest, people frequent zoos because they want to see exotic animals. There is little financial motivation to release these creatures to the wild where they will be much more difficult to watch.

Are they happy? Are we safe? Determining whether zoo animals are happy is a difficult task. Most visits to zoos reveal no outrageous behaviors such as self-mutilation or obsessive behaviors such as spinning or pacing, but how can we be certain that animals who engage in those behaviors weren't taken off display or removed entirely? But are we humans safe? As I conducted research for this chapter, a tiger escaped her enclosure at the San Francisco Zoo, killed one zoogoer, and mauled two others. In light of this event, it doesn't seem fair to suggest that zoos are patently safe for humans; indeed, after this tiger escaped, many people argued that dangerous animals should not be held captive at all.

What is at stake with such an argument, I suggest, is the future of many species on earth today. Do we really want to be the generation that ushers in the total eradication of many species from our world? Can't we find or create a better way of sharing the planet with them?

While one strategy for improving the conditions of captive wildlife is to call for increased public funding of accredited zoos, we should also explore other settings and arrangements for captive wild animals. Both private owners and broadly defined sanctuaries (which might also be described as roadside zoos or menageries) currently hold many more wild animals than the AZA-accredited zoos here in North Carolina. In both of these zones, the keeping of the animals is funded through private money (private owners own and care for their exotics as "pets," and broadly defined sanctuaries fund their endeavors usually through donations and various formulations of adoption and sponsorship). But if the motivation behind keeping wild animals in zoos is to educate, what do private owners and sanctuaries think they're doing? And what is the effectiveness of those motivations? And of course, our perennial questions: Are these animals happy? Are we safe?

Zone Three: Private Owners

The driveway up to the house was long and narrow, but paved. I was about thirty-five miles north of Durham on my first exotic pet visit, and I must have expected a run-down double-wide trailer with junk cars on the front lawn, because I was quite shocked to see a house that could have been found in any upscale suburb in America. The property was rural and wooded; the house was a fancy split-level brick, probably built in the 1950s and very well maintained. It was both large and charming, with hanging plants and wind chimes hovering over a beautifully groomed landscape. From the outside, you wouldn't think by looking at it that a tiger lived inside.

Sally met me on the front stoop. A thin wiry woman who could have been anywhere from forty to sixty years old, dressed in tie-dye and jeans, she was deeply tanned (even though it was the middle of December) and had blond streaks in her hair. She wore loads of silver jewelry that looked like it never came off. At first, I thought she might be from California, but the minute she opened her mouth it was clear she was a Southerner, born and raised. Inside the house, I was surprised at how nice her furniture was and how clean everything was. (It looked a lot better than my house does with six-plus dogs and three cats.) I thought the tiger must be outside only, but Sally then pointed to a double-sized futon on a frame in the corner and told me that was Charles's bed. We sat and talked for about half an hour before I met the animal.

I learned about Sally and three other local private exotic owners through three different listservs on the Internet, and also through a bi-weekly publication called *Animal Finders Guide*. One listserv and the AFG are largely devoted to buying and selling exotics, the other two to discussing particular problems people were having with their animals. I sent e-mails or called over a hundred folks living in North Carolina to see whether they would be willing to talk with me about why they owned exotics, any trouble they had gotten into with either the animals or the law, what they thought about the new proposed Inherently Dangerous Animals bill, and mostly asking if I could meet them and their pets. Seventeen people answered my queries. Several immediately explained that theirs is a fairly tight community of exotic owners, many of whom had been burned by the press and were reticent to allow journalists into their lives. I cajoled and begged and tried to explain that I wasn't writing a journalistic exposé but rather a scholarly chapter that tried to think about what, if anything, humans owed to wild animals. Most were happy to e-mail with me, but all except four refused to have me visit. My impressions and thoughts about these exotic owners were formed through these conversations and visits.

Sally told me that she had grown up with tigers and that tigers especially were a true Southern tradition. Although they weren't for everyone, they made great pets, she claimed. They were much smarter than dogs and could really communicate with humans. Charles was three years old and was the fourth tiger she'd lived with by herself. Other humans drove her crazy, but having a tiger around was better than having a husband, she said. Charles was big and beautiful and could protect her better than any man. Her other tigers had all lived to be at least fifteen years old and one had lived to be almost twenty. She thought that was longer than they lived in the wild anywhere. Charles did not receive vet care as it was illegal for her to take him off her premises (that required a special permit, which she did not have). They were very healthy creatures, she told me, and they didn't need what she called "heroic" vet care like most dogs and domesticated cats. A vet tech came out every few years to give him his rabies and other vaccines, and otherwise she just doctored him herself. He ate meat, lots of it, and Sally spent a significant amount of time combing country highways for roadkill. She also bought downed cows and pigs for him at the slaughterhouse. Owning a tiger, she laughed, meant that you had to spend a lot of your time handling meat. She got Charles from a breeder in eastern North Carolina and felt there was no problem with inbreeding among the tiger population. It's only when you got into the white tigers or the "crazy monster crosses" like ligers that genetic problems appeared, she said. For a regular old tiger, the captive gene pool was very healthy. Charles cost three hundred dollars in 2004, and she brought out his "cub book" to show me what he looked like when he was an infant. He now weighed about four hundred pounds.

North Carolina law prohibits the public from touching privately owned tigers directly, and she didn't have insurance anyway, so I could meet him but would have to stay on the deck. He had never ever been aggressive to humans, but as she put it, why risk it? (I agreed wholeheartedly.) We went through a very nice kitchen (with two full-size freezers of meat for Charles) to the backyard.

The scene was kind of unbelievable. Her yard was maybe an acre surrounded by a fence that was about six-foot welded wire (with another foot on top caving inward so Charles couldn't climb out). There in the middle of the yard atop a huge Great Dane–size doghouse was a tiger sleeping in the sun. He was really big and I wondered whether he could actually fit in the doghouse. I sat on an Adirondack chair on her deck and watched Sally enter the pen and proceed to play with Charles as if he were a big dog. He fetched a ball for a few minutes; then she got him to do some tricks (sit, stay, down, jump on his house and sit, roll over); then she sat down on the ground and just petted him, which he clearly loved. We talked through the fence. All cats needed to be trained not to hurt humans, she said. She showed me his enormous paws, which looked like dinner plates with claws the size of jumbo shrimp. They learned pretty quickly to keep their hands and claws away from you, Sally said. You had to use a lot of positive reinforcement when they were young, and some negative training if they were slow learners. I asked about the negative training. Squirt bottles were her favorite tool, she said, but she did have a shock collar to help guide the tiger if he needed it. "You have to think of it like this," she said. "When they're little, like six to eight weeks, they're this helpless ball that bonds to you and just wants to please you and make you happy. During that time, you have to establish the fact that the human is the boss. If you miss that lesson when they're young, you can't ever really make them into a safe pet." I was to hear such ideas about training over and over. What Sally seemed to be saying was that she sort of tricked the animal into not recognizing his own size and power by establishing dominance when he had neither. When the tiger got big, bigger than human size, it simply didn't understand that it had the power to kill us.

Sally said that Charles's biggest danger to humans was actually his size. If he rolled over on her during play, he could crush her (she weighed maybe 150). Her last cat was a smaller female who only weighed 200 pounds. That cat, Esmeralda, slept with Sally, but Charles had to sleep in his own bed because of how big he was. Charles spent most of every day outside, unless it rained or snowed and then he was in the house. She exercised him every day by having him run around the perimeter of the pen for at least forty-five minutes. He did not get exercised on rainy days.

Watching Charles lean over Sally to get his belly rubbed, it occurred to me that no one could interpret this as animal abuse. He was majestic and powerful, and under her caress, he became so docile, it was almost as if they were lovers. Indeed, the overriding thought I had watching them was that these two creatures loved each other, and shutting that kind of love down would surely diminish both the human and the non-human animal. Yes, maybe Charles was a little bored a large part of the day; he didn't have to hunt for his food or protect his area. But how many dogs are left home alone all day to snooze and dream their ancestors' dreams of hunting rabbits? And how great is the joy when their owners return home to love and play with them? What kind of world would it be without such deep bonds?

After a few photos, we returned to the house, where I asked Sally about the proposed legislation. I got, as we say in the South, an earful. Animals were personal property, she stated baldly, and she blanketly opposed all legislation that restricted the private ownership or use of animals. She went on with a diatribe about how individual humans had rights to do whatever they wanted to animals. They were property, she said over and over. I was taken aback. The words she used now seemed to have nothing to do with the way she petted and talked to the creature outside, and I couldn't help feeling that she had adopted this language about ownership because she thought it would defend her from having to move to another state or worse, give up Charles. I left feeling somewhat confused about the disconnect between the human-animal relationship on the one hand and the "owners' rights" justification for it on the other.

The next weekend, my first visit was to a woman who bred and sold servals and savannahs. Servals are small cats (about forty-five to sixty pounds) native to Africa, and savannahs are the hybrid product of the domestic cat and the serval. They are smaller, weighing maybe twenty pounds, but the best ones have the leopardlike wild coat of the serval. Nancy, a perky woman in her midthirties dressed casually in J. Crew–type clothing, ran a business, and although the cats were all tamed and appeared well loved, none were allowed in her house. Her cats were all out back in a very clean cattery, with an outdoor pen that had a wire mesh roof to ensure no escapes. Nancy's breeding stock consisted of four female servals and maybe a dozen or so male domesticated cats (most of them were large and looked like Maine coon cats to me). I would classify Nancy's house as more suburban than rural; you could see the neighbors' houses on either side of her and there was much less wooded area than at Sally's. Nancy had a husband who worked and three kids, all in school; the cats were just her hobby. Once in a while she bred serval to serval, she said, but the market there was limited. The big market, she said, was in savannahs, and Nancy couldn't keep up with the demand. Her kittens could sell for a thousand to five thousand dollars, and well-marked ones, she said, could occasionally bring fifteen thousand dollars. Everyone wanted a savannah because they were easy to keep and small but still had a wild look, she explained. She shipped her kittens all over the East Coast, where they lived successfully in homes as well as apartments. She apparently didn't know about the rule that the public couldn't interact with exotics because cats climbed all over me the entire duration of my visit. Some of them were about the size of some of my smaller dogs, and it was interesting to see how outgoing and loving they were. I never once feared that any of them would attack me. Although I did feel a bit uncomfortable about the intentional breeding of these animals when so many cats were dying in local shelters due to lack of homes, it wasn't any different from the concerns I had visiting reputable dog breeders. In the end, I concluded that these animals were being born into a world where they most likely would be surrounded by care and love.

The next day I visited a family who owned a wolf and a wolf hybrid. Chuck, the father, was the primary enthusiast, although all four family members loved "the dogs," as he called them. Chuck lived in the most urban setting of the four sites I visited; his house was large with lots of light. The wolves, Sasha and Pansy, had a large fenced backyard and full access to the house. The whole family met me, but mom and teenage sons left soon after my arrival, so I really only got to see the wolves interact with Chuck. They did seem very much like regular dogs, I noted. They are regular dogs, Chuck explained. Dogs and wolves are not different species, he said, but wolves do have a greater protein need than dogs. As a result, Chuck's wolves ate a raw meat diet of BARF (biologically appropriate raw food), which although very costly, was, Chuck said, the only kind of food wolves really could live on. Sasha was bought from a breeder in Oklahoma who was well known for breeding very tame pets. Sasha was 100 percent wolf. Pansy was her daughter, bred to their friend's purebred golden retriever. While Sasha did look pretty wolflike, Pansy definitely had some golden in her; she kind of looked like a yellow German shepherd. Both dogs got regular vet care and were licensed and registered with the local wolf registry along with animal control. Chuck said they were hoping one day to breed Pansy with a male wolf; the offspring then would be 75 percent wolf, which would make them, as he described it, "high content." Both wolves were eager to meet me and smelled my legs and feet for sniffs of my dogs, but quickly settled down (they were very well mannered). They slept on L. L. Bean dog beds in strips of sunlight while we talked.

Chuck was part Lumbee Indian, he stated, and keeping wolves felt like a sacred act to him. He loved Pansy but really wanted high-content wolves because they had a special spirit about them. When I asked him if living with wolves was like living with dogs, he answered, "I kept dogs all my life. They were all OK. Wolves are a lot more work, but they give a lot more back." Chuck said that playing with and walking and feeding wolves opened up a spiritual channel for him. He felt he was walking the same path of his ancestors by having them around. He kept apologizing for "how hard it was to explain," but he said he was in balance when the wolves were around, that they protected him against evil, and that living with wolves was part of his heritage. They were a lot of work, he said repeatedly. They would get into everything if you left them alone too long, and you had to constantly work to soothe their aggression and territorialism. But it was work he liked to do. Chuck said he spent at least twenty hours of every day with the wolves (he worked from home) and about four hours a day playing and working with them in the yard, focusing directly on them. He wasn't interested in obedience training or any other "tricks," he just wanted to watch their eyes and have them watch his; they ran and fetched and wrestled and did whatever, nothing in particular but just quality time spent together. If the Inherently Dangerous Animals bill passed, Chuck would either have to rehome the wolves, buy insurance for them (which he thought would cost about seven hundred dollars a month), or euthanize them. He didn't think any of these choices were viable options and was angry about being put in the situation. He said he felt it was his religious right to own the wolves, that they were part of his native heritage and the core of his spiritual life. In his words, living with them "kept him walking straight."

Driving home from that visit, it occurred to me that private ownership of exotic animals, when it's done well as in the case of Sally, Chuck, and maybe even Nancy, operates on a different model of confinement than zoos. Where good zoos try to make up for the loss of wild spaces by reconditioning zoo environments (i.e., importing "natural habitat"), private owners seek to redress the loss of the wild by taming their animals, or trying to tame them. Instead of running free in the wild, Charles and Sasha and Pansy, and maybe to a lesser degree Nancy's cats, get human connection. They get to be enmeshed in the everyday life of a human family, they get to feel love and care, they get to be tamed. Their animals are not museum pieces like zoo animals; they are in a sense subjects, not objects. If we are going to take them out of the wild, perhaps we owe them something more than making them into objects? For animals who constitutionally feel comfortable striking a bargain to share space and connection with humans, a good home like Chuck's or Sally's can easily be thought of as a better life than being displayed in a zoo.

I am not arguing that anyone can own a tiger or a wolf or any other exotic animal, but rather that the best places in captivity for tigers and wolves may not be zoos. Granted, some zoos have great zookeepers and handlers who do care deeply about their animals and have special relationships with them, but that is not guaranteed. Having a degree in biology or zoology does not determine how well you are able to connect with or even care for the animals. Moreover, in zoo settings, it's often not the handler making decisions about the welfare of an animal but corporate managers who have profit as their bottom line.

Which is interesting. In the state legislative meetings discussing the bill and all the newspaper and e-mail publicity concerning it, criticisms about financial incentives or "money being more important than animal welfare" were almost always marshaled against private owners and never against zoos themselves. Before visiting and e-mailing private owners, I heard over and over that people only owned exotics to make money off them. The impression that was projected was that most exotic pet owners were uneducated, working-class people; they were the kind of people who believed that owning snakes or tigers or wolves would impress or intimidate other people. They were the kind of people who charged neighborhood kids five dollars to have their picture taken with a wolf or ten dollars to pet the tiger; the kind of people who couldn't really afford pets at all, let alone exotic ones. That was the feeling I had about exotic owners before I started visiting them. Despite the fact that zoos are run as corporate businesses that must produce a certain amount of profit to remain afloat, I started this research thinking private owners were the only ones in it for the money.

From the animals I was visiting and the people I communicated with, I was beginning to believe that the opposite might actually be true. Granted, Nancy did make money selling her kittens, but you could see that the cattery cost a lot to build and maintain, and that the sale of the kittens probably just about covered upkeep on the establishment. She was not making a living off those cats. And the tiger and wolves cost a lot of money, probably more than I could afford. I was beginning to realize that people who owned these animals successfully had to have pretty good incomes. Moreover, the folks I was meeting not only had the money to buy the food and fencing and toys and beds and care those animals required, they were also fairly educated and had done a great deal of reading and thinking about what their animals needed to be happy. These people didn't own the animals to make money; they were involved with the animals because they loved them.

Two things were becoming clear to me as I thought about my interactions with exotic owners and my own preconceived notions about them. First, exotics cost a lot of money and most of the people who own exotics have a great deal of disposable income to spend on them. And second, I wouldn't have believed that fact before I started this research. Before, I thought I knew that the keeping of exotics was a lower-class phenomenon; I thought Sally and others would live in trailers and shacks. Where did I get that impression? And why? Perhaps it was simply zookeepers and animal rights propaganda, and I unwittingly got sucked in? When I started this research, why did I believe exotic owners were less than legitimate? And was it really the case that the reverse could be true?

These were the questions that occupied my thinking as I went on my last visit. Joanie and Bill had devoted their lives to big cats and big-cat rescue. I could tell by their presence on e-mail lists and at legislative meetings that they weren't just owners, they were advocates and leaders in the local exotic community. A sign posted at the end of their driveway alerted me to the fact that this was a different setup: "Caution Regulated Animals on Premises. Enter at your Own Risk!" The area was very wooded; the dirt roads had handmade signs, and the road up to their place was long and hard to follow. I worried that if I made the wrong turn, I wouldn't be able to turn my van around in such a narrow space. But I didn't make any wrong turns, and I finally found the small but nice contemporary house with active solar panels and floor-to-ceiling windows. Bill came out to greet me and walk me around the back.

I knew from e-mailing with Joanie beforehand that these folks didn't just have one or two, but eight medium-size cats: two lynxes, two bobcats, two caracals, one panther, and one serval. What was unique about them, though, wasn't exactly the number of animals they had but the fact that only one of theirs came to them as a kitten; all the rest had been rescued from other owners, which meant they were to one degree or another fairly damaged and needed rehabilitation. Most of the cats did not have proper training as kittens; they missed that lesson where they were tricked into thinking humans had all the power and size. These animals were the homeless, unwanted ones, the equivalent of my much beloved shelter dogs.

We went right to the cats who were outside in separate pens. Bill explained that they were at different stages of being trained and different stages of being tamed. He didn't trust any of them (except the one lynx they had raised from a kitten; he was in the house) enough to let them interact with the public. That was fine by me. All the cats were born in captivity, Bill told me. The market in exotics across the country was so big no one ever needed to trap wild animals any longer, and in most parts of the world, most of these species were threatened or endangered. Because these cats were all captive born, however, none of them could really fend for themselves in the wild. They inhabited a middle ground between being tamed and able to live in a family, and being wild and able to fend for themselves. Most of the animals came from people who thought they wanted an exotic cat but then didn't have the time, the money, or the passion to establish the kind of connection that would tame an animal. It was a lot of work, Bill kept saying, and you had to be 110 percent behind it to make it happen. The taming also had to happen when the cats were very young because once they got big it was infinitely more difficult to establish that connection. It was not impossible, he said, and they were trying their best. But most of the cats had missed being tamed in the crucial stage.

The caracals, for example, both came from the same home, a young woman who thought she was going to breed them, but as they grew they pretty much destroyed her house. She tried working with them for almost a year before giving up. Now they fought with each other and needed to be housed in separate cages. Bill had been unable to establish contact with either one yet. They were very angry, he said. As we walked by all the pens, the stories got jumbled in my head. The bobcat came from a wealthy guy who had a menagerie but not enough time. The serval was one a breeder had that she couldn't sell or breed and was going to euthanize. The panther was rescued and brought here when she was young; she came from an experienced owner who had been successful with other exotics; this cat just refused to be handled, even when young. She perhaps could survive in the wild, but the breeder didn't have the right permits to release her (even though she was virtually extinct in her native Florida). The cats were all at different levels in their training. Some could be touched by Bill, some by Joanie; some of them could only be touched sometimes, which meant you had to read their moods and intentions very accurately. Both Bill and Joanie had been scratched to the point of needing stitches, but neither had ever been bitten. "Thank God for that," Bill said, as he pointed out that a sixty-pound cat can kill you five times faster than a sixty-pound dog.

Eventually, we went back in the house, where I met Joanie and their tame lynx, Dream. I liked Joanie a lot. She was down-to-earth and very charming. Dream didn't even get up to greet me, and after hearing how much damage these cats could do, I had no urge to pet him. "A lot of people think we're trying to be martyrs," Joanie said, "but we're not. I just can't see the sense of killing these animals. I always want to try." Both Joanie and Bill had serious doubts that any of the cats out back would ever be real pets, or ever be able to come in the house. But as they put it, "At least they know a little human kindness." They felt their lives out back weren't terrible and mostly I concurred. Their situation was similar in my mind to dogs kept alive in good no-kill shelters. When I asked them about the proposed bill, they responded with vehemence. As with Sally, there was a disconnect between the way they spoke about the animals themselves and the language of rights they used to justify owning them. Animals were property and what we did with them was nobody's business, they argued. Bill and Joanie strongly opposed the language of pet "guardianship" for this reason. "We are owners," they repeated, "and we want to defend ownership rights." They worried that the language of "guardianship" would leave openings for groups to monitor their treatment of their animals, and possibly even seize them if they were being mistreated. Guardianship, Joanie stated, was the first step on the animal rights' agenda to abolish all animal ownership from our lives. They feared anything associated with animal rights as leading to a world without animals, and they said the only way to protect their cats was to argue that they were private property.

Driving home I reflected on this disconnect: how such an intense love for animals could be set right up against a discourse about how they were simply property to be owned. Even though my hosts all defended themselves with the language of ownership and private property, what I found in those visits were people who had such amazing passion and love for the nonhuman world that they were willing to negotiate living arrangements with wild animals. That, I realized, was the kind of affective connection animal people seek; it is the same revolutionary love that calls us to make untold sacrifices in our quest to connect with nonhuman life. It is the recognition that animals are not objects to be displayed but subjects to be communed with; it is the foundation of the shift that this book calls for. But instead of descriptions of a magical and life-affirming connection, what comes across when you talk to these people about the Inherently Dangerous Animals bill (or even the possibility that private ownership might be regulated) is anger and hostility toward anything that infringes on their rights as owners. I strongly believe that the people I visited have a better way of making their argument than solely on the basis of property rights.

The law requires us to think of our animals as property despite the fact that those of us who live with pets know that they are much more than property. They are more like partners, children, or extended family than they are like objects. Pet owners in many locations are turning to the language of "guardianship," not because it's the first step toward abolition of human interaction with animals, but because guardianship more accurately reflects the kind of relationship we have with our pets. We don't own our pets like slaveholders owned slaves; we share our lives with them and do our best to guard them against danger. This was also certainly true of the four homes I visited; the people were not, in my opinion, "owning" these animals simply because they had a right to. They were living with them because doing so was intensely rewarding.

I couldn't help but wonder whether part of the reason most of the public thinks private exotic owners are poor or crazy isn't related to the fact that they all seem to rely on property rights as the sole justification for their practices. The people I met and conversed with cared for their animals very well and fostered the kind of connection I advocate in this book, but they misrepresent themselves in the public sphere by formulating their arguments as property rights. As a result of the emphasis placed on private ownership and animals as property in their arguments, their websites, meetings, and lists, they come across as potential animal abusers. Statements like "these animals are my property and no one can dictate what I do with my own property" alarm other animal lovers who don't have the benefit of visiting their homes and seeing the situation for themselves. The general public hears statements like that and imagines that exotic animals in private homes must be living in horrendous conditions. If they are thought of as only property, the public assumes that when the animals get too old or become useless they are treated as unwanted property and simply sold or discarded.

Moreover, arguments that center exotic pet ownership on property rights quite possibly attract the wrong kind of person to exotic ownership, that is, people who buy exotics not because they love animals but simply because they have a right to. Every spring, the North Carolina State Fairgrounds in Raleigh hosts an exotic pet show that features mostly reptiles and snakes and insects, along with booths of stuff for general pet ownership. This show is always on the same weekend as the annual gun show, which is housed in the building right next door, not twenty feet away. The discourse of property rights ties these two events together: people who are interested in defending their right to do whatever they want to their pets are often the same kinds of people who want to own guns. In both cases, why you would want to own an exotic or a gun is configured to be "nobody's business." Such an attitude completely obscures the kind of love and devotion I found on my field trips; it hides the unique human-animal connections in those households.

I am not saying there are no private owners who treat their animals cruelly and neglectfully; of course there are. And I'm also sure that there are many who off-load their old or sick animals to canned hunts. Indeed, I'm sure that the people who were willing to engage in electronic conversation with me about their exotics are probably the most conscientious owners, and that those who allowed me to visit them were probably the best of the best; folks who had problems with their animals or kept them in less than acceptable conditions wouldn't respond with such openness. But my point is that arguing against this proposed bill solely on the basis that you have the legal right to own animals both attracts potentially uncommitted owners (who think they should exercise that right also) and obscures the larger lesson that living with exotic "wild" animals, although difficult, can be a rewarding experience for both human and nonhuman animals. A better way to argue against the proposed bill, I believe, would be to open up the discourse on the human-animal connection.

The other problem with basing arguments solely on ownership rights is that it has become inextricably combined with the idea that there should be no oversight of these relationships at all. Accountability is important for all animals, whether it's working for legislation against chaining dogs, monitoring conditions of all breeders and shutting down irresponsible puppy millers, visiting the family farm where you buy your meat and eggs, or evaluating the living conditions of exotics. Animal people need to find a way of supporting and endorsing the relationships that Sally, Nancy, Chuck, Joanie, and Bill have established with their animals, and condemning the guy who keeps the tiger locked up in a shed or spare bedroom. We need to figure out how to separate good guardianship from bad. Do I think everyone needs a tiger or a monkey or a wolf? No. But there are people who are capable of taking care of these animals and should be allowed to do so if we put reasonable regulations in place and if they follow those rules. One of the central tenets of this book is that this sort of accountability must be instituted for all animals, not just exotics.

Along with such accountability, we need a great deal more education. Anyone who approaches animals as objects or as cute furry beings that will be there for us only when we want to interact with them is in for a rude awakening. All animals, whether a pet rat, dog, cat, tiger, or wolf, are subjects of their own needs, affects, and desires; they respond to the world on their own timetable, not ours. If animals are valued for their ability to provide intimacy and connection only at our whim, they are at risk when they fail to live up to expectations. Getting your mind in the right place before you agree to live with any animal is essential. They make demands, and failing to meet those demands leads to neglect, abuse, and relinquishment. This does not mean that we should condemn all pet owning, but rather that we need to be as clear as possible that living with any animal takes work and adjustment. The bond created as a result of that work, that comes when you start to see the world as nonhumans see it, can be one of the most rewarding of life's experiences. It can change your orientation toward everything. But it takes time, energy, education, money, and support.

Animal lovers of all stripes need to figure out ways of supporting people who want to live with wild animals, I believe. Exotic owners need to drop their defensive posture and help all of us figure out how to support them. They need to stop making arguments that sound like "I have a right to own these animals and what I do with them is my business," and start telling us what it's like to live with a wolf or tiger, and how we can help them on their journey with these creatures. We also need to support rescues, sanctuaries, and other institutions that help exotic owners who do get in over their heads. People make mistakes about their capabilities and we need to forgive those mistakes and, as a community, provide care for the animals they acquired but can no longer keep. I say this because the answer to the first of our significant questions—are the animals happy?—is often yes. Charles, the servals and savannahs, Sasha, Pansy, Dream, and the other rescues he lives with are leading fairly happy lives, I think. Again, this is not to say there aren't many exotics in miserable conditions that live outside the purview of the public eye. I'm sure there are, but animal people have got to come up with a way of sorting good homes from bad. We need just systems of oversight that help us figure out how to make these distinctions. We need to fight against abuse and neglect of all types, and we need places to put the animals who are now living in substandard conditions.

But are we humans safe? As I have claimed, there doesn't seem to be much evidence supporting the idea that animals in private ownership are more dangerous than those in zoos, or even those in the wild (especially given habitat encroachment rates). In zoos, the shrinking wild, and private homes, wild animals do attack humans. In my limited experience, however, private exotic owners are not the untrained, irresponsible owners accredited zoos and animal rights people make them out to be. There are undoubtedly irresponsible exotic owners just as there are irresponsible zookeepers and irresponsible dog owners, and again, we need a better system of oversight and regulation for identifying and shutting them all down. But in the end, the private owners don't seem to fare worse than their more public counterparts. Living with animals—whether dogs or big cats—can be dangerous, but we don't reduce that risk by prohibiting and outlawing the relationship. Systems of education, regulation, oversight, and support are the only way to increase the safety of the public.

Zone Four: Sanctuaries

If we hope to leave our children and grandchildren a world that contains such things as tigers and wolves, we need to start thinking more creatively about where and how to keep them alive, safe, and reproducing. I believe this is an important project because many of these animals are essential components of our imaginations. While we define our human selves against them, they are also critical for biodiversity, for teaching us to see the world from different kinds of sensory perceptions, for our spiritual practices, for imagining what it would be like to live like they do, for the comfort of their companionship. We need solutions for their continued well-being and we need them fast.

In the past few decades, a new formation has emerged to respond to homeless wild animals. Sanctuaries are popping up all over the United States, housing every kind of animal imaginable; animal people are stepping up and caring for these exotics because of their special connection to these particular types of animals. Sanctuaries constitute a new zone that glorifies wild animals rather than gawks at them, engenders respect for the otherness of animals, and provides a view of nature that is about relationship rather than domination. These sanctuaries make it clear that it is possible to create captive situations in which animals can enjoy a life that is healthier, more comfortable, safer, and longer than they might have had, even in the wild. Humans who work in sanctuaries in both paid and volunteer positions get to know the animals not only by their species but also individually by their unique personalities. Committed donors "adopt" a specific animal and provide the funding necessary for their upkeep. Sanctuaries are allowing many people to experience close contact with wild animals, and, to my thinking, they are fostering the kind of affective shift necessary for the continued existence of many endangered species.

Over the winter of researching this chapter, I visited six different sanctuaries throughout North Carolina: one for bears, one for wolves and wolf hybrids, three for big cats, and one mixed-species compound that housed about a hundred different kinds of animals. I've seen transformation happening in every sanctuary I visited. Animal-identified people come out of the woodwork and jump at the chance to form a bond with a real animal. They get to know what the animal likes and is like, whether she's lazy or likes exercise, whether he likes treats of chicken legs or frozen beef patties. I've seen volunteers working with aromatherapy to stimulate and entertain animals, folks who think every animal needs "a job" or something to accomplish in order to feel fulfilled. I've talked to people who spend hours hiding food in enclosures so that animals have to "hunt" to find it. I've met people who make toys for big cats, people who hold Native American ceremonial fires so wild animals can howl at the moon and communicate with otherworldly spirits and ancestors, people who communicate with animals psychically or who hire psychic animal communicators to both tell the animal stories about humans and listen to the stories animals themselves tell. I've met working-class people who take overtime shifts to make enough money to "adopt" one of these wild animals even though that means they can only visit their friends twice a month rather than twice a week, and I've met rich people who visit their animals every day and plan to leave their entire estate to the sanctuary. I've met volunteers who live down the street from the sanctuary, and others who travel hundred of miles to work there for a few weeks or months. I've met people who pay hundreds of dollars to have their animal's paw print framed, and others who've erected shrines to their animals at home. At the wolf sanctuary, I met potential and former adopters who extend the logic of dog rescue into the realm of wolves, people who wanted to adopt homeless wolves and take them home and rehabilitate them rather than breed new ones. I've met sanctuary owners and founders who've devoted their entire lives and incomes to the cause of rescuing animals from death, or from fates worse than death. Some of them are running out of money and are desperate for the next donation to pay the vet bill (they are quick to note, though, that the money always comes through because people out there really love the animals). I've met owners, founders, and volunteers eager to show you scars of bites and scratches, and in the very same breath tell you that working with these animals is their dream come true. While sanctuary animals may have lost something for not living in the wild, they have also gained something, and that something is affective connection with humans. Animal people give freely of their time, money, and hearts to see that their special animals have all they need and more. In a world where we humans are separated from daily contact with wild animals and are quickly losing appreciation of other kinds of beings, sanctuaries are giving many of us the space to reconnect with them.

All the sanctuaries I visited have different histories, policies, and funding structures. While they are all housed on large plots of rural land (usually ten or more acres), and none of the sanctuaries I visited had any visible neighbors, the similarities pretty much end there. Some only take animals being retired from zoos, some take them only from other sister facilities, some take them from private owners, some breed them, and some acquire animals from combinations of some or all of these sources. (No sanctuaries that I know of take animals out of the wild.) Many of the animals in these sanctuaries have been through countless homes and some in a number of zoos. They were locked up in closets and garages or dumped out in the country to fend for themselves. Two full-grown tigers from one facility were found walking down the streets of downtown Charlotte. Some sanctuaries charge a placement fee, some don't. Some charge an admission fee of anywhere from five to twenty dollars (for the public to view animals); others operate on donations only. One sanctuary I visited was founded by a scientist at a local university who needed a place to retire his research animals. Another was founded by a wealthy couple who had made a killing in the dot-com rush and started their compound to fulfill a lifelong dream. A third was started by a guy who was really just an animal collector at heart; thirty years ago, his operation would have been called a menagerie or roadside zoo. By calling it a sanctuary he gets both volunteers and donations, which allow him to collect more animals and keep them in better conditions. The fourth sanctuary was also closer to a collection, but its owners only collected one species. That compound had been in their family for four generations, dating back to the turn of the twentieth century (the enclosures were a lot smaller back then, the tour guide assured us). The fifth place was started by a young woman who had a lifelong dream of rescuing tigers because she felt she could speak with them in her mind. When her parents died and left her about $250,000, she bought the land and started collecting tigers; she now owns about thirty and the public is invited to watch her psychically communicate with them (we can even ask them questions through her). A Native American woman started the final sanctuary; she had started out as a wolf breeder who had a lot of pets returned to her. When word got out that she took back wolf pups that were too much for new owners, she was inundated with requests to take failed pets from other breeders as well. She ended up on twenty acres with more than seventy homeless wolves.

Unlike in zoos, a lot of the animals in these sanctuaries are less than perfect. Some are old, many have broken tails or three legs, they walk funny or act funny or are somehow deformed, a few were cross-eyed. Unlike in zoos, these animals don't get sold or killed if they don't show well. Many are aggressive, some as a result of abuse, some by nature. Volunteers and staff clue you in to those problem animals quickly, and many of the worst aggression problems aren't on the public tours. In most sanctuaries, however, even the most aggressive animals get visited and often have treatment plans and progress reports made for them. Most of these sanctuaries have a makeshift, homespun feel to them. Dirt paths lead from enclosure to enclosure, the driveways don't have enough gravel. Hunters and volunteers drive up almost daily depositing carcasses and roadkill to be chopped up into food. Toilets—if there are any—are port-o-johns. The enclosures are not bars of steel but welded wire fences that tilt and list in ways that can make you a little nervous if you think about it too long. But the volunteer tour guides have learned not be scared; they have built a rapport with the animals and trust many of them enough to hand-feed them. Most of the animals in the sanctuaries I visited were creatures nobody else wanted. While it's true that most sanctuaries buy and breed some animals, those numbers are very small compared to the number of animals who are there because nobody else wants them. In these sanctuaries, though, no matter how broken or aggressive they are, they are wanted and they are loved. In *The Lives of Animals*, J. M. Coetzee wrote, "The question that . . . occupies the rat and the cat and every other animal trapped in the hell of the laboratory or the zoo, is: Where is home, and how do I get there?"[26] I believe the animals in sanctuaries have found their way to the best kind of home humans can give them.

And, as I've noted, if the proposed bill passes in North Carolina, all these sanctuaries will be shut down. A few of the animals may have the good fortune of finding a space in another sanctuary in one of the few remaining states that doesn't have exotic bans, a few of the better-looking ones may possibly get sold to zoos, or maybe one of the sanctuaries will scrape up enough money to close themselves to the public and still maintain a funding base. All the other animals will be either humanely euthanized or sold to canned hunting facilities to pay off outstanding debts.

Behind the conviction that these places need to be shut down is a tangle of ideological compromises that originate with the strange bedfellows of the bill's progenitors. Animal rightists in general and Animal Protection Institute in particular, as I've said, believe wild animals belong only in the wild. They recognize, however, that existing exotic animals can't be released into the wild and therefore do need a place to go, so they are willing to make exceptions for sanctuaries approved by the Global Federation of Animal Sanctuaries or the American Sanctuary Association. Both organizations espouse abolitionist ideology on their websites. The policy upshot of these abolitionist convictions is that no approved sanctuary can breed for any reason except U.S. Fish and Wildlife Services–authorized reintroduction to the wild. Intrinsically related to this abolitionist platform is the idea that the public should not have access to these animals because all viewing and interaction is seen as exploitation. In the abolitionist mind-set, these animals have been used for human entertainment much too long and the sanctuary is the space of retirement and rest. Thus, while visits to some (not all) accredited sanctuaries may be arranged, no admission fees can be charged. Public contact is discouraged or banned, even if the animals enjoy it. No animals can be rehomed or traded or studied or even abstractly "adopted." As one website claims, "A true sanctuary is a lifetime home for animals once they arrive to ensure that they are ALWAYS in a safe place and treated well."[27] These abolitionist beliefs construct the sanctuary as a space set apart from the workings of the world where animals can retire peacefully. They never need to breed or perform or interact with humans or do anything they don't want to do. Driven by the belief that they should not have been brought into the sphere of captivity at all, such a retirement is seen as compensation for their captivity. Where release or reintroduction is impractical, this utopia is seen as the next best option.

From a certain angle, this model of sanctuary is laudable, idyllic even. However, it is deeply impractical in today's world where value is construed in relation to circulation. Approved facilities require funders with deep pockets who agree with abolitionist ideology. Because they eschew part-time volunteers, these sanctuaries require full-time trained staff members willing to work for lower wages than they could make in accredited zoos. Put simply, these ideal sanctuaries are hard to maintain; as noted, there is not one ASA-approved sanctuary in all of North Carolina. Moreover, these sanctuaries do nothing to perpetuate future generations of threatened and endangered species. And while some animals may prefer the life of solitude offered by these sanctuaries, many animals prefer the kind of stimulation found in more public, community-based sanctuaries like the ones I visited.

At the other end of the impetus behind the bill, the Association of Zoos and Aquariums is invested in shutting down these unapproved sanctuaries because they are cutting into accredited zoos' market share. The public would rather pay to interact with animals up close at these local sanctuaries (and provide a much needed funding base) than travel across the state to view animals in more corporate settings. This is apparent when you look at the activity of these competing institutions. To get a tour in a local unapproved sanctuary, you need an appointment that sometimes takes a few weeks, especially if you can only visit on weekends. These sanctuaries limit the number of people coming through each week because they are primarily interested in the well-being of the animals. And in my experience of these sanctuaries, the public is more than willing to wait a few weeks to see the animals up close. The reservation books are filled for weeks in advance. Meanwhile, the parking lots at accredited zoos seem increasingly empty.

The proposed bill is putting unapproved sanctuaries in a bind. They either need to get on board with the conflicted message imbedded in the bill (i.e., it's wrong to exploit animals at all but if we're going to, we should only do it in a corporate setting), or they face an uphill battle to become accredited with limited resources. Locally, you can see this conflict played out in the one sanctuary that is trying to become accredited. I had two tour guides the first time I visited that sanctuary. The first guide, a woman, talked about the sanctuary in a way that was in keeping with the bill. "Private ownership of these animals is wrong," she said, "and we need to outlaw it." As she took us through the compound, she highlighted the kinds of abuse that many of the animals had suffered at the hands of private owners. One tiger lived her whole life locked in a shed, she told us; another was beaten because he defecated in the house. She insisted that the goal of the sanctuary movement was to put itself out of business. "We don't want to see animals suffering like this," she implored. "Someday there will be no need for sanctuary." She rehearsed the idea that private owners were bad and that we should end the animals' suffering by shutting the private exotic industry down. Halfway into the tour, though, the other guide, a man, spoke up and disagreed. "If it weren't for private owners," he said, "our sanctuary would go out of business, and that would be a very bad thing. We love these animals and they are now leading very good lives here. Some people can care for exotic pets just fine, others can't. People make mistakes. I'm just happy a place like this exists so I can come visit the tigers." The tension between the two guides was palpable.[28]

    To my thinking, there are only two theoretically unassailable positions in this debate. Either we need to, as the abolitionists suggest, stop displaying, breeding, and trading in captive wildlife in all arenas, including zoos and high-profile sanctuaries (which will lead to the imminent extinction of many species), or we need to create rules and regulations whereby anyone can own, care for, interact with, display, and possibly even breed these animals in ways that are healthy and productive for both the individual animals themselves as well as for the long-term well-being and survival of their species. Only this second option guarantees that our children and their children will grow up on a planet that includes tigers, wolves, and other charismatic megafauna. Unless current rates of deforestation and environmental degradation are reversed immediately such that animals routed for extinction start springing back, a democratic approach to conservation is our only reasonable option. Anyone who can provide a healthy and fulfilling life for exotic animals should, in my opinion, be allowed to.

Democracy does not imply a blank check, though, and we must continue to fight for legislation that monitors and regulates the conditions under which these animals should be kept. Currently, while U.S. Fish and Wildlife Services monitors human interaction with threatened and endangered species in the wild, captive-bred exotics have only the poorly conceived and enforced Animal Welfare Act (AWA) to guard them. The AWA is primarily designed to give minimal protection to pets and guarantees them reasonable amounts of food and water, protection from an extremely harsh climate, and enough space to stand up and turn around. It is administered by the U.S. Department of Agriculture and is not really adequate for the protection of dogs and cats, let alone the complex needs of exotic wild animals. Dogs and cats need better regulations (including no chaining, no outdoor-only pets especially in inclement weather, and licensing and vet care for free-roaming cats), and wild animals need much more than that. They need room to roam, uncontaminated food, standard vet care, minimal exercise standards, and regular oversight to guarantee that they are leading full-enough lives. We need systems of education and support to help owners intervene when animals are stressed to the point of self-mutilation, we need systems of removal when those owners are unable to comply, and we need sanctuaries to put them in when they are removed.

I believe the exotic animals living in the four private homes I visited are leading full-enough lives and would pass any test administered by reasonable inspectors. It's the animals in the houses I didn't visit that I worry about, just like I worry about all the chained dogs, outdoor-only cats, and the countless animals in factory farms. People do terrible things to animals. We need to awaken our thinking to the gifts and graces that nonhuman beings offer, and we need to figure out better ways to share our world and its resources with them. We need better legislation and oversight for all animals, especially nontraditional exotics. We need systems of registration, better funding for enforcement, standardized processes for removal and relinquishment, and places to put animals when they no longer have a home. Creating such a network will be expensive and time consuming, and will only be accomplished if and when we learn to love them as they deserve to be loved.

In the meantime, it seems clear to me that community-based local sanctuaries already have in place many of the checks, regulations, and oversights I am calling for here. Because they are open to the public, most of the animals are interacted with on a daily basis; even animals not on public tours garner loads of attention. Tour guides and volunteers work hard to keep the animals safe from any taunting on the tours; the public explores each facility in supervised small groups of eight to twelve, so it's possible to monitor most interactions. In my experience both on public tours and as a volunteer at one site, almost all the animals in these sanctuaries have at least one "special advocate" in a volunteer who has made a connection with them. These volunteers observe the animals carefully, watching for any signs of depression or unwellness. Much to my surprise, my special animal at the site where I work is a lynx named Toby; I thought I would connect more with a big cat as I've always had a "thing" for lions. But alone in his enclosure, big round Toby with his stubby tail and funny beard is the guy who comes to me in my dreams. He definitely knows my voice and smell, and I like to think he looks forward to my visits. I worry about him during the week when I'm not there, and wonder how he's doing and what he's thinking. One Saturday I took him a half dozen free-range eggs from my favorite local farmer, which he ate like a box of chocolates. His picture is on my screensaver. My team manager thinks that by summer I may be able to take him on supervised walks on leash. There's also a binturong named Sebastian that comes down from his tree to greet me; we'll see where that relationship goes. But given the intensity of these connections, there is no question in my mind that any law that threatens to shut this facility down is ill conceived and misguided. The relationships that are happening between human animals and wildlife at community-based sanctuaries stand as examples of the affective shift this book calls for, and constitute the most viable hope for the future of wild animals.

Wild animals come from a different time, a time more friendly toward nonhumans. For two or three centuries now, we've poured our science and passion into improving conditions for humanity. The population of the world has doubled in the last sixty years and will double again in the next forty. We are living longer and growing exponentially. Humans are in charge now, and we rapidly approach a world that looks like something out of a science fiction novel. Where the animals will fit in depends on us. Are we willing to build them sanctuaries? Are we willing to meet them halfway? If they let us tame them, are we willing to accept responsibility for their well-being? If we tame them, can we make room in our human-centered world for their ongoing existence?

> If you tame me [the fox said to the little prince], my life will be filled with sunshine. I'll know the sound of footsteps that will be different from all the rest. Other footsteps send me back underground. Yours will call me out of my burrow like music. And then, look! You see the wheat fields over there? I don't eat bread. For me wheat is of no use whatsoever. Wheat fields say nothing to me. Which is sad. But you have hair the color of gold. So it will be wonderful once you've tamed me! The wheat, which is golden, will remind me of you. And I'll love the sound of the wind in the wheat. . . . Please . . . tame me![29]

Even in a totally human-centered world, we hope there will be wild animals willing and eager to be tamed by us, if we're willing to take on that responsibility. Two roads lie in front of us. The first leads to a world where the animals in the wild eventually disappear and the only ones left will be held like objects in zoos. No one will know the joy of hearing those special footsteps, or the joy of belonging to that one special animal. The other road leads to a world in which communities learn to share space and resources with the wild things, and where special attachments between humans and animals form in sanctuary settings. This road is the road of the heart, where the special connection between creatures is fostered and encouraged. It's not an easy road and it's going to take money and work to figure out how to live safely with these creatures. But those of us who already love animals can make a start and help each other do it better. Even animal people who are opposed to keeping wild animals in captivity should get involved, I think, because they could help us set the absolute highest standards of care.

The fox reveals an essential truth to the little prince: "Here is my secret. It's quite simple: One sees clearly only with the heart. Anything essential is invisible to the eyes."[30] Focusing on affective connection as a major component of animal advocacy gives us a way to name this as truth. To keep charismatic megafauna on the planet with us, we need to learn about them, to feed and care for them, tame them, keep them safe, make them happy, teach them how to be in relationship with us, and, most important, see them clearly with our hearts.

FIVE FROM OBJECT TO SUBJECT
Animals in Scientific Research

NOWHERE IS THE DEBATE ABOUT HUMAN USE OF ANI-mals more incoherent than in the domain of invasive somatic research on animals, also known as vivisection. Scientific researchers and their advocates claim that using live animals in experiments is absolutely necessary to the advancement of science, that without animals, we would not have developed vaccines, antibiotics, and almost all the drugs and products on the market today. Without animals, they say, research and development in medical science would come to a complete halt.[1] Animal rights activists disagree. Some argue that we actually learn very little from experimenting invasively on animals; indeed, these activists say, much of the information we do gather is either not useful or just plain wrong.[2] Others argue that even if we do advance our own knowledge of human medicine through animal experiments, the cost in terms of animal suffering is much too high.[3] Scientists claim that because animals do not have any legal standing, we can and should use their bodies to learn more about the natural world and ourselves. Activists counter that all animals have inherent value and therefore have the right not to be experimented on. Researchers argue that a great deal of experimentation benefits animals themselves (as in veterinary medicine). Activists claim

153

that animals cannot give informed consent and therefore ought not to be subject to invasive procedures. Researchers rebut by pointing out that we do not need their informed consent to give them the medicines we develop for them, from which they clearly benefit. Some activists, so upset both by these procedures and by the lack of communication between researchers and advocates, turn to violence.

All research labs that use animals in the Unites States are required to appoint an internal review board known as an IACUC (Institutional Animal Care and Use Committee) to oversee all experiments on animals. These boards are not concerned with determining the relative value of an experiment; they are solely charged with overseeing the care and treatment of animals (for example, that their cages are big enough and clean enough, that they have necessary companionship and enrichment, proper food). IACUCs must have at least five members, including one veterinarian, one scientist experienced in animal research, one institutionally aligned nonscientist, and one community member unaffiliated with the research facility. Although research labs are federally mandated to establish IACUCs by a 1985 amendment to the Animal Welfare Act, researchers claim they are happy to abide by these animal welfare dictates because well-cared-for animals produce better results; indeed, many researchers believe that the existence and governance of IACUCs constitute a middle ground between unregulated use of animals in science and complete cessation of all use of animals. These researchers fundamentally believe that they are doing the right thing, that IACUCs provide adequate oversight, that their research may someday save suffering humans, and that the painless sacrifice of animals is a small price to pay for human health and well-being.[4]

Most activists feel that animals simply should not be killed or harmed for human benefit. Although rightists advocate the complete liberation of animals from the laboratory (as well as all from environments in which humans own and control them), many advocates adopt the strategy of forcing research facilities to comply with the Animal Welfare Act and their own IACUC recommendations. Thus, undercover reporters and whistleblowers set about identifying, documenting, and publicizing infringements. In the videos that come out of these labs, animals are beaten, nailed down, drilled into, cut open, burned, deprived of all fluids, thrown against walls, electrocuted, starved, suffocated, drowned, gassed, starved, blinded; their bones are broken and their limbs severed; their organs are crushed; and ulcers, paralysis, seizures, and heart attacks are induced. They are forced to inhale tobacco, drink alcohol, and take drugs such as cocaine and heroine; they are infected with every disease imaginable; they are irradiated and frozen; they have parts of their brains surgically removed; and they are kept perpetually isolated from all other creatures. How can this be welfare? animal activists ask.[5] Activists work hard to force facilities to improve care, but according to them, the ghoulish practices only continue. They argue that this IACUC kind of welfare is not now and never will be enough. Some of those activists turn to violence. Like pro-life activists who simply cannot bear to see one more innocent baby "killed" by abortion, these animal rights activists break in, steal animals, bomb labs, burn vehicles, destroy property, and threaten researchers and their families. Governments respond to these activities by treating animal rights violence as domestic terrorism.[6]

How did we get ourselves into such a moral conflict? While there may be some extremists on both sides, the overwhelming majority of people involved in this debate are, it feels to me, good people trying their best to make positive social contributions. Unlike some of the other topics covered in this book, it's hard to identify clear "bad guys" in the debate over vivisection; put differently, both sides take the moral high ground in their writings. That is, unlike the indiscriminate puppy millers and factory farmers who don't even care enough to marshal a coherent defense of their practices, scientific researchers adopt and engage the language of animal welfare. Neither side fosters a necessary predilection for violence; neither side hates either humans or animals. Indeed, if asked, both researchers and activists say their hope is to work together to create a better world for everyone. Both sides want to be heroes, one side saving animals from torture, the other saving humanity from illness and disease. Both sides pursue what they see as best for the world, and because they disagree on the contours of goodness, they end up locked in conflict.

One side has learned to see the use and sacrifice of animals as absolutely necessary to the advancement of science. For them, human exceptionalism (i.e., the commitment that humans are more important than any other life-form) is a concrete reality and the sacrifice of animals for human benefit is warranted. They point to the long history of medical and scientific advancement and make it clear that virtually all Americans have benefited from these experiments. For these folks, breeding and experimenting on rats and mice, or occasionally using dogs, cats, primates and other mammals (only when deemed scientifically necessary by the IACUC, researchers are quick to add), are simply justified by common sense. Who among us has not benefited from modern medicine? they ask.

The other side inhabits a completely different world. From an animal rights perspective, the inherent value of all animals is self-evident and paramount. This side watches the visible suffering of animals in labs and sees little or no good coming from it. Armed with the experience of heartless torture of innocent beings, they see invasive researchers as little more than well-funded sadists. From their perspective, nothing new can be learned from the animal model; it is only allowed to continue because scientists see themselves as above morality and societal control. Researchers are pumped-up demigods who have tricked the rest of us into thinking our lives depend on their research, some activists say. The torture must end, they argue, and many of them are willing to perform acts of violence to intimidate and frighten researchers into ceasing their work. The commitment that all sentient beings have the right to freedom from human enslavement produces a landscape where experimenting on animals is as evil as experimenting on innocent, nonconsenting humans.

These differing landscapes produce different languages for the people who inhabit them. Animal rights proponents say that scientists "kill" or "murder" animals, while scientists say they "sacrifice" them. Animal rightists believe that all animals should have proper names and be referred to as he or she; researchers mostly give animals only numbers and call them "it." No one has an accurate count of how many animals are used for experimental research. Scientists tout numbers ranging from a half million to five million annually, while activists suggest numbers upward of twenty to fifty million, some even suggesting numbers in the billions. Part of the discrepancy lies in the fact that because the Animal Welfare Act excludes regulations for rats, mice, birds, and all invertebrates, their numbers do not need to be reported or tracked.[7] (Most sources claim that anywhere from 50 percent to 90 percent of experimental animals are purpose bred rats and mice.) Another source of discrepancy, though, is the failure of labs to accurately report to their own IACUCs how many animals are being used. Activists claim the labs underreport, sometimes by a factor of 2 or 3.[8] Finally, while researchers say they can't be sure an animal feels pain if it doesn't have the language to identify and understand it, activists are certain that lab animals suffer immensely.

Throughout each chapter, this book has asked readers to look at animals through the lens of affective connection. While it seems clear to me and most animal advocates that the current "blank check" approach we use when dealing with animals is deeply flawed, I've suggested that the ethical strategies of rights, utilitarianism, and welfare could be greatly enhanced if proponents of each position attended more deeply to affective approaches. Through deep human connection to animals, a moderate middle ground can be negotiated where animals come to represent themselves in the political sphere through relationships with humans. But how would this thesis apply to lab animals? How can we connect with those we intentionally hurt? Don't we need to see animals as objects if we're going experiment on them? Isn't it necessary to maintain a distinction between those pets we love and those animals we cut open?

The reverse of all three of these questions must be considered; that is, here in the realm of vivisection, perhaps more than any other arena of animal use, such intimacy and connection are absolutely necessary. I will argue that only by knowing an animal thoroughly and deeply, only by having some knowledge of his character, only by loving her well, can we ask the animal for the kind of sacrifice vivisection entails. I believe both sides of this debate need to shift the way they understand the human-animal connection; while science views animals as objects or models to be manipulated for research purposes, and animal rights sees them as beings to be liberated from human use, I suggest we all need a new landscape, a landscape that sees animals as partners, family members, and friends. The affective power of love can offer a third alternative for using animals in scientific research, and perhaps can bring about some amount of resolution to the animal research wars.

To build a third way that both sides can live with, we first need to examine what the world looks like from inside the worldviews of opposing factions. We need to see what the competing arguments are, who the stakeholders are, how language shapes the world. Only when we recognize what's involved for both sides can we explore new ways of thinking, new formations of what might look like middle ground, new possibilities for animals.[9]

The Landscape of Animal Rights

Animal rights advocates in the strong sense are shaped by many arguments that function to delegitimize invasive experiments. First, they detail the many reasons that experimenting on animals leads to limited benefit for humans: for example, we humans contract different diseases than animals do and use different medicines to combat them; we react to poisons and pathogens differently (what is harmful to one species may not affect another at all); we have different systems with different nutritional needs; the texture and composition of our skin and other organs are different from those of most other animals; we sense the world in different ways.[10] Given all these differences, how much can we actually learn about human medicine from animal experimentation? Some activists, particularly those associated with PETA (People for the Ethical Treatment of Animals), take these allegations a step further and argue that we have never in history learned anything from animal experimentation, or that not a single benefit to humans or animals has come from animal research, or that all current biomedical information could have been developed without the use animals. Data drawn from animal experiments, these activists claim, are never accurate or reliable and often lead to dangerous conclusions; humans are different from other animals and experimenting on animals tells us nothing about humans.[11]

It's not clear where one could stand to evaluate the accuracy of this most radical claim. To a nonscience person like me, it seems patently absurd. It goes against everything I learned in high school and college science classes, where everything from smallpox vaccine to penicillin has been brought to us through the bodies of research animals. In some ways, I believe claims like "we have never learned anything from experimenting on animals" weaken the credibility of the animal rights movement. My point in recounting it here is not to endorse it but to elucidate the shape of the activist worldview. For many followers of PETA and the Humane Society of the United States, I suggest, research on animals is so horrifying, the premise with which they begin their thinking rests in the conviction that evil like this cannot and never has produced anything good.

More moderate arguments and insights against experimentation do exist.[12] Antivivisectionists suggest that the vast majority of animals used in experimentation are not used to find cures for life-threatening illnesses, but rather are used for testing consumer products or producing new and unnecessary drugs. These welfarists point to the fact that drug companies introduce hundreds of new drugs every year that contribute almost nothing to the general health of the population; these new drugs replace those drugs on which patents have expired, since drug companies make less money on generics. Hundreds of thousands of animals die each year in tests for those copycat drugs, these welfarists argue. They suggest that the discovery and production of new drugs are motivated by profit more than human health. Some of these antivivisectionists argue that although animals may have been essential in the early part of the twentieth century for developing medicines and other therapies, twenty-first-century science uses many more animals with much less payoff. For them, modern medicine has lost its way in its quest for human health; the goal of profit has tipped the balance. While earlier animal experiments may have been crucial, what's happening today is different in kind and in scale.

Some people argue that the vast number of animal experiments, especially in the realm of product testing, are relatively useless because many of the drugs and products being tested are already available to the human public, or it has already been proved that the drug or product is harmful. Multitudes of experiments continue to be performed on animals regarding tobacco, alcohol, opiates, and various other chemicals, they say; such data can only tell us what we already know. The more cynical describe corporate greed as the engine driving a machine much bigger than what happens in a lab. For example, they note that after thirty years of fighting cancer with animal testing, cancer deaths are up; people with cancer live longer, but more contract it. Many studies have linked pollution and Western diets to a host of diseases, including cancer. If animal testing funds were diverted to programs that cleaned up the environment or encouraged dietary change, they suggest, we would finally see disease rates plummet. Instead, governments allow toxic waste to be disposed of into our environments and support unhealthy diets so that, in an attempt to combat cancer and other diseases, the animal testing industry can continue to profit.

From the perspective of animal advocacy, an inconsistency exists in scientific thinking with regards to animal models: researchers claim that animal bodies are close enough to ours to provide a valuable test for drugs, products, procedures, and so on. They say, in essence, animals are a lot like us, and if something is harmful to them it will be harmful to humans. The very same researchers also claim, however, that animals are not like us in that they can't feel pain, don't understand what's happening to them, and don't have significant value when measured against humans. How can they be so alike and so different at the same time? these activists ask. Animal advocates claim that researchers want it both ways; they hold that animals are enough like us to experiment on, but unlike us in relation to pain and suffering. But in truth, advocates want it both ways too; they say that because animals are not like us, information obtained from their torture is useless. Animals do, however, deserve rights, these advocates claim, because like us they have intrinsic value.[13]

Some people argue that even if some valuable information is obtained from the vivisection of animals, the cost is too great. Many refuse to take medicines developed on animals; in general this means they do not use Western medicine at all because all patented drugs have been tested on animals (herbs and many homeopathic treatments may not have been tested on animals). Similarly, many activists refuse to use products tested on animals. Again, since virtually all products in mainstream America were at one time tested on animals (or worse, still need to be), advocates committed to a cruelty-free lifestyle must work hard to seek out products on the margins of society.

Animal rights advocates note that although it would produce better science, we no longer perform harmful tests on humans because we now believe those experiments to be unethical.[14] This position claims that a preference for our own kind does not make tests more ethical when performed on animals. Animals are born with inherent rights that ought to be recognized by science, some say, and this presses these advocates into a world where experimenting on animals is as morally repugnant as experimenting on humans. Recall that Peter Singer used utilitarian logic to argue that medical experiments might more rightly be performed on mentally impaired infants than on fully functioning apes.[15] While a strict rights perspective would disallow experimentation on anyone who did not offer informed consent, many animal welfarists also suggest that any animal suffering at the hands of humans is unacceptable.

A small but vocal cross section of activists, mostly associated with the Animal Liberation Front, feel that the only way to be heard in this debate is through the use of violence.[16] The ALF is made up of unconnected underground cells that draw attention to the plight of research animals by destroying property and liberating animals. The ALF is a self-proclaimed community of radicals who believe the scientific testing system needs a revolutionary overhaul. They argue that the government should be ashamed that its unquestioning support for a corrupt system has forced concerned citizens to turn to violence. While some major architects of the animal rights movement have denounced this violence, others endorse it, some wholeheartedly.

These apologists for violence see themselves as part of a revolutionary process aimed at restructuring not only medical science but capitalism and all forms of oppression as well. The forces that allowed slavery to exist in the United States, that caused wars and devastation, are, according to these militant activists, the same forces torturing animals in laboratories. The corruption, greed, and cruelty of corporate animal research are seen as integral aspects of impending global apocalypse. They must be stopped at all costs.

This radical end of the animal rights movement turned to violence as early as the 1970s in England when an activist group called Hunt Saboteurs damaged vehicles involved in foxhunts. Several members of this early group broke off in the late 1970s to form the Animal Liberation Front, an organization focused on attacking research labs, especially those associated with pharmaceutical companies. These ALF activists rescue research animals, but also trash labs where they were kept, vandalize cars, and burn and bomb office buildings.[17] By the mid-1980s, the movement had moved to America (particularly California), and new tactics focused on harassing individual researchers.[18] In the past twenty years, ALF and other radical animal organizations have bombed buildings and cars, destroyed billions of dollars of property, threatened the lives of animal researchers and harassed their family members to the point where some have either stopped experimenting on animals altogether or have moved to other geographic areas that are less politically volatile. While many of these actions are kept out of mainstream media reports, news (and often even videos) of these activities can be found easily on the Internet.

The ALF wants to stop the torture of lab animals. The intensity of their compassion is fueled by a number of sources, I believe. Many of them watch the suffering of research animals on video and are simultaneously told by animal rights authorities—some of them scientists themselves—that such suffering produces no positive outcome or value, that it is completely pointless. Moreover, they are encouraged by some leaders to involve themselves in (often illegal) direct actions against people and businesses that profit from harming animals. The convergence of these three streams produces a landscape in which rage against injustice dominates. While the impulse to fight injustice is good, and turning to violence even sometimes works, in the greater scheme of things such violence has often turned public opinion against the animal rights movement.[19] While many social movements in America have their roots in violent action, no social movement gained legitimacy with the American public until it took up nonviolent approaches. From labor struggles to civil rights, from feminism to the movement for gay liberation, social change was only widely accepted once the average person stopped feeling threatened.

How do most outsiders view animal rights activists/antivivisectionists? In a word: as terrorists. While heated conflicts about animal treatment have been going on for a long time in England, in the last few years, the United States has taken violent actions associated with animal defense much more seriously. Recent passage of the Animal Enterprise Terrorism Act (AETA), signed by President George W. Bush in November 2006, has given all of us who work in the field of animal advocacy great pause. AETA replaced the Animal Enterprise Protection Act (AEPA) of 1992, which criminalized all illegal actions against animal enterprises (even if the crime itself was only a misdemeanor). In other words, the AEPA wasn't about the crime itself, it was about the politics behind the crime. AETA extends that logic and now classifies all actions against animal-based businesses as terrorist; animal activists can be prosecuted under the Homeland Security Act with the same broad principles used against foreign terrorists.

Many commentators on the AETA argue that the act unconstitutionally curtails the First Amendment right to free speech.[20] Under the AETA, even nonviolent civil disobedience (such as a boycott or sit-in) can be prosecuted as terrorism, if the animal-based company experiences a loss of at least ten thousand dollars. In other words, it's risky these days to say anything bad publicly about meat or fur or animals used in research. The effect of the AETA on anyone who writes or thinks about or does anything on behalf of animals has been chilling. Even legal protests can be seen as violations if corporations lose profits as a result of the activity. Supported largely by a combination of animal researchers and agribusiness factory farmers, the AETA is deeply intimidating. It fundamentally prevents individuals from exercising their right to protest for fear of being unjustly labeled and prosecuted as terrorists.

So why aren't most Americans educated about and resistant to this new law that treats protestors at a research lab or meatpacking plant like violent terrorists? Partly, of course, the mainstream media have been resistant to reporting both the passage of the law and the contours of its implications because their news services are owned by conglomerates that use animals. But underneath this, I suspect that most average Americans are somewhat apathetic to the cause of lab animal activism, not because they don't care about animals, but rather because they do not want to be associated with an extremist animal rights agenda. Mainstream media portray activists as anti-intellectual and fundamentally opposed to modern science. When it comes to the laboratory setting, many people view lab animals as just another category of laboratory supply, no different from glassware or computer disks—as "test tubes with tails." From this worldview, anyone who cares about or identifies with research animals is seen as peculiar and sentimental.

I discussed this perspective more generally in chapter 2, where outsiders saw solitary pet owners as pathetic, maladjusted, and lonely. This perception is only exaggerated when it comes to advocates for research animals. Outsiders sometimes see antivivisectionists as using the figure of the research animal to act out a displaced anger at their own helplessness and frustration. In other words, the only people involved in activism against scientific research, according to many outsiders, are people on the margins of society themselves. Their compassion for lab animals is only a reflection of their own disenfranchisement. Because research animals can't "talk back" to the activists, outsiders claim, they function as the perfect cause for the fringe. The wider political left is especially prone to this opinion. If people really want to make a better world, many on the left argue, they would work in coalition with other humans to eradicate racism, sexism, homophobia, classism, and other destructive forces. Choosing research animals as a cause, these outsiders argue, signals that these people can't really get along well with other humans.

These views by and large are narrow and wrong and need to be challenged. But many advocates themselves fuel these misperceptions in several ways. First, making claims and assertions that run against common sense (such as "we have never benefited from research on animals" or "no matter how many humans would be saved, it's not worth the life of even one animal") tends to discredit the validity of the movement in the public eye. Second, violence scares people away. We are not living in a country where anyone wants to be associated with terrorism, and although I understand the desire to make change and be heard immediately, in the long run it alienates more people than it converts. Antivivisectionists need a more positive approach if they want to move the animal rights movement from the margins to the mainstream. I will offer such an approach later in this chapter.

The Landscape of Animal Research

I suspect that those animal rights activists who resort to violence do so because they feel unheard by researchers and experimenters. In my opinion, there is a clear lack of communication not only between researchers and animal activists but also between researchers and the wider public. Readers who have made it to this point of the book will recognize that one of the major styles of my research for figuring out a thesis is to jump in, headfirst, to ask the people on the front lines what they think, how they see the world. Characteristically, then, I sent twenty-three e-mails to researchers at my own and neighboring institutions, contacts I had been given through mutual acquaintances, asking them to help me see their side of the picture and asking for comments about the value of animal experimentation in science today. I received only two responses, both from "noninvasive" experimenters. Each would be happy to meet with me, but the worst crime they could be accused of, they claimed, was keeping animals in captivity; one offered that he wholeheartedly opposed invasive experimentation on animals, especially primates. Twenty-one researchers ignored me. I also contacted the director of Duke's Vivarium (the building where many of the research animals are housed), requesting a tour of the facility. I was denied. The director replied that the Vivarium is under twenty-four-hour armed guard surveillance, and that only authorized personnel are allowed entrance.

In Adam Wishart's documentary on animal research, *Monkeys, Rats, and Me*, one young researcher claims, "Animal activists have absolutely no knowledge of what goes on in the laboratory. I would never hurt a rat; they're here to help me and I would never want to hurt them." There is a significant truth to her claim that animal activists have no knowledge of what goes on in the laboratory; how could we when we are given almost no access and little information? Although Wishart's film focuses on the controversy in the United Kingdom surrounding the building of new animal labs at Oxford University, the wall of silence is just as prevalent in the United States as in England. This chapter might have come out quite differently if I could have visited just one lab to see for myself how the animals lived, or if even just one researcher had stepped forward to help me figure out why using animals' bodies was important. I was able to speak with three graduate students who work in the labs of their advisers, and with two techs who keep cages clean and animals fed. But no primary investigator would meet with me; no animal researcher would show me her lab. The woman in Wishart's film is right: I don't know what goes on in the laboratory. But how can I if researchers won't let me in?

The high security and lack of openness testify to the general tenor of the conflict between researchers and activists today. The closed nature of the scientific community indicates researchers are worried about break-ins, property damage, and violence. The closed nature of these environments also supports the privilege and proprietary disposition many researchers have toward their work. Because they live in a world where scientific research on animals regularly leads to valuable medical information (the story most of us learned in high school science classes), researchers see themselves as victims of abuse and violence at the hands of animal activists. Researchers live in a world where testing and experimenting on animals have consistently brought new and lifesaving benefits to humans in every decade of the twentieth century. Testing on animals brought us, for example, blood transfusions and kidney dialysis in the 1910s; insulin for diabetics in the '20s; anesthetics for surgery in the '30s; antibiotics and whooping cough vaccine in the '40s; polio vaccine and kidney transplants in the '50s; heart bypass, valve, and transplant surgery in the '60s; asthma drugs in the '70s; immunosuppressants for transplantation and protease inhibitors for the treatment of HIV/AIDS in the '80s; and gene therapies in the '90s. Without animals, none of these advances would have occurred. Thus, the kind of violence marshaled against them by the ALF and other groups has caused researchers to mistrust anyone outside their circle of trusted colleagues. Communication between scientists and anyone even vaguely associated with animal advocacy has almost completely shut down. And as activists get more impatient and aggressive with their tactics, scientists seem more defensive and secretive about their work.

As suggested earlier, researchers believe that IACUCs constitute the middle ground and that they are indeed already practicing animal welfare. Animal research is expensive, researchers argue. While random source animals can save money (dogs and cats from animal shelters, for example, might cost as little as fifteen to twenty dollars per animal), the more sought-after "purpose bred" animals range in the hundreds of dollars. The more complex the organism is, the more it costs. And genetically modified "knockout" purpose-bred animals (in which certain genes are knocked out or replaced to foster a particular disease or illness) are very dear. Researchers argue, often persuasively, that their labs run on the lowest cost they can. No lab would use a costly monkey when a rat would do. No lab would use fifty rats if five would do. And no lab would use animals at all if nonanimal models were available. In their minds, then, researchers are embodying animal welfare already and do not need to respond to the harassment of activists. They demand that the public trust their judgment in using animals.

There is another way of interpreting scientists' lack of engagement with the public on these issues, however. Robertson Davies has written, "Science is the theology of our time. . . . The new priest in his whitish lab-coat gives you nothing at all except a constantly changing vocabulary . . . and you are expected to trust him implicitly because he knows you are too dumb to comprehend. It's the most overweening, pompous priesthood mankind has ever endured in all its recorded history."[21] While this is certainly a harsh way of looking at things, there is a sense in which it's true that we are all held captive by science and contemporary medicine. It's not just the animals locked in steel cages, but all Americans who take pills for flaws they don't understand or undergo procedures simply because a doctor says they should. It's the way most of us blindly follow doctors' orders and are unwilling to question these authorities. We have given care of our health over to doctors, and many of them are intricately connected to profit-driven pharmaceuticals and biotechs. It's not that medicine isn't useful, it certainly is; the tools and techniques it has brought us are wondrous. The problem is not with the tools but with the idolatrous attitude that has begun to accompany medicine. In some ways, as Davies suggests, science really has become the theology of our time.

Science's great success has been based on its exclusive and unwavering commitment to "the scientific method." Indeed, by the eighteenth century, objectivity had virtually replaced appeals to divine authority. Yet that very success of objectivity and scientific method carries with it a limitation: if science is seen as the only authority, any process or exchange that cannot be observed, quantified, and reproduced can be overlooked and rendered valueless. But there is still the possibility that not everything has a scientific explanation, and it's reasonable to ask how and why scientific knowledge became so influential that we are inclined to believe something only when it has been scientifically "proved." How did scientific knowledge acquire so much persuasive power? And how much of that power is dependent on what happens in laboratories to other animals? Would we not benefit from a public discourse that understood science as having limits? Could we not recognize that there must be limits to the benefit of research, limits to the struggle against death, limits to relieving pain and misery? Can we not imagine that many things have value even if they are not reproducible by science? Our love for animals, for instance? If scientists could learn to have better conversations with animal activists and the general public on these topics, I think we all might be more open to fresh explorations of the role of animals in science.

Although many scientists want the public to unquestioningly trust not only their use of laboratory animals but the direction of their research agendas as well, something of a sea change is taking place in American public opinion. Cloning, genetic manipulation, xenotransplantation, nano-technology, and other new technological therapies raise concerns, and not just because animals are sacrificed. Are we headed in the right direction with all these new interventions? Our novelists and filmmakers spin horror stories about what the world is going to look like once we all become nonhuman or robotic. Are we simply afraid of the unknown? Or are we, as many novels and films portray, headed for the technological breakdown of humanity and civilization itself? Are these technologies tampering with nature—human and otherwise—in a different and new way?

There is no question, in my mind at least, that medicine had a golden age. The advances for human health made throughout the twentieth century stagger the mind. We owe science a lot. But the critical questions here are these: Does that debt include the kind of trust scientists are now asking for, especially when they refuse to communicate on issues as grave as vivisection? Is medicine still a heroic, caring profession, or has the desire for profit altered the way many of the systems work? Do scientists continue to deserve our loyal respect, or do we need to be suspicious of their motives, especially when living creatures are involved? Has science surged too far ahead of public comprehension? Do we really have any sense of what they're doing in these labs with all these innocent animals?

What is at stake in the question of vivisection, then, is the question of social authority. The vast majority of medical breakthroughs of the late nineteenth and twentieth centuries functioned positively for many humans; people could see the benefits and subsequently paid science its due respect. From antibiotics to vaccinations, from organ transplantation to birth control, our lives were made healthier and longer. But the calculation has shifted for many of us recently, and the thought of all those animals tortured and dying in labs across the nation no longer squares with a new allergy medicine patent, or a new leg-pain drug, or the promise of cloned cows in our meat supply. What we need from scientists today is increased conversation and assurance that these animal deaths are worthwhile; what we're getting, because researchers themselves are scared, is silence.

In what follows, my argument will not be that all scientific experiment on animals needs to stop immediately, but rather that scientists have a moral responsibility to better communicate to the public the goals and projected outcomes of their work. Scientists are part of society, and a wider cross section of society needs to be involved in making decisions about animal use in the development of new therapies. Scientists are not above dialogue, but animal activist violence has helped push them to be less open with the public. I will suggest in what follows that if researchers absolutely need animal bodies to advance their studies, they must do a better job of communicating what they're studying and why. I also believe animal activists must reform some of their strategies and theories to find a middle ground that can begin to heal this conflict. Specifically, I believe animal activists need to eschew violence to allow the possibility of peaceable conversation.

A Proposal for a New Middle Ground

One of the things I find most shocking about lab animal research as it exists today is that the grant writers and primary investigators rarely even meet the animals upon whom their experiments are performed, and they virtually never provide care for them. That work is done by lower-level employees; in university settings, that can be graduate or undergraduate students, but in all corporate pharmaceutical and biotech arenas, that work is done by low-paid technicians. These techs often make close to minimum wage and have very little training; as a result, such work is usually not thought of as a profession. In the United States, the people responsible for caring for animals are usually viewed by researchers and the general public as low-level janitorial staff, responsible for feeding animals and cleaning cages, but nothing else. They are usually members of minorities and often do not speak English (which sometimes makes following complicated directions nearly impossible). Indeed, few credentials are needed to get a lab tech job caring for animals in America today.

A different approach could begin with the conviction that what we do with animals in a lab must be grounded in sustained affective connection with the animals themselves. We must start by demanding that researchers provide care for their own animals. I know that any researcher who just read that sentence probably laughed out loud, but I mean it in all sincerity. If you are going to ask an animal for the ultimate sacrifice of her body, you must first be willing to care for her. By providing such care you will get to know her, you may even learn to love her. If you are going to use animals on humans' behalf, you need to know the animal well before you ask him for such sacrifice.

One of the dominant themes of this book has been resistance to corporate abuse of animals; whether in the pet industry, food industry, or in relation to wildlife, a balanced, moderate alternative to "blank check" animal use seeks to take control of animals out of the hands of the corporate leaders and put it into the hands of animal lovers. This will not eliminate all conflict, as there are concrete differences of opinion over when an animal is happy, what is good enough care and protection, and other considerations. But suggesting that moral decisions about animals *must* be made by people who have a concrete connection to them—by the people who love them—offers a middle ground between the strong abolitionist animal rightist position that currently dominates the movement today, and (IACUCS notwithstanding) what I see as the blank-check approach most industries (including science) employ for dealing with animals today. I contend that the reason why animal research is so much more conflicted than any other area of animal use, the reason we call it a war, is precisely the almost total lack of such connections. There is no middle ground that animal lovers can point to as model research because love has been deleted from the equation. So let's ask researchers to take the first step toward connection by providing care themselves. The animals themselves will respond to that care by loving researchers back. Therein lies the beginning of healing.

Indulge me for a moment here. What if, by federal mandate and culturally accepted practice, researchers became the kind of people who cared for their own animal subjects, in their own homes, for, say, a year before the experiment took place and for the natural life of the animal after the experiment ended (if possible)? What if scientists stepped up and took responsibility for the experiment based on the emotional connection the researcher had with the animal? What if they knew the animal well and deeply before cutting her open or injecting her with chemicals? What if they knew their animals' likes and dislikes, their individual personalities? What if they received love and trust from the animal, and only then made the decision about whether his sacrifice would be worth it?[22] In other words, I am simply asking scientists to make the hard decisions that pet rescuers and local farmers and sanctuary workers make on a daily basis: Is this animal worth keeping? Is her life one that can I make room for? Or is she really unable to make the kinds of connections that deem her as valuable in this setting?

Researchers can only treat these animals as objects because they do not know them. Indeed, many scientists see themselves as so important that they are above providing care, above cleaning cages, above feeding and watching and petting a nonhuman animal. They see themselves as superior to the kind of connection that many humans almost naturally make with animals. Herein lies the heart of the problem. If these scientists had to live with their animals, things would change for the better. There would still be a great deal of disparity and disagreement about which animals could and should be used for experiments, but the debate would shift dramatically to a more animal-centered conversation.

In preparation for this chapter, I read stories of many people who experiment on animals because they really don't like animals at all. Part of me sees this orientation as a defense mechanism—how can they afford to like animals if they are hurting and killing them by the dozens or hundreds? But I wonder, if a scientist really and truly doesn't like animals, should he really be conducting experiments on them? Medical researchers who don't like people usually go into a branch of medicine that does not deal directly with human care; the same should apply to animals (rather than the reverse). Only when you care for and connect with someone should you be allowed to use him or her for your benefit.

I think of my own pack of animals, and wonder what I would do if I were a scientist. Jerome, Duncan, and Madonna are closest to my heart, but they maintain that position because they have characters that are good to their cores. If I thought I could cure cancer by experimenting on one of them, I would do it because I know them, and I know in my heart they would want me to. I would work very hard to make sure that every-one who benefited from my experiment knew their names and honored them deeply. They would be heroes; and knowing them the way I do, I believe they would want to be heroes. Some of the other animals I live with are less present and different calculations would have to be made. Chester's happy if he gets his walk, Hattie's happy if she gets the bed; they don't really want to be heroes. The last foster dog I had, Lewis, was the kind of guy who would jump in front of a speeding car to save a squirrel. He would want to make such a sacrifice. The one before that, William, was a quiet and reserved soul; underneath he was afraid and I think just wanted a safe spot on earth. Experimentation would not be an option for him. These would be very, very difficult decisions, in some ways an educated guess about a creature's character, but they are the kinds of decisions I am called upon to make all the time as a guardian and res-cuer; with this proposal, I am simply asking scientists to do the same. I am asking scientists to look into the figurative hearts of their animals, to discover what kind of being their animals are and whether they might or might not choose such sacrifice for themselves. At first, many may not be able to see the magnanimous spirit of someone like Jerome and will choose the least connected animals to experiment on. But choosing the least connected and engaged will certainly be better than not know-ing the animals at all. And in time, I believe researchers will be able to learn which animals stand out and want to be remembered as heroes.

If this proposal were adopted, I can imagine that there would be a sig-nificant shift in the kinds of experiments conducted. A lot of people might elect to continue working on rats and mice because they don't think the connection they could make with those species would be strong enough to deter experimentation. In a sense, then, the rats and mice would have to fend for themselves, and some might reach out and connect. If they didn't connect, if they couldn't help us transform our feelings toward them, then maybe they would be better off being sacrificed. At the very least, after a year of trying to figure out what an animal's spirit is like, I believe most scientists would try to conduct their experiments in a way that was less harmful and less painful. As I've said before, I don't have a problem with keeping animals in captivity as long as they are treated well and receive love. And I want to get to a point where we animal lovers can trust scientists to say the (very) few animals they sacrificed were the kinds of creatures who wanted their lives to have that kind of meaning. We're all going to die someday. Some human people are born with and develop such a sense of greatness that they will be remembered for generations after their deaths. I believe there are great animals too, of all species. But, in the current structure of science, the world today has no way of sorting who those particular animals are. That's the problem I want to end. I want to know the names of the pigs sacrificed for my insulin or the multitude of animals sacrificed for all the products I use and consume. I would build shrines for them if I knew who they were. We need better stories of the animals sacrificed for our benefit, and those can only come if the researchers using them know and love them.

Animals who do participate in experiments should be allowed to live happy and full lives after the experiments if they are not called on to be sacrificed. In *Thanking the Monkey,* Karen Dawn writes, "If any experiment is deemed absolutely necessary for medical progress, participation in one should earn an animal a luxurious retirement."[23] I couldn't agree more and would like to take it one step further. Animals who undergo experiments for human benefit should be made into public heroes. We should print their photos and tell their stories in newspapers. We should honor them for the gifts they bring to all our lives.

I recognize that this proposal is not the kind of solid abolitionist intervention that the animal rights community hopes for. There will still be people who experiment on animals, but I would hope that the nature of the experiments is different, that researchers would choose and treat their subjects as living subjects and not as objects. It is a middle ground that neither animal rights nor the scientific community is going to like, but it may be one that each side can live with, at least better than the way they're living together now. There are many in the animal rights community who feel that all experimentation must end immediately, but I think the majority of animal advocates feel the problem is that experimentation today is done heartlessly and without adequate oversight. Forcing researchers to activate their consciences by providing care would, I think, alleviate untold suffering and ease the urgency that many activists feel. It might also force scientists into a better mode of communication about their research, breaking down the wall of superiority associated with science. If scientists tell the public about the wonderful sacrifices their beloved animals made for the betterment of the world, maybe we could hear their stories, honor their friends, and still have all the benefits science wants to provide.

Put differently, this proposal will not be acceptable to the extremes on either side, to the animal rights activists who firmly believe humans should not use or interact with animals for any reason, or to the researchers who believe animals are no different from test tubes. They are destined to remain entrenched in irreconcilable conflict. But a lot of Americans already occupy a middle ground; they believe that perhaps some animals could be sacrificed (infrequently) if doing so clearly advanced what they see as legitimate medicine. These people might feel much better about animal sacrifices if researchers were willing to carry the moral weight of experimenting on animals they love and were more open about both the research and the love. The wall between science and the public has to be torn down, and the only beings that can do that, I believe, are the animals themselves. We need a new approach that gives them that chance.

I am advocating that to treat lab animals more fairly, we must make their affective subjectivities more visible through the power of connection. Rather than treating them as objects, as "test tubes with tails," we ought to treat them as subjects, with temperaments, desires, and personalities. Advocates of animal research tell us that every drug we take and virtually every product we use has been tested on an animal (certainly for safety, if not for efficacy). I believe them. But what I want to know is that animal's name. I want to know her species, where she lived, what her sacrifice looked like. We know the names of many researchers (or can look them up quite easily); if we don't know their names, we can be fairly assured that they were (hopefully) compensated financially for their work. What we don't know is the names of the animals who gave their lives for our safety, animals who received no compensation whatsoever, no honor, no memory, nothing. This is what needs to be corrected. This information will establish the connection that current practices work so hard to obscure.

Glimmers of Hope

Several students I spoke with helped me understand that some connections between lab techs and animals do happen already.[24] One student told me that he went into the lab every day to play with a dog who had been involved in blood chemistry experiments a few years before. According to the rules of this lab, he explained, all animals used in an experiment must be killed after that experiment was complete (as researchers fear the animals might carry diseases or toxins into the general public). This student, however, had convinced the researcher to keep the dog alive after the experiment was officially over by arguing that long-term studies of aging and blood chemistry might prove informative. He told me that the real reason he made the argument wasn't about blood or aging but that this was a good dog that didn't deserve to die. He wasn't sure what was going to happen after he graduated and planned to ask the researcher if he could take the dog with him. Other students and lab techs have "rescued" rats and mice from completed experiments and taken them home to happier lives. There seems to be an almost underground network of advice and support for lab workers in relation to animals; these students learn from others that establishing bonds with the animals can be rewarding, if only because the animals themselves are more likely to cooperate with procedures if they are administered by someone they trust. Several students told me they took their animals special treats from home, read to them, or played music for them in off-hours. These kinds of practices, I think, are a beginning. In a sense, what I am asking is that primary investigators also try to see the world from the perspective of their research animals. Whether it's a frog or a dog or a rat or a primate, they must try to imagine what his or her life inside a steel cage must be like. From that point of connection, they will be in a better position to ask three questions: Can they use fewer animals and save others? Can they make the lives of the animals they do use any better (i.e., give them more enrichment and socialization and less pain)? And finally, can they move to a world where they can conduct their research without animals at all?

Scientific organizations including the National Academy of Sciences, the Institute for Laboratory Animal Research, and many antivivisectionist organizations, including the American Anti-Vivisectionist Society and the Animal Welfare Institute, have developed a program they call "the three Rs": reduction in the number of animals used in any given experiment, refinement of the experiment to limit the suffering of animals to the minimum necessary to accomplish the experimental goals, and replacement, whereby animals are eliminated from experiments when non-animal models such as computer programs will do. Indeed, for many of these organizations, the strategy of complete replacement of all use of animals is the ultimate goal; much of the discussion regarding replacement revolves around the increasing viability of stem cells and cell lines for research purposes, as well as the use of invertebrates in some of these experiments. Following a report issued by the NAS in 2008, a number of agencies have been working toward making this goal a reality in the next twenty to thirty years.

The goals of the three Rs—especially replacement—are laudable and should be supported. Entering the affective world of lab animals will prompt all researchers to ask the kinds of questions that will bring about these goals more quickly. Greater attention to connection with lab animals can and will not only help speed the progress of these agendas, it will also help us more clearly understand our place in the world. If we believe animals are different from us and hold the possibility of teaching us new kinds of ways of being in the world, then we need better ways of communicating with them. A change of heart concerning animals entails a full recognition that all animals understand the world in their own way. That understanding, granted, is not the same understanding shared by humans. Animals live in different worlds, with different levels of awareness, contours of reality, and ways of sensing their surroundings. They are not only different from us, they are different differently. They have other scales and methods for comprehending, shaping, and producing reality. They live in worlds we can't quite imagine because our senses have not shaped our reality in a way that can easily comprehend theirs. Although we all share the same space of earth, we inhabit vastly different psychic landscapes. I've talked about my dogs' sense of smell; imagine the world from the body of a rat, a monkey, a bat. We have to start figuring out how to honor the knowledge they live with, even if we may never have complete access to it. We can never enter the full inner life and private experiences of another human being, but we continue to try our best to understand their worldview, especially if they are loved ones. The same should hold for nonhuman animals.

Some people will argue that what I am suggesting here is sheer anthropomorphism—the attribution of a human form, human characteristics, or human behavior to nonhuman beings or things. In a sense, the charge of anthropomorphism has its roots in scientific method; that is, because we can't prove beyond the shadow of a doubt that animals think or feel or communicate, this criticism goes, we must assume they don't.[25] Anything that is not reproducible and measurable, anything that we can't prove exists, is, in this mind-set, not worthy of our attention. The effect of the criticism of anthropomorphism has been unbalanced. In fear of making animals too much like humans, we often err in the opposite direction and make them into objects. But again, anyone who lives with animals knows that they are not things, that there is a presence behind those eyes that cannot be denied. Indeed, an exaggerated fear of anthropomorphism is as unscientific as being unaware of the need for caution in attributing feelings and intentions to other species. We are all part of a great chain of evolution and existence, and to believe that consciousness and connection only evolved in "man" is folly. Surely closely related species perceive the world in similar fashions. Those who refuse to recognize these similarities are guilty of "anthropodenial"; in other words, people who insist that humans are exceptional and superior to all other living creatures do not sufficiently understand the implications of evolution. We are more alike than many want to admit.[26]

In his 1974 essay "What Is It Like to Be a Bat?," Thomas Nagel elucidates the complicated world of sonar to convince us that, in short, we simply can never know what it is really like to be a bat; we can never think like a bat because sonar is not similar to any human sense. While I agree that it is hard to imagine what it means to "see" the world through sound, the essence of my argument here is that we should use our imaginations to try. No one can ever fully know what it's like to be another person either, say, a starving child in Africa or a Chinese peasant caught in a flood. But morality dictates that we try to see the world from different perspectives, that we walk a mile in the shoes of another. We need to do the same for animals. It's impossible here to think like a bat *only* if we believe it's impossible. We may get it wrong at first, and we may get it wrong all the way through, but if we are ever going to understand animals, we must try.

German biologist Jakob von Uexküll used the term *Umwelten* to describe the limitations of understanding the worldviews of other creatures.[27] As he outlines it, each creature is trapped inside something like a soap bubble, an *Umwelt*, a world of understanding that is developed through differing senses and the habits that accompany them. As he writes, "Picture all the animals around us, be they beetles, butterflies, flies, mosquitoes or dragonflies that people a meadow, enclosed within soap bubbles, which confine their visual space and contain all that is visible to them."[28] They—and we—are permanently locked into their own subjectivity, unable to escape; we cannot fully occupy the world of another, he says. Each and every leap of the imagination inevitably falls short of complete understanding. Within that reality, though, Uexküll reminds us that the world of the other—be that a human, animal, or plant—is always bumping up against and connecting with our own, much the way soap bubbles do. Whether in the form of pollen or manure, friendship or food, other beings intermingle with and are connected to us; the soap bubbles are not solid, they change their shape and open onto other worlds. We can see into them, if only distortedly. For Uexküll, we are enfolded in the limits of our own particular niches, but finally not entirely confined by them.

To find our place in the world, we must try to push through to the *Umwelten* of other animals. What matters in connecting with other beings is not a shared identity or background of experiences; rather, what matters is the kind of involvement with another that produces affection. To connect with others means doing our best to understand them and to love them; this is true for other humans as well as for animals. By not searching out affective relationships with lab animals, and not basing our advocacy work on the experience of those relationships, the animals themselves go unrepresented. To advocate for lab animals, we need to know them, we need to listen to them, we need to love them, and we need to talk and write about them in ways that bespeak who they are. As Uexküll proposes, we may not always get it right, but we always need to try.

On Language, Affect, and Communication

The philosophical mechanism that allows us to perform medical experiments on human beings is called "informed consent." Put simply, an individual has to understand the possible outcomes of a new drug or intervention and fully and freely agree to the risks involved. We do not experiment on children or mentally disabled people, because we believe they cannot give informed consent. We do, however, experiment on animals without informed consent, because we don't believe they have the kind of selves that require consideration. We don't exactly assume that consent is present; we overlook its absence because we assume animals are not really interactive or conscious.

In addition to supporting the three Rs, then, one way to approach the question of the Umwelten or worldviews of lab animals is to teach them our language. Although the history of animal language studies is long and complicated and beyond the scope of this book, many scientists agree that great leaps in interspecific communication have been made with both great apes and parrots in controlled scientific settings.[29] Sue Savage-Rumbaugh has taught a bonobo named Kanzi to use a keyboard and lexicon to give voice to his desires and inner emotional states.[30] Kanzi knows hundreds of symbols and uses them correctly in a wide variety of settings. He has also been successful at crafting rudimentary knives out of stone. Roger Fouts taught a chimp named Washoe over a thousand ASL (American Sign Language) signs for communication; Washoe in turn passed many of these signs to other chimps she shared an enclosure with.[31] Although Washoe died in 2007, Fouts continues to observe the dissemination of ASL throughout the chimps Washoe knew. Irene Pepperberg's African Grey parrot Alex learned to correctly identify objects according to color, substance, shape, and number at a success rate of more than 90 percent.[32] Alex also died in 2007, but Pepperberg continues her work with another African Grey named Griffin. Watching videos of these animals communicate with humans using our language inspires the possibility that someday we may actually be able to simply ask animals whether they would like to offer themselves as research subjects; we possibly could obtain from them the same kind of informed consent we require for human subjects.[33]

But until that happens, or until the third R of complete replacement of animals in labs becomes the norm, I suggest another approach that can begin to heal the world for lab animals immediately. That is the path of affective connection. Here, the goal is not simply for them to learn our language but also for us to learn theirs, to move forward together by developing new modes of communication. Although full replacement stands as the ultimate hope, until all scientists agree that animal experimentation is unnecessary, we need a better way to understand the worldviews and subjectivities of lab animals. And while it would be ideal if we could talk to them in the manner of Doctor Doolittle, such unmediated language exchange is, right now, not a possibility. We need to be more creative in our modes of communication with other animals. Remembering that we may not always get it right, we also recognize that we need to try. Affective connection is the place to start such a project.

But what do these alternate forms of communication look like? What could it mean to share an *Umwelt* or soap bubble with a nonhuman animal, even if only partially and temporarily? In her *Songs of the Gorilla Nation,* Dawn Prince-Hughes exemplifies such a connection with a captive gorilla named Congo. At one meeting, he offered Prince-Hughes a twig through the bars of his cage. At first she did not understand the gesture, but soon he motioned for her to throw her apple over the wall to him. She suddenly saw the exchange of the twig for the apple as a way for Congo to mark friendship and connection. She writes, "It is clear to me that not only do apes have a language that is complex and holistic, but by communicating with us, they illustrate that it may be we who are less skilled at the art of sharing true subjective experience."[34]

The concept of affective connection gives us a way to name the sharing of subjective experiences and a way to recognize a broad range of interspecific communication, even those that fall outside the realm of language. Think about the fact that when you love another human person, you often know what he or she is thinking without exchanging any words. It's the way he holds his body, the way she looks at you, the feeling you get being around him. A similar thing often happens between people and their pets. Julie Ann Smith describes this affective connection in her life with pet rabbits:

My rabbits execute actions all the time that convey their understanding that they are in a relationship of some kind with me. They constantly shove their noses under my hands to demand petting. I have seen them work out relationships among themselves in ways I would call extended performance: endless marking, bodily postures, directed gestures—all designed to produce a response that will elicit a counter response, which will be modified to evoke a slightly different response. When the rabbit Rose sometimes runs circles around my chair before she plops down beside it, she performs her recognition of our relationship by referencing the ancient ways of rabbit courting. Does she see me as her partner, and, if so, what does partnership mean to her? Has she borrowed an act from another context to express something about the two of us here and now?[35]

It is this kind of curiosity about the *Umwelt* or worldview of the other that affective connection seeks. It is the knowing that happens through living together. It does not have to be about the English language, but about shared soap bubbles that make coexistence pleasurable. It is about watching, wondering, imagining, and loving the way another performs her place in the world.

As I argued in chapter 3, one of the central aspects of affect is the notion that our physical bodies are inextricably bound up with our feelings, sensations, and sentiments; there I argued that as a result of culture, habit, age, and genetics, different bodies needed different kinds of food. One of the easiest ways to affectively connect with other animals, then, is by learning from them how and what to feed them. In the wake of the 2007 pet food recalls, I switched my dogs from processed kibble to home-cooked meals. Even though none of my dogs were infected with tainted food, the whole scare made me realize that good (local, organic, free-range, sustainably and humanely raised) nutrition had changed my life, and I wanted them to experience a similar transformation. Cooking for my dogs deepened my relationship with them in ways that fostered the kind of greater affective connection I am striving to describe here. It inspired the same kind of curiosity that Smith describes with her rabbits. In short, it allowed me to see more clearly into their soap bubbles.

I started with recipes that basically subscribed to one-third (free-range, grass-fed, pastured, local) meat, one-third whole grain, and one-third organic or fresh vegetables. I would cook up a stockpot of this recipe once every few days, altering it with different meats, grains, and vegetables at each cooking. My dogs let me know—and fast—what they liked and didn't like. I just have to watch them eat to understand the complexity of their selves and their desires. Jerome absolutely loves any meat. He pulls it out of the mixture and eats it with such relish; no matter what it is, if it came from an animal, it is, for him, delectable. I found my local farmers to be great resources for very affordable cuts of meat that don't sell well because most humans often don't eat them. Organs, feet, ears, backs, testicles, necks, wingtips, hearts, tongues—Jerome loves them all. He literally smiles while eating. (The farmers are thrilled to offload these unpopular items; as one of them put it, "With your dogs, you are literally practicing nose to tail eating!") Conversely, Duncan often leaves the meat chunks aside and goes instead for the vegetables and grains. The week I served them oatmeal, Duncan went wild. This is a guy who didn't really ever seem to care about food, but when oatmeal is on the menu he prances and dances for his food and comes alive in new ways. One day when I didn't have time to cook grains, I served them free-range scrambled eggs with cottage cheese, and Duncan loved that even more. The girls are pretty easygoing, but Jubilee needs a lot more of this food than she did of the kibble. She loses weight fast when fed the same amount as other dogs and will steal anything at all that she can eat. And Hattie hates vegetables. She picks through her bowl as if sifting for diamonds, and leaves even the tiniest piece of carrot or okra to the side (and yes, sometimes she even buries them in my bed). Chester likes everything and is visibly thrilled to be off kibble.

After a few weeks, I realized this new food program was giving them another way to communicate with me; in responding to their desires, I communicate back. Whereas before this, they had all gotten the same kind of kibble in varying amounts, now they had preferences and appetites that were clear and apparent. This new food program made them more distinct from each other. They became even more themselves, in my eyes. If I force meat on Duncan, he quickly develops diarrhea and is not happy. If I feed Jubilee the same amount as the others, she loses weight. And if

Jerome doesn't have his local meat, he is miserable; his head hangs low. Slowly I started tailoring their meals to their preferences. Jerome now gets almost all meat with a little bit of grains and vegetables on the side. Duncan gets grains and vegetables, and lots of eggs and dairy; he also loves almost any fruit (which no one else will even consider). Chester and the girls get the standard one-third, one-third, one-third recipe, although I take Hattie's portion out before I add the vegetables. And I always give Jubilee a lot more than I think she needs. She is still thin as a reed but seems less frantic about life in general now.

It's hard to explain, but even this communication around food helps me formulate ideas about their character, and whether or not any of them would want to be sacrificed for legitimate scientific progress. As I said, I believe Jerome and Duncan have the kind of souls that, if they were human, would be destined to be great. Although Jerome's head hangs low when there's no meat in his bowl, he eats what is given to him because he accepts the world as it is. If the world called upon him to make the sacrifice of his body, I believe he would comply willingly. Similarly, Duncan eats meat even when it gives him diarrhea. He wants to be stoic and wants to be a hero, even if it upsets his digestive system. Hattie, Chester, and Daisy just want what they want; they don't have designs on being great. They are just here, enjoying life; they pick out the things they don't like and move on. And Jubilee, well, I'm still trying to figure her out. I don't make these observations about their character based solely on food, but food is another avenue of communication that deepens my perception of them greatly.

People who don't live with animals may not appreciate the kind of connection that food affords, but for me it was like opening a new channel of contact between us. It isn't about language exactly; they don't order from a menu or name what they want for dinner in words. But close observation, coupled with love, reveals much. I understand their bodies better and I am able to accommodate their desires in ways that deepen our connection. My affection for them makes the cooking a pleasurable experience; after all, I am doing something that makes the people I love the most infinitely happier. How could I see that as a chore? And they are now so much happier when dinnertime rolls around. I know them better. I attend to their desires and they reciprocate by being even more in love with me. They make eye contact much more now; they seek me out when meal times come around; they knock against my elbow as I type as if to say, "What's on the menu for me today? Might there be an egg for Jubilee or some blueberries for Duncan or some liver for Jerome?" I feel as if I am more magical to them now, and in turn, they are closer and more special to me than ever before.

Communication is a journey we are all on together, and learning about their desires makes me—and them—indescribably happy. One of the easiest ways to understand another animal is by attending to her food preferences. Many pet guardians, farmers, exotic animal owners, and sanctuary and zoo workers already know this. Attending to animals' dietary preferences renders their subjectivity more visible; it makes them happy to see us, and happy to be seen in this special way. They connect better as a result. Food, of course, is just one of many ways we can be affectively involved with other animals; I use it here as an illustration of the kind of shared subjectivity we all should strive toward. It's that intermingling of lives, that shared communication that stands outside language, that I think needs to be embraced in the laboratory.

Scientists might say this way of connecting seems silly and sentimental. Animals themselves don't deserve such recognition, they say; they are "only" animals. Their lab animals are not pets; they do not even have names, only numbers. This is precisely what we need to correct. We—all humans who benefit from experimentation on animals—need to come to grips with the real, somatic sacrifices lab animals made and make on our behalf. We need to figure out a way to honor those sacrifices. The worst exploitation science performs on animals is not cutting them open but rather believing they don't possess preferences, desires, consciousness, or character. I have argued throughout this book that the human-animal connection can become the new starting point of worldmaking. It can heal the rupture we have with nature; it can help check the human ego and keep our place on the planet in perspective. Nowhere is this connection more desperately needed than in the laboratory. Scientists should only continue to experiment on lab animals if they can learn to recognize that they too have meaningful, subjective lives. Living in embodied ways with other animals helps us know them in mystical and spiritual ways. Lab animals are in great need of such recognition and connection, partly because they make the most supreme of sacrifices any being can make in this world, and partly because they are so terribly hidden from our gaze. Imagining a new reality for lab animals, one where they choose their own food, or where the humans around them develop a curiosity about their preferences and worldview, begins in the request that researchers live with and care for them. Coupled with the three Rs and further studies in language acquisition, affective connection will change the world for lab animals. Understanding affect gives us a way to make the world a better place for them. And as I will explicate more fully in the next chapter, it also gives us a way to understand their sacrifice and our interconnectedness more deeply.

SIX CLOTHING OURSELVES IN STORIES OF LOVE
Affect and Animal Advocacy

THE FIFTH AND FINAL WAY WE HUMANS USE ANIMALS to enhance our lives is through clothing. Debates rage between abolitionists, utilitarians, and welfarists on questions of fur, leather, and wool; animal products are also used in the production of lotions, perfumes, and hair-care products. For the most part, positions taken up by various stakeholders mirror the arguments made elsewhere about the human use of animals. While orthodox animal rights proponents often wear no leather, wool, or fur, and work hard to avoid not only products that use animals but also ones tested on animals, utilitarians and welfarists often take more moderate positions.

Rather than rehearsing these debates, this chapter uses clothing as a metaphor for a new way to think about ourselves—our "selves"—and our relationship to animals. Clothing becomes a tool that can lead us to a better understanding of how we make our worlds. Through dressing in certain ways, we send messages to others about who we are, what we believe, where we belong. Clothing helps us produce our identity, and it is this process of identity production that is the focus of this chapter. Indeed, I push the metaphor far beyond the shirts and pants we carry on our bodies into the realms of habit, comportment, emotion, and affect. I am looking for new ways to dress and perform our selves that will produce deeper and more meaningful relationships with the earth and her animals.

What if we could think beyond our bodies and the clothing that wraps them to a larger understanding of selfhood? What if we told the story of our subjectivity by focusing on the matter that surrounds our blood and bones? What if we could manage to convince ourselves that in addition to food, our bodies also really needed clean air and water to flourish? What if we understood that the best way to care for the self is to care for wildlife? What if we understood that if the birds and creatures of the earth thrive, so too shall we? What if we constructed our sense of selfhood around the idea that we share this space and time and breath with all animals? What if we could see the ground that holds us up as part of us as well, the air and the sky as part of our lungs? The boundary between the rest of the world and our selves wouldn't rest or hover around our skin and clothes, but would reside instead out there somewhere, in the world. While traditional philosophy posits the human being as the center of everything important, the metaphor of clothing, and the liminal space it occupies, can help us tell a different story. That story could focus on the environments we share with other creatures; it could remember that we too are animals; it could help us recognize that if we don't take proper care of animals, we stand to lose the very world that sustains us.

To unpack this metaphor of clothing, I suggest that we need to expand the discourse of animals into a new affective domain where rationality and emotionality are connected, where "the head" and "the heart" are not two separate entities. We need to remember that affect is also about bodies and corporeal conflict, and finally that reason, emotions, and fleshliness, especially when they connect to others, often create something larger and more awe inspiring than any of the separate parts. Affect helps us see ourselves as different kinds of subjects that not only possess reason, emotion, and bodies but can also chase wonders and create new worlds. Clothing ourselves in affect means recognizing these gifts; it understands that the head and the heart tell the same story from different angles, and if we can get the heart to recognize a different story, if only a little, the head will change too.

The Concept of Affect

The concept of affect means many different things in many different places; so let me be clear about how I am using it. A number of new works on the role of affect have emerged recently.[1] In sometimes very dense prose, they suggest we take the affective realm more seriously as a form of both politics and knowledge. In the humanities, affect claims a deep lineage in contemporary theoretical work including postmodernism, post-structuralism, and psychoanalysis. It is built on the shoulders of Foucauldian theories of social construction, on Derrida's work on deconstruction, as well as on insights about emotions found in the work of Freud, Lacan, and Deleuze. In the social sciences, affect refers to both positive and negative emotions, and the ways those emotions present themselves in certain bodies and in certain settings. The dictionary definition of affect also has many meanings. As a verb, affect means to act on, to produce and effect or change, to impress the mind or move the feelings of another. As a noun, affect speaks to our feelings and emotions; in psychoanalysis, it also sees those emotions as having a basis in our physical bodies and our corporeal habits. Finally, the dictionary tells us that affect also has an obsolete usage; in the nineteenth century it meant affection, passion, sensation, tendency, inclination, inward disposition or feeling. I want to use all these ideas in a way, but let me begin by showing precisely what the concept of affect rejects and replaces.

From eighteenth-century Western philosophies associated with the Enlightenment, many of us inherited a view of ourselves that is dominated by concerns about things like personal freedom and individual responsibility. The philosophers of the Enlightenment turned the thinking of the Western world away from blind adherence to monarchs and religious leaders, and onto the idea that every human individual housed his or her own moral authority. The founding fathers of our country used these ideas as blueprints for citizenship. As Americans, most of us are taught to believe that each person is finally ultimately responsible for his or her own destiny. Many of us derive a great sense of hope from this ideology; we believe we can succeed if we work hard. This sense of individualism very much relates to the way René Descartes theorized us as uniquely rational beings. Most of us were taught to believe that something—though we're not quite sure what—makes us different from all the other animals on earth. We learned that we alone have hopes about the future, anticipate death, have deep thoughts about the meaning of life, and possess free will.[2] We were taught to think of ourselves as whole beings, as having some sort of core essence that is unaffected by the world around us. What we buy, how we entertain ourselves, the choices we make about our personal lifestyles, what we eat, even our actions in general aren't really "who we are"; they may reflect our characters in some ways, but they can't be said to constitute the core of our existence.[3]

The concept of affect tells us that this sense of a self that transcends culture and nature somehow now seems wrong. We are, affect suggests, thoroughgoing products of the worlds that surround us. We are constructed, and that sense of rationality that seemed above or outside culture and nature no longer holds. Or put differently, if we do view ourselves as superior to everything else around us, it is not because there is an intrinsic, inherent, objective difference inside of us, but only because our particular culture tells us this story. Categories of race, gender, sexuality, ethnicity, class, nation, religion, and so on operate to mark us as separate and different from each other; however, because these categories are only used to construct and identify human characteristics, they also function to produce a strong divide between humans and all other creatures.

One way to understand this idea of affective construction is to imagine that we humans really don't have the kind of freedom or free will the Enlightenment philosophers thought we had. We don't choose our own destiny in the same profound way Descartes thought we did. We're not fully determined beings either, of course; that is, our lives in Western society aren't mapped out for us from birth. Rather we are constructed, or hampered if you will, by the shape of language and culture into which we are born, and the ways we do or do not connect with everything around us. We can't think things that don't have words; we can't act on things without some basic understanding of them. These theories use the word "constructed" instead of "determined" because it signals not only the loss of absolute freedom in the Cartesian sense but also a positive aspect: that is, we are who we are because the world around us made us this way, because we have these particular affective connections. Without these enmeshments, we would have no language, no way of being in the world, no sense of understanding or awareness. Because we are social creatures, we would not exist without these hampering connections and relationships. We make choices, of course, but only within the cultural logic we have available to us. The way I think of constructed subjectivity is that it is as if we were characters in a good novel. You never know what will happen when you turn the page, but what can happen—in a good novel, at least—is structured by all the pages that came before. That is, the narrative will only be persuasive if we see and understand its development as a product of its environment. The next page is possible only because of what preceded it.

The pragmatic outcome of Enlightenment philosophy is the tool of rights. In a liberal society, the "true self" that each individual allegedly possesses is protected by a catalog of agreements we make with other, equally rational citizens; this catalog is called rights. Each individual person has the freedom to pursue her own desires and interests in whichever way she wants; rights function to facilitate these individualized visions as much as possible by making sure that one person's good does not infringe upon that of another. In Enlightenment philosophy, each individual, then, is believed to be a self-contained, autonomous, and self-determined unit, protected by agreements called rights. The concept of affect challenges that view and suggests instead that we are creatures bound to each other by the fluidity of habits, language, and culture. In this frame, there is no sense of self that precedes this construction. We human subjects are not exactly born with rights, then, but rather we are born into a culture in which one dominant story that constructs us is the story of rights.

Taking the concept of affect seriously means recognizing that the ideology that advocates for animal rights is in some ways moving in the wrong direction. Animal rights is trying to take the tools produced by Enlightenment thought and extend them into the domain of animals. From this perspective, the exclusion of animals from righted protection is a mistake that can be rectified by granting animals similar protections. However, the concept of affect helps us see that the tools of the Enlightenment are deeply flawed. I contend that even if we could extend rights to animals, Enlightenment philosophy advocates a very problematic kind of subject; it advocates beings that are separate, autonomous, and unconnected—beings that are primarily responsible for themselves alone. It does not attend to interconnection and dependency. The ideology of rights fosters a kind of self-centeredness, especially in relation to entities that aren't thought to possess rights—like air, water, sky, earth, and, currently, nonhuman animals. Even if we could grant rights to animals, such a project would have little effect on environmental problems. It would do nothing to protect natural habitat of wild animals. What we need is a sense of selfhood that teaches us to view ourselves in a much larger frame, that constructs our interests much more broadly to include the well-being of fellow travelers and the environments that sustain us all. We need a view of our own subjectivity that highlights affective connections and identifications with the other. Affect opens the door to that kind of subjectivity by recognizing the power of connection and enmeshment.

Granting animals rights leads us to an abolitionist policy toward them. If a strong rightist agenda succeeds, we would not be able to keep them as pets or on farms; we couldn't "own" them or use them or be in relationship to them. If we follow the logic of rights all the way to its conclusion, we humans end up in a world that has no animals, with the possible exception of wildlife (if we manage not to destroy their habitats). This is exactly the opposite of what we need, I believe. The problems we are experiencing in the world today with regard to environment and animals stem from the fact that humans and animals have fewer and fewer meaningful relationships. Affect gives us the tools to mark those existing relationships as important; it prompts us to rediscover many different kinds of connections with animals and thus helps us poke through into a new kind of reality.

Affect does not demand that we abandon reasoned debate. Rather, it recognizes that reason, emotion, flesh, and spirit are inextricably intertwined. Descartes and many Enlightenment philosophers tried to pull them apart by valorizing only rationality, but the concept of affect recognizes that all are at play in the production of our lives. It challenges the idea of detached rationality; being is no longer a question of "I think, therefore I am" but a project of being immersed in culture, language, and narrative. Affect provides openings for the movement of the heart, and uses those openings to galvanize political action. It allows us to form a social movement that uses the current popularity of pets as a foundation for sustained animal love, and teaches us how to extend that love into other domains. Affect tells us that the role of stories is critically important, as stories function as a central way of forming connections and interweavings with others.

I use the concept of affect as a portal that can allow us to move into a kind of fanciful and powerful world around animals. In grasping toward a practice that allows us to see animals as commanding beings, affect gives us the language to see them in such a different light. Through stories and deep connection, we can understand animals not as objects or property but as bearers of talents, sensibilities, and powers that we have too long overlooked. Through the language of affect, we can see animals as subjects that, whether we know it or not, affect us. We make our worlds in relation to them; how we treat them matters because they are watching and interpreting us, and their worldviews matter. They contain mysteries and truths that we need to move forward. Affect allows a "being with" animals that recognizes what animals see and know is the only path for a sustained humanity. The concept of affect helps make this visible, especially in the emotional bonds many of us feel with pets, farm animals, or wildlife. These bonds are not add-ons to an already established human identity; they are circuits of exchange that direct our actions and ethics. These relationships change us on the deepest level. The concept of affect also highlights the embodied nature of our relationship with animals. We exchange flesh, air, water, and love with them, and they and we emerge as different beings as a result of the relationship. The openings that affect afford us point toward a more deeply spiritual way of being in the world with other animals. A practice that strives toward mutual recognition and intermingling can easily be accessed once we open our thinking onto affect.

Several thinkers suggest that the kind of spiritual relationship I seek to describe here has been lost as a result of human domestication of animals. In his *Hunters, Herders, and Hamburgers,* historian Richard Bulliet argues that hunting communities were by nature more spiritual toward animals. For him, the hunt itself produced a kind of balance with nature whereby the animals commanded human respect, and killing them inspired a feeling of profound admiration. Bringing down a wild animal not for sport but for sustenance is, according to Bulliet, an honorable and spiritual way to procure meat and clothing. The wildness of the hunted animal ensures that it had a good and natural life, and hunting returns the human to a more natural and primitive mind-set as he pursues his prey. For Bulliet, the spirit of the thing rests on the fact that the animals are wild and must be chased and hunted. The hunt is not easy; it takes work, and that work reconciles the hunter with his essential nature. As he is hunting, the hunter must ask himself questions about his own self-worth and wonder about why his life is more valuable than his prey's. These questions and internal dialogues help produce a sound ethical orientation toward other living creatures. The hunter and the hunted deeply affect each other.

In *Coming Home to the Pleistocene,* naturalist Paul Shepard makes a very similar argument.[4] For him, the fundamental nature of humans was formed by our hundreds of thousands of years as hunter-gatherers, and that our subsequent lifestyle as herders and farmers has been very destructive not only of our lands but also of our psyches. Hunting, according to Shepard, renders us one with nature and all creatures. The best way to love animals is to enter their world and become one of them, says Shepard. Indeed, the hunt allows humans to be fully aware of the substantial exchanges that happen between animals and us, and only in hunting does killing and eating animals become the ultimate act of respect for animals. That spiritual connection we have with nature is lost once we tame it for our own uses, Shepard says. When we see ourselves as something above or outside nature, we lose sight of the fundamental things that keep us affectively connected. Only through hunting for meat and skins, according to Shepard, can our natural balance with earth and animals be again achieved.

The spirituality that emerges in these descriptions of hunting is filled with claims about the role of affect in identity production. Subsistence hunters (as opposed to sport hunters) kill animals with an orientation toward connection and interrelatedness. Hunting inspires awe and incurs guilt. Meat is not something to be consumed often or mindlessly; it is a celebration of the sacrifice an animal made so that humans may live. Hunting communities often identify themselves in terms of the types of animals that constitute the bulk of their food; "deer people" or "buffalo people" in some symbolic ways become the animals they eat. The concept of affect highlights these deep corporeal connections between humans and animals, and points the way to a new dimension of animal advocacy.

The connection the hunter has with his prey is driven by hunger and deep passion. In many settings, the hunter puts himself at risk to procure this meat; even if there aren't predators like wolves, jaguars, or alligators waiting to make the hunter himself food, accidents happen, snakes bite, rivers flood, hunters get lost. Being part of a hunt means accepting vulnerability. In this world, the animal and the human exchange both risk and flesh as part of a sacred food chain. Awareness of emotions involved for both parties is crucial. Subsistence hunting demands that we recognize that part of using an animal's body ethically means that we understand the sacrifice entailed. Hunting for meat is a deep way to connect with an animal's spirit. Hunting makes the human more ethical because, by virtue of the task in which he is engaged, he must reconcile himself to the spiritual dimension of his own animality. The hunter gives thanks for the life of his prey, and that action restores a certain meaning and morality to the human use of animal bodies.

While Bulliet and Shepard believe that this spiritual balance can only be achieved through hunting, affect theory gives us a way to imagine similarly reciprocal relationships in many different kinds of connections with animals. On many small farms, there is definitely a sense of spirituality in the farming and sacrifice of animals; local farmers are not raising chickens, cows, and pigs in a way that makes those animals into products or objects. The farmers and the animals, along with the soil, the rain, and the sun, are all part of the same system. The small farmer isn't above nature in the sense that she dominates it or sucks all life out of it for her own profit. She is part of nature, and revels in the connections she makes with plants, animals, soil, and all that surrounds her. When I speak with my local farmers they are keenly aware that their relationships with the land and the animals are sacred.

These sacred connections can also be achieved in other relationships with animals. As wild animals lose their natural habitats, they are forced to sacrifice the ways they've lived for centuries. In shifting their sensibilities to adjust to captivity, their affects—their senses of self—must change profoundly. They no longer range fully free; they can't hunt; they must be managed. But what enables some of them to accomplish this transformation are the deep bonds of love and affection they may develop with their human keepers and guardians. It is a shift in affect, a shift in their desires, predilections, attachments, habits, and tendencies, that finally may allow many species to remain extant on this crowded planet. In return, the humans who love them must be willing to make great sacrifices for these attachments. Exotic pet and sanctuary managers must be able to see their own futures in the happiness of their animals; they must be willing to offer them the best care possible in return for such love. Focusing on affect does not mean that everything comes out happy; private owners, especially, must make hard decisions about whom they can connect with, and they must admit that sometimes those connections fail. Using love as the basis of a new form of advocacy is not a utopian fantasy; it is about what is possible. And sometimes limitations arise that make living with certain other beings ultimately impossible, no matter how hard we want it to be different. That's why sanctuaries are so important.

Even in the troubled world of scientific experimentation, I hold that such affective connection may be possible. Some animals may be willing to sacrifice themselves for our benefit. In order to accept that sacrifice in a balanced way, we must pursue greater methods of communication with them. We must become more affectively attuned to them, and be willing to listen to their emotions, languages, needs, predilections, tendencies, desires, wishes, and hopes. The natural outcome of becoming affectively connected to lab animals will mean better ways of treating them. Such a deep bond in the realm of experimentation will push us all to honor their gifts and sacrifices in a more public manner.

Such affective bonds already exist between many people and their pets. In striving to make ourselves worthy of our pets' affections, our sense of self often shifts. When seen in the frame of affect, human-pet connections are not systems of domination; rather we live with our pets simply because we love them and they love us back. In affective love, they teach us things we could not learn if we only strive to dominate them: things like how to watch a good sunset, how to be excited about a long walk or a good treat, how to fight our own fears and phobias and trust the world, how to run as if no one is watching. They teach us how to see the world from a different viewpoint, how to look outward in nature and find communion with many different species.

In these interpersonal, affective enmeshments, something magical happens. One night last winter, my dogs and cats and I were sitting around the fireplace. I was reading, we lost electricity, and the lights went out. As I sat looking into the eyes of all these animals reflecting the fire, I had a profound feeling that we were more than just family. It was more as if we were all one organism, different sets of eyes looking out at each other from the same body. It was an enchanted feeling, as if I wasn't inside my own skin anymore, but "I" was all the living creatures in that whole room. I also understood in that fleeting moment that if I were to see the world in the most animal-friendly way possible, "I" was also in the shelter with those dogs whose eyes stared back at me, and in the cows and pigs "I" ate, and in the gorillas and elephants and tigers dying to the point of extinction because we humans have taken their land. "I" was the animal staring back at myself from cages in labs everywhere. Affect gives us a way to honor and display these realities.

Religion, Spirituality, and Affect

It is critical that we distinguish this sense of affective connection and even spirituality from organized religion, particularly Western Abrahamic traditions. Based on both ancient Greek and Roman thought, Judaism, Christianity, and Islam primarily teach us that animals exist for human use. In some fundamental way, Western religion argues, we can use animals any way we want because only human life really matters. For example, Thomas Aquinas taught that morality was something only humans possessed; thus, human beings could not morally harm creation because it was made for our use and didn't have its own moral framework. Indeed, Aquinas went so far as to argue that animals are not even worthy of our charity or love. Four centuries later, Descartes translated these ideas into the concept of "soul." Humans are the only organisms to possess a soul, he claimed. Animals are like machines; their only value comes in how they can serve us.

While some scholars of religion attempt to interpret these traditions through the lens of animal rights, the kind of affective interconnectedness I advocate is of a different order.[5] A spiritual enmeshment based on affect is not about dogma or ritual, not about God or scripture or ecclesiology.

What it shares with some aspects of religion is the hope that we can transcend ourselves by becoming part of one another. While organized religion locates that enmeshment either between members of a particular congregation, community, or tradition, or between humans and deities, animal advocacy based in affect aims to forge similar connections between humans and other animals. It hopes to reset the boundaries of our awareness to possibly include all living creatures, and it advocates transcendence beyond human exceptionalism. As we look into the eyes of another, the concept of affect allows us to see ourselves more clearly; through loving that particular animal we become fulfilled. Loving animals is a practice rooted primarily in going beyond ourselves through connection with animals.

Affective connection with animals stands to the side of organized religion; however, they can exist together. For example, a recent book by conservative Christian Matthew Scully stands as a powerful example of what I'm calling affective connection. *Dominion: The Power of Man, the Suffering of Animals, and the Call to Mercy* calls on Christians to act more compassionately toward animals for reasons not associated with rights. For Scully, God loves the world in such a way that there must also be some divine love for animals. As he puts it, "We are called to treat [animals] with kindness, not because they have rights or power or some claim to equality, but in a sense because they don't; because they all stand unequal and powerless before us."[6] For Scully, then, the very heart of what it means to be a Christian rests with the idea that Jesus loved and helped the oppressed, the outcast, and the disenfranchised. Christians should treat animals better, Scully believes, because God demands careful stewardship of his creatures.

What is so striking about Scully's work, though, is not his call for mercy or his Christian orientation. Rather it's located in the kind of affective connection he has with real animals, a connection that produces affective change for his readers. Scully's argument embodies the kind of affective dimension I am trying to identify. This is quite ironic; on practically every other social issue imaginable—from abortion to homosexuality to war—Scully and I probably stand at opposite ends of the political spectrum. (I'm a queer, anticapitalist, academic, bleeding-heart liberal; he's a leader in the Republican Party. I was brought up Catholic, then became a lefty Protestant, and now am not at all religious; he's a conservative evangelical.) Yet, I page through his book over and over again and what draws me to it are his descriptions of real animals. The way he sees them and writes about them is utterly moving: the baby pigs falling through the gestation crates into the waste pits on a factory farm, and the horrible look in the mother's eye as she realizes what's happening; the fright on the face of the animal about to be shot by a hunter who only wants his head as a trophy. Scully is able to see the world from inside that animal's skin, and from that place he pleads with us for her life. He is connected to them at a spiritual level. When other people describe the same scenarios, it's as if you're watching it from a distance, or through some kind of filter. With Scully you are right there with the animals, smelling them, feeling their pain, wanting more than anything to build a world that gives them a better life. Scully is not invested in helping these animals as a result of a commitment to a principle. He is doing this because he literally loves these animals. They make him who he is. I teach this book to my most militant women's studies students and they come away transformed. They, like me, are able to temporarily put other politics aside and share in Scully's dream because he has narrated an affective connection with the animals he's studying. It's gut-wrenching, disturbing reading, but he communicates his emotional attachment to the animals, and his readers are forever changed. In the most fundamental way possible, he is affected by and affects the world of these animals.

Affective connection with real animals is critical in transforming the human-animal relationship. As Scully suggests, we need to practice compassion toward animals not only because such activity will make us better people but also because the animals deserve it, because we ourselves are animals, and they are a part of all of us. But also like him, we need to put ourselves at risk to make these connections. What it's going to take to change the world for animals is for us to get down on the ground with real animals and experience their lives and their suffering—not as observers but as participants. We need to make these kinds of deep connections with them in order to see the world from their eyes, in order for them to become their own advocates through relationships with us. To tell their stories well, we need to let them affect us. That is part of what I mean by affect. We have to see our lives as enmeshed with the dogs in the shelters; the chickens, cows, and pigs on factory farms; the elephants and primates and tigers losing miles of habitat every day. Our journey on this earth is their journey too; our fate is entwined with theirs. As Scully suggests, they are not for us, they are with us. A new way of seeing ourselves, a new theory built on affect, can help with this process of building bonds with animals.

The concept of affect can also help us see animals as enchanted, awe-inspiring, respectful, generous, magical, and gracious. Partly this is because of the tremendous sacrifices they have made for humans for centuries. Despite all its faults, Christianity can help us discern the meaning and value of this sacrifice: "Take and eat this in remembrance of me." Indeed, the communion feast is said to be the event that sets the world right with God, but we have mostly forgotten how to think of animals in this sacrificial register. We usually don't think of our meat as coming from an animal that made a sacrifice; we don't see the animals living in zoos and sanctuaries as making a sacrifice; and the animals in our labs are so hidden from us, we don't see them at all. Premodern people's beliefs regarding animal sacrifice were akin to (the Christian) God's sacrifice in the Eucharist; that is, its life was a gift that was freely given by the animal but it had to be accepted with gratitude and care, with the heart of the receiver in the right place. Sacrifices are made through affective connection. Whether it be in the hunt, on the small farm, with our pets, in sanctuaries, or in labs, we can attend to all animals better if we understand that they make sacrifices to be with us.

In recovering this sense of sacrifice, affective theory helps us clearly recognize that we must also make sacrifices for them. We can continue to breed them poorly for pets or food, we can crowd them in cages and CAFOs, and we can lock them away and forget about their affects. We have the power to continue to ruin the planet, torture animals, tear down habitats. We can take it all for our selves, for the cells floating inside a limited sense of our physical bodies, for the fattening of our bankbooks. Nothing is stopping us; there is no final authority that mandates our compliance. We can destroy it all for personal gain. But that's not power, really. That's tyranny. Real power exists in the capacity to realize that we no longer need that kind of isolated human exceptionalism, that we have gone too far already in taking from the planet and other creatures, without proper care or thanks or sacrifice on our part. Affect focuses on the ways we affect each other and calls for greater care and commitment in our relationships with animals.

The Role of Stories

The world we live in is deeply shaped by imagination and entertainment, and thus the stories we produce can help us move toward a more affective and effective advocacy for animals. Because we are constructed, connected creatures, we can participate in the making of a new and better world by manipulating the narratives that capture us to attend to these larger questions. Affective theory suggests that we are not consumers of images, fiction, and film, but are in many ways also consumed by them; we learn to love and hate and become who we are in large part through our participation in stories. We perform a world we learned through narrative. Leslie Marmon Silko expresses it like this: "Stories aren't just entertainment. Don't be fooled. They are all we have to fight off illness and death. You don't have anything if you don't have stories."[7] The production of affect—of our orientation to the world—depends on stories. This is true whether we are aware of it or not.

A quick example that may illustrate the power of stories: if you are persuaded by my argument about ethical meat eating—it's not *that* we eat animals but *how* we treat them—the logical conclusion to that premise, in keeping with Bulliet and Shepard, may very well be that the most humane meat is perhaps that which is procured through hunting. Most of us, though, don't hunt; indeed, the idea of hunting may actually repulse some people, even those of us who eat meat. Why? I suspect that it's not that the logic of wild animals having the best life is wrong; something else is at play. That something else, I suggest, might be Disney's *Bambi*. Many of us have the view that although it may be right for primitive peoples to hunt, those of us in the developed world wouldn't consider it, largely because we have been profoundly affected by the story of one very cute little deer who was orphaned because a hunter shot his mother.[8] While I can't prove that *Bambi* shaped our cultural orientation toward hunting, this simple example is meant only to highlight the fact that stories can shape our moral intuitions about everything. They teach us, through our affective identifications, what is right and wrong, and who we want to be in the world. They help us form the boundaries of our bodies and figure out what is and is not morally acceptable for our "selves." The shape of the world changes as a result of the stories that form us.

The power of stories in forming our moral framework means that we can change the world by shifting representations. Changing the story changes the world. Something happens to us when we enter a good story. The lines and squiggles on the page, or the images captured on film, open us onto a new landscape of imagination. While we inhabit that world, its worries become our worries, its characters our circle of friends. When this happens, the shape of our self becomes more malleable, the boundaries of our place in the world blurred. When a story is good, it momentarily changes the person we are; when it is very good, it permanently marks us. One way to concretely improve the world for animals, then, is to improve our stories. Doing so can lead us back to a place where our relationships with animals are balanced, where our sense of our own subjectivity expands to include other living creatures. Once we are able to identify ourselves as people who see ourselves in nonhuman animals, the practices that improve their lives will follow more easily.

Pets, stories, affective connections with animals, and new ideas about our own subjectivity are the materials I am using to call for a new kind of animal advocacy. I am not primarily interested in changing laws; I am invested in changing people's hearts. An affective approach requires us to see ourselves as part of the world of animals; it requires us to pay more attention, to understand their value differently, to see them as subject rather than object. Animal advocacy thus far has mainly been constituted by projects that try to get animals recognized within existing philosophical constructions of subjectivity. This book asks us to step outside that system, that Western way of thinking, into a territory where we connect with animals at very corporeal levels, and then to make ethical decisions from inside that connection.

Many people would argue that learning about animals through stories is wrong; in stories, they say, animals are anthropomorphized and viewers aren't given an accurate sense of what animals really are like. As I argued in the preceding chapter, we need to use our imaginations affectively to occupy the world of animals in order to represent them in culture.

Without stories, our relationship to animals will truly be jeopardized. Other critics will say that stories are childish and sentimental, and couldn't possibly contribute to animal activism. But why do we see deep affective connections with animals as an activity only appropriate for children? Why do we so forcefully insist that successful transition into adulthood requires leaving animal love behind? Why do we mark human maturity as the capacity to distance ourselves from animals? Why does growing up always entail the ability to overlook the regularized abuse of animals? One way to think about a politics of loving animals, in other words, is through the lens of stories. The stuff that moves our hearts, or scares us, or makes us happy or sad or lonely can be harnessed to transform us into better relationships with animals.

Others will say that any approach that hinges even in part on emotion, affect, and love is too "soft" to succeed in producing change. They think of emotion and affect as inferior or unreliable only because they believe reason to be objective and universal. Attending to capacities like love and spirituality may indeed not feel "hard" as in objective or universal, but the affective realm is one of the basic ways in which we become who we are. When our hearts are moved by something, when our spirits are awakened by another's struggle, we are compelled to act. In other words, understanding political change as something that only happens when laws are changed, or when objective, rational arguments are made, neglects the full spectrum of existence. In many cases people change because they feel something new and different. That's the kind of transformation this book advocates. If we can change the stories that change our hearts, we can change the world. With public sentiment on the side of the animals, legal and policy advances for animals will be accomplished much more easily.

I've told some stories in this book: about the ways my dogs sense change and feel love, about the way it feels to visit Mary and Joseph and care for their friends on the farm; I've told about people who live with and love tigers and wolves, and the myriad creatures locked in labs who, perhaps more than any other animals, require our attention. They are not sidebar illustrations of a point or principle; they constitute the work of thinking about ethics and advocacy. When we get it right and when we get it wrong can only be portrayed through narrative. Stories can remake our world with other animals by helping us forge wondrous, imaginative, and reciprocally affective connections, by instructing us about who they are and what they desire. Stories can illustrate and underscore the value of being involved with animals at the level of the heart. They can help us know when we're living with animals in a balanced way, and when we're not. They can help us open ourselves to the possibility that other animals are agents in the world, and that we are all forging our worlds together. Stories belong as central players in the project of animal advocacy.

Affective connections, and stories that shape and represent those realities, are exceedingly powerful tools that could be put to much better use in animal advocacy. As it stands now, the philosophical tools that guide our movement at best overlook the power of affect and stories, and at worst diminish these connections by calling for complete abolition of the human-animal relationship. A worldwide transformation is needed to change the affect of people around animals. We need to be more curious about their desires and needs; we need to see them as full subjects in the world; we need to learn to love them better and remake the planet into a more hospitable home for them. When we do call on them to make sacrifices on our behalf, we must also figure out how best to honor those sacrifices. We need to soften our hearts to their plights, to allow ourselves to awaken to their spirits, and to shift our thinking in ways that invite the revolutionary power of love to enhance the existing animal advocacy agenda. Such transformation is not only possible, it is absolutely necessary. Their lives, and ours, depend on it.

CONCLUSION
TROUBLE IN THE PACK

I'VE TOLD LOTS OF STORIES IN THIS BOOK BECAUSE I believe affective connection is the basis for mass change, and because those connections are often best displayed through narratives. Just as I was finishing this book, an event at my house drove home the critical importance of "being with" animals in a way that is based on affect. So let me end this book with one more true and heartfelt story. It illustrates well, I think, why paying attention to affect is so necessary.

It happened Easter weekend 2009. My next-door neighbor and I often host "Dog Park" and open the gate between our yards to let our dogs play together, happily, exuberantly, as dogs will. We had done this hundreds of times before. On that particular day, for reasons beyond human comprehension, the pack of medium- to large-size dogs ganged up on my little old beagle, Daisy, and almost killed her. If you've never seen a dogfight, it will be hard to comprehend the emotional intensity involved; it's like something out of a horror movie where people that otherwise seem civil start attack another smaller, older, weaker person for what looks to you like no reason at all. Just to kill her, because it's fun. That's what happened that Saturday. I wasn't outside when the fight started, but my neighbor says the reason for the fight was imperceptible. It was as if a wind blew through the yard and everyone all at once decided to attack the defenseless old animal, to eliminate her from their ranks. These were dogs that had successfully cohabitated for over three years. There were no fosters or outside dogs; nothing at all had changed. They all knew each other well. But on that particular day, something in their affect shifted, and that shift changed us all.

I heard the fight from the bathroom and went running out in my robe. My neighbor was yelling already, but I started screaming, and most of my dogs responded immediately. Jerome, Duncan, Chester, and Hattie pulled away from the pack immediately, but my pit bull mix Jubilee and my neighbor's Plott hound, Calvin, refused to release Daisy. They each had an end of her and were biting her, pulling her apart, she was bloodied in many places, howling terribly. Everyone who works with multiple animals is taught never to stick her hands into an animal fight; when a human is bitten by an animal, the law gets involved, and the consequences are much graver. So my neighbor and I grabbed sticks and chairs and screamed and cried at Jubilee and Calvin. After a few minutes (which seemed like hours), both dogs released Daisy. She lay on the ground, bloodied and moaning. Within a few seconds, though, to my total horror, Jubilee went back after Daisy for one more bite. A young, very scrappy teenager visiting my neighbor, who didn't know the unwritten rule of animal management, emerged and took control of the situation. She grabbed the screaming beagle from Jubilee's jaws and took her inside. It is a miracle the girl didn't get bitten, and I am forever indebted to her. If Holly hadn't intervened, Daisy would certainly be dead now.

I took Daisy to the vet immediately. She had multiple bite wounds that would require drains. "A lot of damage," my vet said, as he shook his head. I was pretty much numb for two days, not knowing what had happened, or how to think or feel about it. I actually don't remember that Easter at all. I picked up Daisy from the vet on Monday. Almost immediately it was clear she wasn't going to be able to be around the other dogs without supervision. It wasn't just Jubilee (the one who had inflicted the majority of the wounds) who seemed excessively curious about her drains and wounds; all the dogs did really. I didn't know if they were smelling blood and responding to some innate attraction, or if as a pack they really had decided to remove Daisy, and now they were just looking to finish the job. I wasn't really even sure they intended her harm; we never came even close to anything like a fight, but the tension was palpable. Daisy could feel it, I know. She would stand at a distance from the rest of the pack, shaved, bandaged, and bruised, waging her little tail for dear life. She would look at me with a face that said, "Please get me out of here." It was utterly heartbreaking.

For two weeks as Daisy's wounds healed, I never left her alone with the other dogs. When I taught classes I either crated her or took her with me to school. I canceled everything else. I knew I couldn't go on like that. I contacted a trainer that I had relied on for over twenty years, someone I knew well and trusted. When I told her the story about how Jubilee just wouldn't let go, she advised that I euthanize Jubilee immediately. In her mind, although a pack mentality might have started the situation, the fact that Jubilee did not respond to my command meant she was essentially a dangerous dog. I was heartsick. By the trainer's estimation, Jubilee would hurt again sooner or later, and I should humanely eliminate her from this world now. I was distraught. I called many friends and talked it all out from every angle, but kept coming back to the advice of this trusted trainer. For this trainer, Jubilee was the instigator and needed to die.

In an attempt to take the advice of this trainer, I made a vet appointment to have Jubilee killed. I didn't sleep the entire night before, and although I got her in the car, looking at her happy unknowing face, I found I could not stop crying enough to drive. I sat in the car for hours that afternoon, sobbing. A neighbor walked by and saw me sitting there. I poured out the story to her, and she contacted a friend she happened to know in beagle rescue about the situation. I know things have to get worse sometimes before they get better, but the way the rescue got involved early on was truly devastating. Within hours I received an e-mail from them saying that because I was harboring "a dangerous dog," they were going to come over and remove not only Daisy the beagle but also Hattie the bloodhound mix I had adopted through them. If I did not kill Jubilee, they said, I would have to give up two of my other dogs. I was panicked, fluctuating between hiring a lawyer to fight the decision, and running from the state with all the dogs to keep my family from being separated.

That evening, my dear friend Madeline came over; Madeline was Daisy's original foster mother and we had stayed friends throughout the years. Maybe there was another way, Madeline offered. Maybe there was a way to let Jubilee live. I couldn't think what that would be. I was terrified for Daisy and so unsure of my decisions, I was almost paralyzed. Madeline suggested we all needed time to cool off and so offered to take Daisy back to her house for a few days, to give me time to think. (She didn't offer to take Jubilee, and I think it was because she was a little afraid of her.) It would only be temporary, Madeline said, until the right path became clear. Daisy got in her Blazer that Wednesday evening; I didn't know it then, but it was the last time I would ever see my little beagle.

After countless tears, many therapy sessions, and hundreds of hours of soul-searching, I decided to relinquish Daisy to be adopted again through beagle rescue. Despite the fact that beagle rescue had been so callous in the way they initially dealt with the situation, I had worked with them for many years and I did trust they could find her a new home, a home at least as good as mine in general, and now certainly even better. I made this decision for a number of reasons. First, although Jubilee had clearly been aggressive, I wasn't really sure what started it, and more important, I wasn't at all certain that removing Jubilee would end the aggression against Daisy. My sense during her final two weeks with us was that all other dogs threatened Daisy. She didn't trust them not to hurt her, and I didn't either. Perhaps she deserved a new life where she wouldn't be picked on. Second, of all my dogs, Daisy was the one who was least affectively connected to me. Beagles often have a different way of looking at the world, a way that is lighthearted, easygoing, and loving, which is why they make fabulous pets. But the flip side of that is often a dog who isn't quite tuned into family dynamics. Over the seven years I lived with her, given any opportunity at all, Daisy would run away. She dug out of the fence regularly and was always up for an adventure. It's not that she didn't want to live with me; she just smelled and imagined a world that was a million times more exciting than anything in her own backyard. I knew with total certainty that it mattered less to Daisy where she lived than it did to any of my other dogs. My other dogs were in love with me, but Daisy was in love with life. The third reason I decided to surrender Daisy had to do with Jubilee herself. Jubilee has been with me since she was tiny, but she grew very big very fast and is now the largest dog in my pack. She is extremely strong and has no real sense of her own size. She's about a hundred pounds of pure muscle, but she acts like a small dog. If you could meet her you would see that she does not have a mean bone in her body; she simply does not know her own strength. Part of me believed that what happened was more a miscalculation on her part than an act of sheer aggression.

The fourth reason I decided to surrender Daisy was the immediate change in my pack in her absence. It's hard to describe, but there was a serenity that took over the household. Everybody was immediately more comfortable, even the first night of her absence. Because Daisy was the dominant female, she always got the best chair, she got to sleep next to me in bed, she ate first. When we were having group training sessions, Daisy did fine with sit and down, but utterly refused stay, come, or heel. She lived out a model where compliance to stay, come, and heel was optional; the other dogs sensed this and followed suit. If she didn't have to do these things, why should they? In no way do I blame Daisy for this dynamic. It was my fault. She was always just so cute and cuddly; I let her get away with things I refused to let the big dogs get away with. And that created tension; my inconsistency created conflict. In their minds, Daisy got away with things because I allowed it; she got special treatment because I protected and defended her. With her gone, it was as if the rest of the pack heaved a sigh of relief. Finally, it seemed that, in their minds, things were now fairer.

People who live with only one or maybe two dogs may not have a sense of this, but when you have six or more, something like a pack mentality takes over. I may mostly be in control, but there's a will of the pack that cannot be denied. With this many, some primal force seems to rule and pack behavior becomes the law of the land. In wild wolf and dog packs, decisions are almost always made that strengthen the pack, and this incident was possibly a distant reflection of that phenomenon. Scientists disagree about why animals work together; pack behavior is a particularly elusive concept. While some researchers claim that animals work together only in a sense of "reciprocal altruism" (i.e., an "I help you and you help me" kind of trade), many suggest that the beginnings of a more generalized morality can be found in the group behavior of great apes and other social animals, even in canine packs. Some suggest that pack behavior is indeed akin to our own sense of "culture."

I have come to believe that such pack culture was at work in eliminating Daisy from our family. It's not as if they held a meeting and decided to get rid of her, but she pushed a little too hard here, rubbed this one the wrong way there, got a few too many goodies that others wanted; finally they had had enough. If she had been the biggest dog, or had been younger or extremely charismatic, she could have done all these things and everyone else here would have acquiesced to her, accepted this world as the way life was. But she was the oldest and by far the smallest and her teeth had been worn down to nubs since before I got her. She wasn't a leader and didn't care too much about pack alliances. The main thing Daisy had going for her was that she was cute and cuddly. I would swing her in my arms, singing "Daisy, Daisy, give me your answer do, I'm half crazy all for the love of you." The other dogs were all too big to swing.

So when Jubilee came of age and into her own at eighteen months, I think she made a decision that makes complete sense from the perspective of pack mentality; she made a play to become more dominant. Jubilee is very charismatic and, unlike Daisy, cares a lot what the other dogs think of her. For eighteen months she had developed relationships with the males and the big female hound mix. She was the initiator of many games; everyone loved her and most of them would have followed her through fire. She is a natural-born leader. I know for certain that if any foster dog had gone after Daisy or one of the cats, Duncan and Jerome would have been on them in a minute, fighting to defend their family to the death. But when it was Jubilee fighting, they just stood and watched. Granted, it all took place in less than two minutes, but the fact that the other dogs didn't defend Daisy, I realize now, reveals a lot. The pack was ready to move the matriarch out and make way for new leadership.

The final reason I decided to relinquish Daisy was because it was the only way everyone could live. Although I believe life itself is not always the most valuable way to resolve moral dilemmas, in this case I was thankfully given an option whereby both my animals could remain alive. And, quite frankly, I just could not find it in my heart to kill Jubilee. I was flooded with memories of her winning the "watch me" contest in her puppy class, and the way she sought out my eyes when something new appeared on a walk, or the way she chose my grandmother's rocking chair as her favorite place to sleep, long after it was even reasonably comfortable for her. There was no way I was going to find a new home for her quickly, as pit bull mixes are very hard to place. With her history now, no one in his right mind would take her. She did not come through a rescue, so there was no one to return her to. In addition to being a pit mix, she also had some greyhound and some Great Dane in her, so she was fast and strong and somewhat wild. She could not tolerate ever being confined to a crate, and she chewed everything from pens to books to furniture. She was a handful and I knew enough about dog rescue to know that it would take months or years to find her a new home, maybe never. Conversely, Daisy was small and cute and endearing, and could (and did) find a great wonderful new home through beagle rescue. (Realizing that Hattie was almost as big as Jubilee and fit in well with the pack, beagle rescue withdrew their threat to seize her.)

Fundamentally, my intuition told me Jubilee needed just one more chance. My general rule for problems between foster dogs has always been "if you create trouble you can't stay here." Like the words of Audrey the hog farmer, "If you can't get along with others here, you've gotta go." I broke this rule for Jubilee. For a long time I developed explanations for this exception, but there's really only one reason why I made such a choice, and I didn't see that clearly until a few months later. I met a real nice guy when I was helping out at an adoptathon for mixed-breed dogs; things were slow and we sat talking for three hours, during which I proceeded to rather obsessively go through the whole narrative about what had happened. This guy was not your typical dog fosterer; he was big and uncomfortable, he had on overalls and a ball cap and was very country. He lived alone and was fostering a border collie mix named Luke. But he had a front porch philosophy that was indeed profound. After listening to me go on and on, he finally broke his silence with two sentences that put everything in perspective. "You just fell in love with this one dog and want to do everything you can to save her. That's what rescue is all about." Yes. You don't really love dogs in general. You always love the particular.

When it comes to Jubilee, it's a funny kind of love that draws me to her. It's not the devotion I feel from Jerome, or the joy I feel with Duncan, or even the hang-in-there nature I love about Hattie. Jubilee is certainly not a pretty dog; she's fawn colored, a pit bull head but with the pointy nose of a greyhound, on a smallish great Dane body, kind of wobbly and unstable. She's not at all cuddly, never licks me, never sleeps in the bed. She knows her commands and will perform them for me, but unlike Jerome and Hattie, who get the greatest joy from hitting the floor hard when I say "down," Jubilee goes down reluctantly, sort of in stages, rolling her eyes each time her feet move a few inches farther out, as if to say "not this crap again." She comes the same way, slowly stopping to smell a few things before she gets to me. She usually stops and takes a whiff from the air, turns and looks at me and takes her time deciding whether to obey or not. She always does, but almost every time, she makes it clear that she's sitting or staying or coming because *she* has decided to.

All this makes her sound headstrong, and that's not exactly accurate. She's big and doesn't understand how strong she is physically, but she's not exactly strong willed. It's more that she is just very complicated. More than any other dog I've known in my life, Jubilee has an interior life that is rich, self-directed, and often visible. One ten-year-old human boy who walks her occasionally says about her, "There's more there, there." She is wickedly funny and I truly believe understands the meaning of satire. She still chews things in the house at almost three years old, but it's more as if they are forms of communication than acts of destruction, because she always picks really quirky things. For example, when I got a new area rug in the living room, I sat and talked with her for a long time, telling her "no chewing on this, chewing is bad," blah blah blah. She got the message that she shouldn't chew the rug all right, and to let me know she got the message, the next time I left the house, she pulled the rug back and totally chewed the pad underneath. She seemed so happy with herself when I got home. I was certain that she had chewed the pad because it must have had a particular smell or something, so I bought another one made of different material entirely. The same thing happened; the rug was pulled back and the pad chewed. I bought a third kind. She chewed the corners of that one and then I think got bored with the game. But to this day, almost every time I return to the house, the area rug is pulled back to reveal the pad, making a statement something like, "Okay, I won't chew this rug. I get it."

Where my other dogs are content to just be, Jubilee is often scheming, usually interpreting, and always thinking. It's not so much that I kept her alive because I loved her, then, although I do love her. It's more that I wanted to get to know her better. I want a deeper connection to her. I wanted to let my life be affected by her. She has the most curious spirit and does things slightly differently than any dog I've ever met; she curls up in places that are much too small for her, and when you say, "Jubilee, what are you doing there?" she throws her head back and makes this sort of noise that's halfway between a silly howl and a gravely bark. "Argh Argh Argh. Aren't I just the funniest thing you've ever seen, sitting here in this little cat bed?" She is always stealing my iPod and hiding it in my bed (undamaged); she grabs some of the other dogs by their collars and drags them around the yard and they appear to love it; she has eyes that not only make contact with you but dance for you. It's very hard to put into words, but if you could meet her, you would see what I'm saying. The girl next door says she has a "cartoon face," and by that she means her features and expressions are so exaggerated they appear to be drawn on her head with magic marker. If ever an animal deserved a second chance at life, it was Jubilee.

So although it broke my heart into a million pieces and I cried for months, I let Daisy go to let Jubilee live. As I've said, my dogs seemed to adjust to Daisy's absence immediately, and eventually the persistent healing spirit of the world took over for me as well. I now spend even more time with the five I have left, mostly because I'm pretty sure I could not bear the untimely loss of another one any time soon. Jubilee has made it through her Canine Good Citizen class (and passed), and we "play" obedience for at least an hour every day. The dogs and I walk together now. I talk to them incessantly. They are a more integral part of my life than when I started this book. The summer after I lost Daisy I met a lesbian who had just moved into my neighborhood; I liked her a lot. We had a few dates, I spent several nights at her house and soon a sweet romance began to develop. But within a month, I felt the lack of connection with my pack of dogs. They hated being left alone and were on edge; I know they felt the lack of my emotional presence. They were less apt to look me in the eye or cuddle in bed, and soon several good shoes were found chewed (probably not by Jubilee). One morning I woke up and realized I could not start a new relationship; I was already "involved."

It's not easy to break up with someone really nice because of your dogs, but animal people will know what I mean. I chose my dogs over her as my life partners. I like to think I would have made this choice even if I hadn't lost Daisy, but Daisy's absence was a poignant reminder that I could lose them all if I weren't fully present. When I got involved with my first long-term partner well over twenty years ago, I had an older dog that I loved very much, named Flannery O'Connor. Once my ex and I moved in together, well, Flanny never really quite fit in. I tried to be grown up about it—she was, after all, "only a dog"—but she failed to thrive very long in our new family. I simply did not want that to happen again to these people around whom I had built my life. This is not the fairy tale ending that most books prescribe, the "and the two humans lived happily ever after" effect, but the reality is that my dogs offer me more than enough of everything good I want from loving relationships. After all, it's that human-centered fairy-tale ending I am trying to rewrite in this book. I am trying my hardest to get nonhuman animals into that script.

This story is about loving animals in all its permutations. Affect begins not with an abstract commitment to a philosophical principle, but with love for and connection to other beings, in particular for me with the love for these five dogs and Daisy. There was no way principles (such as "if you can't get along, you gotta go") would work in resolving our conflicts. Life is too complicated and sometimes you have to put your principles aside to do what is right.

Affective love is about bodies, about the way we perform with our bodies, about Daisy's chewed and mauled body, but also the way she looked at me that cried to be released from the terror of living with animals that had hurt her. It was about my body and its anguish over losing her, and about the bodies of the other dogs who got what they wanted (for example, Jubilee as dominant female), and along with that, a sense of fairness. Our mingled corporeal existences crashed into each other in the fight and its aftermath; sometimes embodiment does that. Bodies affect each other in ways that both mind and emotions sometimes can't quite control. Allowing ourselves to be a part of one another means, in this case, bumping up against the harsh realities of pack behavior and figuring out how to live from there. It means putting everyone at risk.

This new approach to advocacy, then, isn't only about love and happiness, it's also about tragedy and sorrow and loss. Sometimes you have to love them enough to let them go. Asking Daisy to live inside this pack was wrong for her and wrong for them, but it doesn't mean I've stopped loving her. It does mean I love the ones I have left even more. I believe this connection is as right and true as any bond that has ever existed on the face of this globe. It's the kind of love that is willing to live with bad breath, chewed shoes and couches, frozen shoulders, and compromised knees; these are small concerns when placed against the wet tongue that licks tears away, the joy of a dance with a dog, the miracle of having this other being love me. An affective approach is one that takes responsibility for all kinds of losses because the life it shares with other species is the foundation of everything that is good, everything that has value. It means being open to the risk of sacrifice—ours and theirs—because we follow the hope of connection. It means understanding that being together—in the best way we can—is a sacred endeavor. Sharing the stories of our heartaches attends to the tragic side of affect. It means remembering others well, even through loss. It means attending to the fact that loss and desire are the terms that move us forward in the world.

Finally, of course, affect is about the recognition of the passions, inclinations, and tendencies that make us who we are. This approach to advocacy is about loving animals and understanding that love as enchanted. The current animal rights agenda stakes its claim for the most part in reasoned debate, and although reason is important, coupling it with sustained attention to affect will only make it more robust. It is with the tools of affect and narrative that we can display why we care so passionately. We need more stories like Daisy's, stories that interpret the world through affective connection, complete with both love and sacrifice.

Beagle rescue found Daisy a great home. She now lives with a retired man whose wife died recently and one other beagle. I get reports from them through the rescue periodically. Her new guardian loves the fact that Daisy sleeps in bed with him, as his other beagle won't. He takes both dogs on long walks and vacations. Although I wish I could turn back the pages of time to that day and prevent that fight from ever happening, given the fact that it did happen, this—what we have right now—is the best outcome. As much as we might want, we cannot always control the world, and that world includes the nature of our family members and ourselves. The best we can do is wrap ourselves in stories of love and use those stories to dream ourselves into a better world. Inside that love and dreaming, we can transform the world for animals.

ACKNOWLEDGMENTS

Books that take a decade or longer to gestate and be born accrue a lot of debts. Here is my chance to acknowledge the people who helped make *Loving Animals* possible.

For unwavering support of my animal fanaticism, I thank the following humans: Anne Allison, Nancy Barrickman, Marc Bekoff, Val Bletner, Kendra Boileau, Jackie Boyden, Jenny Campbell, Jane Caputi, Katie and Greg Christo, Judi Clark, Elizabeth Clift, Margo DeMello, Marc Fellenz, Marilyn Forbes, Susan Fraiman, Mary Fulkerson, Cindy Giovagnoli, Pete Glickenhaus, Liz Grosz, Michael Hardt, Eva Hayward, Hal Herzog, Sharon Holland, Leslie Irvine, Robin Kirk, Beth Anne Koeltsch, Kathy Lanier, Michelle Lennon, Jane Marshall, Lisa Mason, Madeline Maturo, Karen McCall, Richard Musselwhite, Negar Mottahedeh, Jen Naylor, Dana Nelson, Diane Nelson, Laura Ratchford, Louise Ratkoski, Laura Rhodes, Frank Rudy Jr., Ken Shapiro, MJ Sharp, Thomas Sherratt, Irene Silverblatt, Kelly, Tom, and Linda Steitler, Kristine Stiles, Randy Styers, and Kate Turlington. Whether I know you through academia, the animal world of Durham, or some other venue, your support and connection have been centrally important to this project.

My women's studies department at Duke University has been gracious and unparalleled as I approached this new subject of animals. Ranji

217

Khanna and Robyn Wiegman both deserve profound gratitude for supporting me in this project. They served as chairs of the department during my long years of researching and writing, and I can safely say that without their expansive understandings of exactly what "women's studies" is (and should be), this book would not have happened. Tina Campt, Ara Wilson, Kim Lamm, Frances Hasso, Lillian Spiller, Cassandra Harris, Melanie Mitchell, Gwen Rogers, and Marialana Weitzel helped me every step of the way. Kathi Weeks deserves a nod of thanks for accompanying me to visit many of those tigers.

A special shout-out goes to my editor, Richard Morrison. He was a masterful and patient midwife to this book, and I am deeply grateful for his guidance. Under his editorial advice, I felt as if I had finally found something like a big brother who had only my best interests at heart. Thank you, Richard.

This book is dedicated to my parents, Rosamond and Frank Rudy. If you knew them at all, you would know that I come by all this animal love quite honestly. The world they created for my brother and me was filled with consummate love for all nonhuman creatures, and the ability to love like that is perhaps their greatest gift to me.

Finally, for me it's always all about the animals. Although they do not read (yet), from the bottom of my heart I thank Cameron, Eeyore, Chester, Daisy, Jerome, Duncan, Hattie, Jubilee, all the foster dogs who moved through my house to find their way home, and even the cats, Langston, Madonna, and Satine. Thanks, people, for opening your hearts and doing your best to educate me about the shape of your worlds. I am in it for the long haul because of you.

The names of most of the human people in this book were changed to protect individuals' privacy. Most of the nonhuman animals, however, got to keep their real names.

NOTES

Introduction

1. I am indebted to Leslie Irvine's work for this concept of connection, a notion that includes love and emotion, but also points toward a broader affect that could capture understanding and commitment. See Irvine, *If You Tame Me.* See also Harbolt, *Bridging the Bond.*

2. Many new works in science support these assertions. See Balcombe, *Pleasurable Kingdom Animals and the Nature of Feeling Good;* Bekoff, *The Emotional Lives of Animals, Animals Matter,* and *Minding Animals;* Masson, *Dogs Never Lie about Love.*

3. See, for example, Shepard, *Coming Home to the Pleistocene;* Berger, *About Looking;* Mason, *An Unnatural Order.*

4. For an extended conversation on naturecultures, see Haraway, *The Companion Species Manifesto.*

5. White, "The Historical Roots of Our Ecological Crises," 1206.

6. Haraway, *When Species Meet,* 85.

7. McElroy, *Animals as Teachers and Healers,* 98.

8. Williams Bianco, *The Velveteen Rabbit.*

1. What's behind Animal Advocacy?

1. For a more complete understanding of animal rights in this sense, see the essays in part I of Sunstein and Nussbaum, *Animal Rights*. See also McKenna and Light, eds., *Animal Pragmatism*. Although animal pragmatism is not exactly the same as animal rights in this weak sense, the essays in this book shed light on the limitations of certain formulations of rights and offer concrete solutions to stronger agendas.

2. See Regan, *The Case for Animal Rights* and *Empty Cages*. There are many different formulations of animal rights, of course, and a full review of their philosophical differences is beyond the scope of this book. For other models, see Cavalieri and Singer, *The Great Ape Project*; Cavalieri, *The Animal Question*; Dunayer, *Speciesism*; Hall, *Capers in the Churchyard*; Patterson, *Eternal Treblinka*; Wise, *Rattling the Cage*. For a model of animal rights based on a contractual theory of rights, see Rowlands, *Animals Like Us*.

3. Francione, *Rain without Thunder*, *Introduction to Animal Rights*, and *Animals as Persons*.

4. See, e.g., Marjorie Spiegel, *The Dreaded Comparison*.

5. For introductory writings of these women see Goodall, *In the Shadow of Man* and Fossey, *Gorillas in the Mist*. Although much has been written by and about these women, one of my favorite overviews is Sy Montgomery, *Walking with the Great Apes*.

6. In speaking about animal welfare here, I refer to the way welfare is used in the general public. There are several excellent books and thinkers that advocate welfare in a much stronger vein than the common one. See Preece and Chamberlain, *Animal Welfare and Human Values*; Rothfels, *Representing Animals*; Scully, *Dominion*; and Rachels, *Created from Animals*.

7. For a paradigm that supports my separation of welfare and utilitarianism, see DeGrazia, *Animal Rights*.

8. Francione, *Rain without Thunder*.

9. Jamieson, *Singer and His Critics*.

10. For further elaboration on this point, see Rollin, *Animal Rights and Human Morality*.

11. Singer, *Practical Ethics*, 60.

12. Ibid., 26.

13. Haraway, *Simians, Cyborgs, and Women*, 152.

14. Wolfe, *Animal Rites*, 1.

15. See Regan, *Empty Cages*.

2. The Love of a Dog

1. Grier, *Pets in America*.

2. Brady and Palmeri, "The Pet Economy."

3. Haraway, *The Companion Species Manifesto*.

4. Haraway, *When Species Meet*.

5. Wolfe, *Animal Rites*.

6. Welty, "Animal Law."

7. The organization In Defense of Animals (IDA) advocates for and monitors these shifts. IDA, *The Guardian Campaign*.

8. For critiques of pet keeping, see Nast, "Critical Pet Studies?" and "Loving Whatever"; Tuan, *Dominance and Affection*.

9. For histories of pre-Stonewall lesbian experience, see Faderman, *Odd Girls and Twilight Lovers*; Kennedy and Davis, *Boots of Leather, Slippers of Gold*.

10. Donovan and Adams, *The Feminist Care Tradition in Animal Ethics* and *Beyond Animal Rights*.

11. It is beyond the scope of this book to review the literature of feminist care theory, or to rehearse the complex feminist theory debates about essentialism, constructionism, radical feminism, and postmodern feminism. Readers interested in animals will find these conflicts off topic, I believe. That said, there are aspects of care theory that deeply resonate with the kind of "connection" I call for in this book. While to some extent I quarrel with both the foundations of care theory (briefly that women are essentially more caring creatures) and with the outcome of care theory (that animals are not ours to use), the impulse behind feminist care ethics is very attractive because it places the weight of social change in the affective, emotive register (rather than in rationality). I hope to revisit these questions in my next project. For more on feminist care theory, see Gilligan, *In a Different Voice*; Noddings, *Caring*; Held, *Justice and Care* and *The Ethics of Care*; Kheel, *Nature Ethics*; Luke, *Brutal*.

12. For an excellent description of this process, see Probyn, *Outside Belongings*.

13. Hall, "Subjects in History," 291.

14. Hearne, *Bandit*, 14.

15. Queer theory is a huge field of study and beyond full exposition here. The texts that most inform my thinking in queer theory are Foucault, *The History of Sexuality*; Sedgwick, *Epistemology of the Closet* and *Tendencies*; Butler, *Gender Trouble* and *Bodies That Matter*; Doty, *Making Things Perfectly Queer*; Warner, *Fear of a Queer Planet*.

16. Of course the process of domestication and the history of dogs itself is much more complex than this short summary. See Derr, *Dog's Best Friend* and *A Dog's History of America;* Thurston, *The Lost History of the Canine Race;* Serpell, *The Domestic Dog;* Coren, *The Pawprints of History;* Sanders, *Understanding Dogs;* Schwartz, *A History of Dogs in the Early Americas.*

17. For example, see Tattersall, *Becoming Human;* Cartmill, *A View to a Death in the Morning.*

18. Clothier, *Bones Would Rain from the Sky.*

19. For an interesting ethnography of homeless cats, see Alger and Alger, *Cat Culture.*

20. Although the remainder of this chapter is largely informed by my volunteer experiences, several important books shed much light on the ways I think about shelter culture. These are Irvine, *If You Tame Me;* Harbolt, *Bridging the Bond;* Hess, *Lost and Found.*

21. www.aspca.org/adoption/pet-overpopulation.html; www.humanesociety.org/issues/pet_overpopulation/facts/overpopulation_estimates.html. Sites accessed July 12, 2010.

22. For example, see Glen, *Best Friends.*

23. This point is quite interesting in light of the fact that many kennel clubs and dog shows, in an attempt to do right by homeless pets, recommend that show dog owners find companions for their champions at local shelters. Fanciers with unaltered pets who try to adopt dogs out of shelters or rescues are often puzzled when they are turned down for adoption.

24. Derr, "The Politics of Dogs."

25. For more information on puppy mills, see www.humanesociety.org/issues/puppy_mills. See also the Best Friends "Puppies Aren't Products" campaign: network.bestfriends.org/campaigns/puppymills/pages/about-the-campaign.aspx. Sites accessed July 12, 2011.

26. Haraway, *The Companion Species Manifesto.*

27. See Arluke, *Just a Dog;* Winograd, *Redemption;* Arluke and Sanders, *Regarding Animals.*

28. The longer a dog is held in a kennel without serious socialization and training, though, the more she is likely to deteriorate. Thus, according to shelter workers, even the good ones have to be "put down" or "put to sleep" when they develop kennel madness. That is, if a dog starts spinning or snapping or growling, no matter how attached she is, shelter workers feel it's their duty to release the dog from her miserable life.

29. For more on temperament testing, see Sternberg, *Successful Dog Adoption.*

30. Grandin and Johnson, *Animals in Translation.*

31. Many works speak to this element of training. See McConnell, *The Other End of the Leash* and *For the Love of a Dog;* Clothier, *Bones Would Rain from the Sky.*

32. I am deeply indebted to reviewer Dana Nelson for helping me better articulate this point. When she read the manuscript for the press, she said, right here, "I just don't buy it." She pointed out that training is a "reciprocal pathway of respect and communication" and shared a really lovely story about her dog Sadie. Although Nelson knew that Sadie didn't really like water, she had wanted a picture of her standing in water; one day when Nelson was without her camera, Sadie got in the water and posed. The next day with camera in hand, Nelson gently placed Sadie in a shallow stream to get a quick shot, but Sadie jumped out and ran away. And although Sadie had a very reliable come, she didn't come then. Nelson writes, "It BUGGED me—and I kept chewing on it all night—'why didn't she come to the whistle???' not seeing what is obvious to everyone who's heard the story. I finally realized the next day and it stopped me dead in my tracks. She was training ME. She was training me not to violate her trust, not to make her do things that were gratuitous and about my whims. She is not a dog who likes water and she won't become one for me—not even for a good photo. She's not my (puppet) dog, she's my (equal) dog." That is exactly right. Training isn't about obedience, it's about relationship.

3. The Animal on Your Plate

1. For excellent descriptions of CAFOs see Kirby, *Animal Factory;* Foer, *Eating Animals;* Mason and Singer, *Animal Factories;* Pollan, *The Omnivore's Dilemma.*

2. Indeed, Ford's assembly-line model actually inspired the disassembly lines in the Chicago meatpacking industry at the turn of the twentieth century. For a beautiful illustration of this, see the Upton Sinclair novel, *The Jungle.*

3. This chapter is about farmed land animals, and hunting and fishing are beyond its scope. But a quick word needs to be said about each. In regard to fishing, recent reports in mainstream media say that our oceans will be empty by 2050. Fishing with nets, although dominant in the fishing industry, is incredibly inefficient. Over half of the creatures caught in nets are not edible and are thrown back into the sea; the industry calls this bycatch, and those creatures die for no reason. Unless wild fish are caught by individual lines, the overall sustainability of the oceans is being harmed. "Aquaculture" (farming fish in concentrated fashion either in land-based pools or containers or in netted areas in the ocean itself; this is the equivalent of factory farming for fish) has emerged

as a huge industry in recent years. While some commentators believe that aqua-culture is the best option to save the dying oceans, most people feel that aqua-culture fish—who are also fed hormones and antibiotics like factory-farmed animals—taste different, smell different, and have a funny texture. The issues in-volved in aquaculture mirror the problems of factory farming: cleaning and filter-ing tanks causes pollution of surrounding areas, the chemical- and drug-filled fish itself is often not healthy for human consumption, and life in a polluted tank can't be much fun for the fish. As for hunting animals for meat, I do believe that some forms of subsistence hunting, especially when they have a spiritual root, are sustainable and moral. Trophy hunting and other uses of wild animals intended only to display dominance over nature and other animals are, of course, deeply problematic. For further discussion of hunting, see chapter 6.

4. "Locavores" argue for the value of eating local, sustainably grown food as a better model for both human health and the environment. Although food writer Jessica Prentice coined the term locavore only in 2006, the concept has so appealed to Americans that the label almost immediately took on a life of its own. By 2007, the *New Oxford American Dictionary* chose "locavore" as its word of the year. Since then, the concept of eating locally has gained national attention.

5. The carbon footprint is the measure of the amount of carbon dioxide and other greenhouse gases produced by a given product. Local foods have a much lower carbon footprint both because of the sustainable ways they are raised and because they require much less shipping energy.

6. For an overview of these shifts, see Berry, *The Unsettling of America.*

7. As a result of mutation and natural selection, many farmers are now forced to battle herbicide-resistant weeds. This development parallels the development of superbugs such as antibiotic-resistant strains of bacteria (e.g., MRSA). Most scientists agree that these developments are the result of the over-use of herbicides and antibiotics in industrial agriculture. See "Farmers Cope with Roundup-Resistant Weeds."

8. For an excellent analysis of the role of GMOs in the global food crisis, see Shiva, *Earth Democracy.*

9. For an interesting thesis that substitutes fermentation for microwav-ability, see Katz, *The Revolution Will Not Be Microwaved.*

10. Many of the harms of fast food—especially fast-food meat—are bril-liantly portrayed in Schlosser, *Fast Food Nation.*

11. For a full exposition of the role of profit in corporate food culture, see Simon, *Appetite for Profit.*

12. For an accessible and brilliant analysis of farm bills, see Pollan, "The Way We Live Now: 4-22-07" and *The Omnivore's Dilemma.*

13. There are many great works condemning the development of factory farms and industrial slaughter. Among them, see Eisnitz, *Slaughterhouse;* Marcus, *Meat Market;* Mason and Singer, *Animal Factories;* Mason, *An Unnatural Order;* Rifkin, *Beyond Bee.* See also this chapter, note 1.

14. There are many wonderful books and articles about local eating; these are some of the ones that informed my politics early on: Halweil, *Eat Here;* Kingsolver, Hopp, and Kingsolver, *Animal, Vegetable, Miracle;* Petrini, *Slow Food Nation;* Winne, *Closing the Food Gap;* Wirzba, *The Essential Agrarian Reader;* Pollan, *In Defense of Food;* Friend, *Hit by a Farm.*

15. Berry, *The Unsettling of America,* 62.

16. Simon, *Appetite for Profit.*

17. Petrini, *Slow Food Nation.*

18. *Satya* magazine is no longer being published, but articles and interviews have been archived at www.satyamag.com. See also Rowe, *The Way of Compassion.*

19. For a theorization of love as a critical conceptual tool for political revolution, see Sandoval, *Methodology of the Oppressed.*

20. LaVeck, "Compassion for Sale?"; Lama, "Sadly, Happy Meat"; Bauston, "It's Not a Black and White Issue." For more information on Tribe of Heart, see www.tribeofheart.org. For more on Farm Sanctuary, see Gene Baur, *Farm Sanctuary.*

21. Lama, "Sadly, Happy Meat," 15.

22. LaVeck, "Invasion of the Movement Snatchers."

23. Pollan, "Engaging with the Omnivore," *The Omnivore's Dilemma,* and *In Defense of Food.*

24. Singer and Friedrich, "The Longest Journey Begins with a Single Step." See also Singer, "Singer Says"; Singer and Mason, *The Way We Eat.*

25. As you might guess, rightists are enraged by Singer's endorsements; their focus on complete liberation from human use is unwavering. Ultimately, they feel betrayed by Singer. See Lama, "Sadly, Happy Meat."

26. Williams, *The Divided World.*

27. Bauston, "It's Not a Black and White Issue," 18.

28. Allen, "Can Vegetarianism Save the Planet?"

29. Singer, "Singer Says"; Singer and Friedrich, "The Longest Journey Begins with a Single Step"; Singer and Mason, *The Way We Eat.*

30. The exchange between Mackey and Pollan can be found in Pollan, "My Letter to Whole Foods."

31. Part of the issue at stake, again, is scale. As consumers we have been

conditioned to want meat at every meal, and small suppliers cannot possibly meet our demand. A central part of the locavore movement continues to educate consumers about the need to eat less meat and to eat it less frequently. Until we fully grasp that central claim, we will be dependent on mass-scale producers to meet our desires. That said, new independent, nonprofit organizations are emerging to help us sort out the kinds of claims both local and corporate meat producers make. Foremost among these are Animal Welfare Institute (which certifies small producers under the banner AWA: Animal Welfare Approved). For the stringent requirements of AWA certification, see www.animalwelfareapproved.org. See also Farm Forward (www.farmforward.com), and Global Animal Partnership (www.globalanimalpartnership.org). All sites accessed July 16, 2010.

4. Where the Wild Things Ought to Be

1. Adoption here means something close to sponsorship and costs a thousand dollars per year per animal. In this facility, when you adopt an animal, you can visit it whenever you want, but cannot take it home. Other sanctuaries, as we'll see, do actually adopt out their animals into private homes.

2. Birds, reptiles, and snakes were included in the original draft of the bill but were subsequently excluded, mostly as a result of pressure from the reptile lobby.

3. As will become clearer as this chapter unfolds, I am not arguing for deregulation of exotic species. Regulation is critical both in curbing exploitation and in guaranteeing that existing habitats are not disrupted. However, I believe that oversight and regulation need to be approached through the lens of affective connection. That is, laws and standards need to be put in place to help many different kinds of people flourish with their animals outside zoo settings.

4. In 2008, API merged with the international organization Born Free. For a history of both organizations and rationale for their merger, see "Born Free/Animal Protection Institute" at www.bornfreeusa.org/d_about.php.

5. The Association of Zoos and Aquariums, available at www.aza.org.

6. Several North Carolina aquariums are members of the AZA, but fish and reptiles are beyond the scope of this chapter.

7. For analyses of the role of nature films in American culture, see Mitman, *Reel Nature*; Chris, *Watching Wildlife*; Bouse, *Wildlife Films*.

8. For an argument that details why confined animals disappoint and are less than whole, see John Berger, *About Looking*.

9. Adams and McShane, *The Myth of Wild Africa;* Bulbeck, *Facing the Wild;* Bonner, *At the Hand of Man;* Oates, *Myth and Reality in the Rain Forest.*

10. My aim here is not to diminish the work done by conservationists. Indeed, new approaches to conservation are saving habitats in many areas worldwide. Of particular interest is the development of protected corridors and conservation easements that allow animals to migrate through areas dominated by human development. See Adams, *The Future of the Wild.* That said, conservation is much less successful in relation to apex predators like big cats and wolves. On this topic, see Stolzenburg, *Where the Wild Things Were;* Berger, *The Better to Eat You With;* Rabinowitz, *Jaguar.* For works that demonstrate the multiple difficulties of conservation of large animals, see Webber and Vedder, *In the Kingdom of Gorillas;* Goodall, Maynard, and Hudson, *Hope for Animals and Their World.* For an argument that life in captivity may be better for some animals than life in the shrinking wild, see Budiansky, *The Covenant of the Wild.*

11. My thinking is informed on this point by the essays in Cassidy and Mullin, eds., *Where the Wild Things Are Now.*

12. Sutherland, *Kicked, Bitten, and Scratched.*

13. Coppinger and Coppinger, *Dogs.*

14. I am not making the argument that all wild animals will be happier if tamed and brought into human care; I do contend that those who tolerate close proximity to and interaction with humans have better chances of long-term survival.

15. Baratay and Hardouin-Fugier, *Zoo;* Rothfels, *Representing Animals.*

16. Wolch and Emel, *Animal Geographies.*

17. Donahue and Trump, *The Politics of Zoos.*

18. Some progressive zoo spokespeople argue that captivity may not be acceptable for all species. Debates ensue about animals that are large, need large roaming territories, or are too closely related to humans, e.g., elephants, dolphins, whales, and all great apes; while such animals are kept by some zoos, others have moved existing animals of these types to sanctuaries or refused to acquire new ones. My argument in this book, again, is *not* that containment and human connection with all living beings is possible or desirable, but rather that those animals who can bear to live with us may fare better in impending ecological crises.

19. Hancocks, *A Different Nature;* Bostock, *Zoos and Animal Rights.*

20. Malamud, *Reading Zoos;* Hanson, *Animal Attractions.*

21. DeBlieu, *Meant to Be Wild.*

22. Norton, *Ethics on the Ark.*

23. Mazur, *After the Ark?;* Norton, *Ethics on the Ark.*

24. See Green, *Animal Underworld.*

25. In canned hunts, hunters pay a certain fee (usually thousands of dollars) to shoot at close range exotic animals who have become accustomed to humans and literally have nowhere to run. See Scully, *Dominion*.

26. Coetzee, *The Lives of Animals*, 30.

27. American Sanctuary Association, available at www.asaanimalsanctuaries.org/AboutASA/aboutASA.htm.

28. Nationally, this conflicted message can be found in high-profile sanctuaries such as Tippi Hedren's Shambala in California and Carole Baskin's Big Cat Rescue in Florida. Both Hedren and Baskin own and run huge, lucrative sanctuaries with hundreds of cats in each, and both speak and work against private ownership of exotic animals. The message they transmit contains the same internal conflict as that of our proposed legislation here in North Carolina: it's fun and rewarding to work with exotics such as big cats, but only certain people (like us) should be allowed to do it. Both Hedron and Baskin have cast themselves as martyrs for their animals; while they decry private ownership for the general public, they see themselves as the exception to the rule that exotic animals should not be held in captivity. They say they are simply fixing a problem they didn't create by rescuing these cats from miserable lives and making them available for public viewing and interaction. While on the one hand they suggest that the goal of sanctuary should be to put itself out of business, on the other they believe it's acceptable for them to breed and buy exotics because the public loves to interact with them.

29. Saint-Exupéry, *The Little Prince*, 60.

30. Ibid., 63.

5. From Object to Subject

1. See, e.g., Conn and Parker, *The Animal Research War*.

2. See, e.g., Greek and Greek, *Sacred Cows and Golden Geese*.

3. Donnelley, "Speculative Philosophy."

4. See, e.g., Orlans, *In the Name of Science*.

5. Bekoff, "Why 'Good Welfare' Isn't 'Good Enough.'"

6. For historical development of this movement, see Sperling, *Animal Liberators*.

7. Rudacille, *The Scalpel and the Butterfly*.

8. I checked my own institution's public veterinary IACUC report for 2006, which did note that there were three more primates and seventeen more dogs than existed on file. Whether the lives of three primates and seventeen dogs matter depends on the landscape one inhabits; researchers grant that mistakes

are sometimes made but that they are minor and statistically insignificant, while activists say IACUC reports that overlook twenty animals in just one institution are virtually meaningless.

9. See also Groves, *Hearts and Minds.* Groves maps the competing sentiments and emotions on both sides of the lab animal controversy in ways that I found very helpful.

10. Fadali, *Animal Experimentation;* LaFollette and Shanks, *Brute Science.*

11. Greek and Greek, *Specious Science* and *Sacred Cows and Golden Geese.*

12. See the essays in Gluck, DiPasquale, and Orlans, eds., *Applied Ethics in Animal Research.* See also Rowan, *Of Mice, Models, and Men.* For an evaluation of the cultural conditions that promote animal experimentation, see Birke, Arluke, and Michael, *The Sacrifice.*

13. It's interesting to note how many of the strands of argumentation in this debate rely either on "they are like us" or "they are not like us" thinking. What I will offer later in this chapter is a way of understanding animals beyond the "like us/not like us" dichotomy. This way will entail the necessity of getting to know them.

14. Guerrini, *Experimenting with Humans and Animals.*

15. Singer, *Practical Ethics.*

16. Nocella and Best, *Igniting a Revolution* and *Terrorists or Freedom Fighters?*

17. Sperling, *Animal Liberators.*

18. Newkirk, *Free the Animals.*

19. Many animal rights activists agree with this assertion, i.e., that violence is an unacceptable political strategy. See, e.g., Hall, *Capers in the Churchyard.*

20. See, e.g., Potter, *Green Is the New Red.*

21. Davies, *What's Bred in the Bone,* 16. See also Rollin, *The Unheeded Cry.*

22. Indeed, I suspect this approach may already be happening in some lab settings. My evidence for this claim can be found in Davis and Balfour, *The Inevitable Bond.*

23. Dawn, *Thanking the Monkey,* 267.

24. Again, see Davis and Balfour, *The Inevitable Bond.*

25. Kennedy, *The New Anthropomorphism.*

26. See Rachels, *Created from Animals.*

27. Jakob von Uexküll (1864–1944) was the first phenomenologist of animals, and some suggest he is the father of ethology. The central point of his writings is that every living thing has a perceptual relationship to the world, enabled and limited by its senses. Although still fairly unknown in biology and animal studies, his work has been rediscovered by philosophers such as Giorgio Agamben, Martin Heidegger, and Gilles Deleuze and Félix Guattari.

28. Uexküll, "A Stroll through the Worlds of Animals and Men," 28.

29. There are many animal language studies that fall outside the scope of scientific authority. In most cases, researchers are criticized for not having enough controls in place or not following through with peer-reviewed publications. For examples, see Hess, *Nim Chimpsky*. See also the case of Koko the gorilla (www.koko.org). Some researchers suggest that even the most scientifically sound experiments render incomplete results; these approaches suggest that language is not available to other animals, that animals that appear to have language are really just responding to training.

30. Savage-Rumbaugh and Lewin, *Kanzi*.

31. Fouts, *Next of Kin*.

32. Pepperberg, *The Alex Studies* and *Alex and Me*.

33. While the world of scientific animal studies still continues, it is fraught with conflict. As a result of these conflicts, in recent decades many in the scientific community have moved toward animal cognition studies. These researchers are not seeking to teach animals human language but rather to better understand the minds of animals. Although this work is moving, valuable, and scientifically accepted, much of it does not represent the kind of two-way communication I seek. I contend that there's something unique about living with another animal and loving that animal that cognition studies do not fully capture. For a sampling of new works in cognition studies, see Bekoff, Allen, and Burghardt, *The Cognitive Animal*; Pearce, *Animal Learning and Cognition*; Wasserman and Zentall, *Comparative Cognition*; Wynne, *Animal Cognition*.

34. Prince-Hughes, *Songs of the Gorilla Nation*, 136.

35. Smith, "Beyond Dominance and Affection," 195.

6. Clothing Ourselves in Stories of Love

1. See, e.g., Sedgwick, Frank, and Alexander, *Shame and Its Sisters*; Sedgwick and Frank, *Touching Feeling*; Probyn, *Blush*; Cusset, *French Theory*; Cvetkovich, *An Archive of Feelings*; Brennan, *The Transmission of Affect*.

2. Recent science on animals suggests that none of this is true, i.e., that we are not the only creatures to experience these thoughts and emotions. See, e.g., Balcombe, *Pleasurable Kingdom* and *Second Nature*; Goodall, *Through a Window*. A recent *New York Times Magazine* story on whale emotions is also instructive and moving. Siebert, "Watching Whales Watching Us."

3. For a sustained critique of enlightenment philosophy with regard to animals, see Wolfe, *What Is Posthumanism?*

4. See also Shepard, *Encounters with Nature*.

5. For Christian-based perspectives, see Linzey, *Animal Rights* and *Christianity and the Rights of Animals.* For an excellent overview of many differing religious perspectives on animal rights and advocacy, see Waldau and Patton, *A Communion of Subjects.*

6. Scully, *Dominion,* xi–xii.

7. Silko, *Ceremony,* 2.

8. For an excellent analysis of the role of Disney in the production and consumption of nature films and culture more generally, see Mitman, *Reel Nature.* For a helpful perspective on the role of *Bambi* on hunting, see Cartmill, *A View to a Death in the Morning.*

BIBLIOGRAPHY

Adams, Jonathan S. *The Future of the Wild: Radical Conservation for a Crowded World.* Boston: Beacon Press, 2006.

———, and Thomas O. McShane. *The Myth of Wild Africa: Conservation without Illusion.* New York: Norton, 1992.

Alger, Janet M., and Steven F. Alger. *Cat Culture: The Social World of a Cat Shelter.* Animals, Culture, and Society. Philadelphia: Temple University Press, 2003.

Allen, Jolia Sidona. "Can Vegetarianism Save the Planet?" *VegNews* (May–June 2007): 31–33.

Apted, Michael, et al. *Gorillas in the Mist: The Adventure of Dian Fossey.* .Universal City, Calif.: Universal Studies, 1999. Videocassette.

Arluke, Arnold. *Just a Dog: Understanding Animal Cruelty and Ourselves.* Animals, Culture, and Society. Philadelphia: Temple University Press, 2006.

———, and Clinton Sanders. *Regarding Animals.* Animals, Culture, and Society. Philadelphia: Temple University Press, 1996.

American Sanctuary Association. www.asaanimalsanctuaries.org/AboutASA/aboutASA.htm.

Association of Zoos and Aquariums. www.aza.org.

Balcombe, Jonathan P. *Pleasurable Kingdom Animals and the Nature of Feeling Good.* London: Macmillan, 2006.

Baratay, Eric, and Elisabeth Hardouin-Fugier. *Zoo: A History of Zoological Gardens in the West.* London: Reaktion, 2002.

Baur, Gene. *Farm Sanctuary: Changing Hearts and Minds about Animals and Food.* New York: Simon and Schuster, 2008.

Bauston, Gene. "It's Not a Black and White Issue: Promoting a Humane World for Farmed Animals; The Satya Interview with Gene Bauston." *Satya,* September 2006, 18–21.

Bekoff, Marc. *Animals Matter: A Biologist Explains Why We Should Treat Animals with Compassion and Respect.* Boston: Shambhala, 2007.

———. *The Emotional Lives of Animals: A Leading Scientist Explores Animal Joy, Sorrow, and Empathy—and Why They Matter.* Novato, Calif.: New World Library, 2007.

———. *Minding Animals: Awareness, Emotions, and Heart.* Oxford: Oxford University Press, 2002.

———. "Why 'Good Welfare' Isn't 'Good Enough.'" *ARBS Annual Review of Biomedical Sciences* 10 (2008): 1–4.

———, Colin Allen, and Gordon M. Burghardt. *The Cognitive Animal: Empirical and Theoretical Perspectives on Animal Cognition.* Cambridge, Mass.: MIT Press, 2002.

Berger, Joel. *The Better to Eat You With: Fear in the Animal World.* Chicago: University of Chicago Press, 2008.

Berger, John. *About Looking.* 1st American ed. New York: Pantheon Books, 1980.

Berry, Wendell. *The Unsettling of America: Culture and Agriculture.* San Francisco: Sierra Club Books, 1977.

Best, Steven, and Anthony J. Nocella. *Igniting a Revolution: Voices in Defense of the Earth.* Oakland, Calif.: AK Press, 2006.

———. *Terrorists or Freedom Fighters? Reflections on the Liberation of Animals.* New York: Lantern Books, 2004.

Bianco, Margery Williams. *The Velveteen Rabbit; or, How Toys Become Real.* Illustrated by Michael Hague. New York: Holt, Rinehart and Winston, 1983.

Birke, Lynda I. A., Arnold Arluke, and Mike Michael. *The Sacrifice: How Scientific Experiments Transform Animals and People.* New Directions in the Human-Animal Bond. West Lafayette, Ind.: Purdue University Press, 2007.

Bonner, Raymond. *At the Hand of Man: Peril and Hope for Africa's Wildlife.* New York: Knopf, 1993.

Born Free/Animal Protection Institute. www.bornfreeusa.org/d_about.php.

Bostock, Stephen St C. *Zoos and Animal Rights.* London: Routledge, 1993.

Bouse, Derek. *Wildlife Films.* Philadelphia: University of Pennsylvania Press, 2000.

Brady, Diane, and Christopher Palmeri. "The Pet Economy." *Business Week,* August 6, 2007, 1–6.

Brennan, Teresa. *The Transmission of Affect.* Ithaca. N.Y.: Cornell University Press, 2004.

Budiansky, Stephen. *The Covenant of the Wild: Why Animals Chose Domestication.* New York: William Morrow, 1992.

Bulbeck, Chilla. *Facing the Wild: Ecotourism, Conservation, and Animal Encounters.* London and Sterling, Va.: Earthscan, 2005.

Bulliet, Richard W. *Hunters, Herders, and Hamburgers: The Past and Future of Human-Animal Relationships.* New York: Columbia University Press, 2005.

Butler, Judith. *Bodies That Matter: On the Discursive Limits of "Sex."* New York: Routledge, 1993.

———. *Gender Trouble: Feminism and the Subversion of Identity.* Thinking Gender. New York: Routledge, 1990.

Carson, Rachel. *Silent Spring.* Boston: Houghton Mifflin, 1962.

Cartmill, Matt. *A View to a Death in the Morning: Hunting and Nature through History.* Cambridge, Mass.: Harvard University Press, 1993.

Cassidy, Rebecca, and Molly H. Mullin. *Where the Wild Things Are Now: Domestication Reconsidered.* Wenner-Gren International Symposium Series. Oxford: Berg, 2007.

Cavalieri, Paola. *The Animal Question: Why Nonhuman Animals Deserve Human Rights.* Oxford: Oxford University Press, 2001.

———, and Peter Singer. *The Great Ape Project: Equality beyond Humanity.* New York: St. Martin's Press, 1993.

Chris, Cynthia. *Watching Wildlife.* Minneapolis: University of Minnesota Press, 2006.

Clothier, Suzanne. *Bones Would Rain from the Sky: Deepening Our Relationships with Dogs.* New York: Warner Books, 2002.

Coetzee, J. M. *The Lives of Animals.* University Center for Human Values Series, edited by Amy Gutmann. Princeton, N.J.: Princeton University Press, 1999.

Conn, P. Michael, and James V. Parker. *The Animal Research War.* New York: Palgrave Macmillan, 2008.

Coppinger, Raymond, and Lorna Coppinger. *Dogs: A Startling New Understanding of Canine Origin, Behavior, and Evolution.* New York: Scribner, 2001.

Coren, Stanley. *The Pawprints of History: Dogs and the Course of Human Events.* New York: Free Press, 2002.

Cusset, François. *French Theory: How Foucault, Derrida, Deleuze, & Co. Transformed the Intellectual Life of the United States.* Minneapolis: University of Minnesota Press, 2008.

Cvetkovich, Ann. *An Archive of Feelings: Trauma, Sexuality, and Lesbian Public Cultures.* Series Q. Durham, N.C.: Duke University Press, 2003.

Davies, Robertson. *What's Bred in the Bone.* New York: Viking, 1985.

Davis, Hank, and Dianne Balfour. *The Inevitable Bond: Examining Scientist-Animal Interactions.* Cambridge: Cambridge University Press, 1992.

Dawn, Karen. *Thanking the Monkey: Rethinking the Way We Treat Animals.* New York: Harper, 2008.

DeBlieu, Jan. *Meant to Be Wild: The Struggle to Save Endangered Species through Captive Breeding.* Golden, Colo.: Fulcrum, 1993.

DeGrazia, David. *Animal Rights: A Very Short Introduction.* Very Short Introductions. Oxford: Oxford University Press, 2002.

Derr, Mark. *Dog's Best Friend: Annals of the Dog-Human Relationship.* New York: Henry Holt, 1997.

———. *A Dog's History of America: How Our Best Friend Explored, Conquered, and Settled a Continent.* New York: North Point Press, 2004.

———. "The Politics of Dogs." *Atlantic Monthly,* March 1990, 49–65.

Derrida, Jacques. *Margins of Philosophy.* Translated by Alan Bass. Chicago: University of Chicago Press, 1982.

———. *Of Grammatology.* Translated by Gayatri Chakravorty Spivak. Baltimore: The Johns Hopkins University Press, 1976.

Disney's Lilo & Stitch. Directed by Chris Sanders and Dean DeBlois. Videorecording. Burbank, Calif.: Walt Disney Records.

Donahue, Jesse, and Erik Trump. *The Politics of Zoos: Exotic Animals and Their Protectors.* DeKalb: Northern Illinois University Press, 2006.

Donnelley, S. "Speculative Philosophy, the Troubled Middle, and the Ethics of Animal Experimentation." *Hastings Center Report* 19, no. 2 (1989): 15–21.

Donovan, Josephine, and Carol J. Adams, eds. *Beyond Animal Rights: A Feminist Caring Ethic for the Treatment of Animals.* New York: Continuum, 1996.

———. *The Feminist Care Tradition in Animal Ethics: A Reader.* New York: Columbia University Press, 2007.

Doty, Alexander. *Making Things Perfectly Queer: Interpreting Mass Culture.* Minneapolis: University of Minnesota Press, 1993.

Dunayer, Joan. *Speciesism.* Derwood, Md.: Ryce, 2004.

Eisnitz, Gail A. *Slaughterhouse: The Shocking Story of Greed, Neglect, and Inhumane Treatment inside the U.S. Meat Industry.* Amherst, N.Y.: Prometheus Books, 1997.

Fadali, Moneim A. *Animal Experimentation: A Harvest of Shame.* Los Angeles: Hidden Springs Press, 1996.

Faderman, Lillian. *Odd Girls and Twilight Lovers: A History of Lesbian Life in*

Twentieth-Century America. Between Men–Between Women. New York: Columbia University Press, 1991.

"Farmers Cope with Roundup-Resistant Weeds." *New York Times,* May 3, 2010.

Foer, Jonathan Safran. *Eating Animals.* New York: Little, Brown, 2009.

Fossey, Dian. *Gorillas in the Mist.* Boston, Mass.: Houghton Mifflin, 1983.

Foucault, Michel. *The Archaeology of Knowledge.* Translated by Alan Sheridan Smith. World of Man. New York: Pantheon, 1972.

———. *Discipline and Punish: The Birth of the Prison.* Translated by Alan Sheridan. New York: Pantheon Books, 1977.

———. *The History of Sexuality.* 3 vols. Translated by Robert Hurley. New York: Pantheon Books, 1978.

Fouts, Roger. *Next of Kin: What Chimpanzees Have Taught Me about Who We Are.* New York: William Morrow, 1997.

Francione, Gary L. *Animals as Persons: Essays on the Abolition of Animal Exploitation.* New York: Columbia University Press, 2008.

———. *Introduction to Animal Rights: Your Child or the Dog?* Philadelphia, Pa.: Temple University Press, 2000.

———. *Rain without Thunder: The Ideology of the Animal Rights Movement.* Philadelphia, Pa.: Temple University Press, 1996.

Friend, Catherine. *Hit by a Farm: How I Learned to Stop Worrying and Love the Barn.* New York: Marlowe, 2006.

Gilligan, Carol. *In a Different Voice: Psychological Theory and Women's Development.* Cambridge, Mass.: Harvard University Press, 1982.

Glen, Samantha. *Best Friends: The True Story of the World's Most Beloved Animal Sanctuary.* New York: Kensington Books, 2001.

Gluck, John P., Tony DiPasquale, and F. Barbara Orlans. *Applied Ethics in Animal Research: Philosophy, Regulation, and Laboratory Applications.* West Lafayette, Ind.: Purdue University Press, 2002.

Goodall, Jane. *In the Shadow of Man.* Boston: Houghton Mifflin, 1971.

———, Thane Maynard, and Gail E. Hudson. *Hope for Animals and Their World: How Endangered Species Are Being Rescued from the Brink.* New York: Grand Central, 2009.

Gorillas in the Mist: The Adventure of Dian Fossey. Directed by Michael Apted. Videorecording. Universal City, Calif.: Universal Studios, 1999.

Grandin, Temple, and Catherine Johnson. *Animals in Translation: Using the Mysteries of Autism to Decode Animal Behavior.* New York: Scribner, 2005.

Greek, C. Ray, and Jean Swingle Greek. *Sacred Cows and Golden Geese: The Human Cost of Experiments on Animals.* New York: Continuum, 2000.

————. *Specious Science: How Genetics and Evolution Reveal Why Medical Research on Animals Harms Humans.* New York: Continuum, 2002.

Green, Alan. *Animal Underworld: Inside America's Black Market for Rare and Exotic Species.* New York: Public Affairs, 1999.

Grier, Katherine C. *Pets in America: A History.* Chapel Hill: University of North Carolina Press, 2006.

Groves, Julian McAllister. *Hearts and Minds: The Controversy over Laboratory Animals.* Animals, Culture, and Society. Philadelphia: Temple University Press, 1997.

Guerrini, Anita. *Experimenting with Humans and Animals: From Galen to Animal Rights.* Johns Hopkins Introductory Studies in the History of Science. Baltimore, Md.: The Johns Hopkins University Press, 2003.

Hall, Lee. *Capers in the Churchyard: Animal Rights Advocacy in the Age of Terror.* Darien, Conn.: Nectar Bat Press, 2006.

Hall, Stuart. "Subjects in History." In *The House That Race Built: Black Americans, U.S. Terrain,* edited by Wahneema Lubiano, 289–300. New York: Pantheon Books, 1997.

Halweil, Brian. *Eat Here: Reclaiming Homegrown Pleasures in a Global Supermarket.* New York: W. W. Norton, 2004.

Hancocks, David. *A Different Nature: The Paradoxical World of Zoos and Their Uncertain Future.* Berkeley: University of California Press, 2001.

Hanson, Elizabeth. *Animal Attractions: Nature on Display in American Zoos.* Princeton, N.J.: Princeton University Press, 2002.

Haraway, Donna J. *The Companion Species Manifesto: Dogs, People, and Significant Otherness.* Chicago: Prickly Paradigm Press, 2003.

————. *Primate Visions: Gender, Race, and Nature in the World of Modern Science.* New York: Routledge, 1989.

————. *Simians, Cyborgs, and Women: The Reinvention of Nature.* New York: Routledge, 1991.

————. *When Species Meet.* Posthumanities. Minneapolis: University of Minnesota Press, 2008.

Harbolt, Tami L. *Bridging the Bond: The Cultural Construction of the Shelter Pet.* West Lafayette, Ind.: Purdue University Press, 2003.

Hearne, Vicki. *Bandit: Dossier of a Dangerous Dog.* New York: Aaron Asher Books, 1991.

Heart, Tribe of. www.tribeofheart.org.

Held, Virginia. *The Ethics of Care: Personal, Political, and Global.* New York: Oxford University Press, 2006.

———. *Justice and Care: Essential Readings in Feminist Ethics.* Boulder, Colo.: Westview Press, 1995.

Hess, Elizabeth. *Lost and Found: Dogs, Cats, and Everyday Heroes at a Country Animal Shelter.* San Diego: Harcourt, 2000.

———. *Nim Chimpsky: The Chimp Who Would Be Human.* New York: Bantam Books, 2008.

IDA. "The Guardian Campaign." 2009. www.guardiancampaign.com.

Irvine, Leslie. *If You Tame Me: Understanding Our Connection with Animals.* Animals, Culture, and Society. Philadelphia: Temple University Press, 2004.

Irving, Judy, and Mark Bittner. *The Wild Parrots of Telegraph Hill.* Videorecording. 2005. www.wildparrotsfilm.com.

Jamieson, Dale. *Singer and His Critics.* Philosophers and Their Critics 8. Oxford: Blackwell, 1999.

Katz, Sandor Ellix. *The Revolution Will Not Be Microwaved: Inside America's Underground Food Movements.* White River Junction, Vt.: Chelsea Green, 2006.

Kennedy, Elizabeth Lapovsky, and Madeline D. Davis. *Boots of Leather, Slippers of Gold: The History of a Lesbian Community.* New York: Routledge, 1993.

Kennedy, J. S. *The New Anthropomorphism.* Cambridge: Cambridge University Press, 1992.

Kheel, Marti. *Nature Ethics: An Ecofeminist Perspective.* Studies in Social, Political, and Legal Philosophy. Lanham, Md.: Rowman and Littlefield, 2008.

Kingsolver, Barbara, Steven L. Hopp, and Camille Kingsolver. *Animal, Vegetable, Miracle: A Year of Food Life.* New York: HarperCollins, 2007.

Kirby, David. *Animal Factory: The Looming Threat of Industrial Pig, Dairy, and Poultry Farms to Humans and the Environment.* New York: St. Martin's Press.

LaFollette, Hugh, and Niall Shanks. *Brute Science: Dilemmas of Animal Experimentation.* Philosophical Issues in Science. London: Routledge, 1996.

Lama, Eddie. "Sadly, Happy Meat." *Satya,* September 2006, 14–17.

LaVeck, James. "Compassion for Sale? Doublethink Meets Doublefeel as Happy Meat Comes of Age." *Satya,* September 2006, 8–11.

———. "Invasion of the Movement Snatchers." *Satya,* October 2006, 18–23.

Linzey, Andrew. *Animal Rights: A Christian Assessment of Man's Treatment of Animals.* London: SCM Press, 1976.

———. *Christianity and the Rights of Animals.* New York: Crossroad, 1987.

Lubiano, Wahneema H., ed. *The House That Race Built: Black Americans, U.S. Terrain.* New York: Pantheon Books, 1997.

Luke, Brian. *Brutal: Manhood and the Exploitation of Animals.* Urbana: University of Illinois Press, 2007.

Malamud, Randy. *Reading Zoos: Representations of Animals and Captivity.* New York: New York University Press, 1998.

Marcus, Erik. *Meat Market: Animals, Ethics, and Money.* Boston, Mass.: Brio Press, 2005.

Mason, Jim, and Peter Singer. *Animal Factories.* Rev. ed. New York: Harmony Books, 1990.

———. *An Unnatural Order: Uncovering the Roots of Our Domination of Nature and Each Other.* New York: Simon and Schuster, 1993.

Masson, J. Moussaieff. *Dogs Never Lie about Love: Reflections on the Emotional World of Dogs.* New York: Crown, 1997.

Mazur, Nicole A. *After the Ark? Environmental Policy Making and the Zoo.* Carlton: Melbourne University Press, 2001.

McConnell, Patricia B. *For the Love of a Dog: Understanding Emotion in You and Your Best Friend.* New York: Ballantine Books, 2006.

———. *The Other End of the Leash: Why We Do What We Do around Dogs.* New York: Ballantine Books, 2002.

McElroy, Susan Chernak. *Animals as Teachers and Healers: True Stories and Reflections.* New York: Ballantine Books, 1998.

McKenna, Erin, and Andrew Light. *Animal Pragmatism: Rethinking Human-Nonhuman Relationships.* Bloomington: Indiana University Press, 2004.

Mitman, Gregg. *Reel Nature: America's Romance with Wildlife on Film.* Cambridge, Mass.: Harvard University Press, 1999.

Montgomery, Sy. *Walking with the Great Apes: Jane Goodall, Dian Fossey, Biruta Galdikas.* Boston: Houghton Mifflin, 1991.

Nagel, Thomas. "What Is It Like to Be a Bat?" *Philosophical Review* 83 (1974): 435–50.

Nast, Heidi J. "Critical Pet Studies?" *Antipode* 38, no. 5 (2006): 894–906.

———. "Loving Whatever: Alienation, Neoliberalism and Pet-Love in the Twenty-First Century." *ACME: An International E-Journal for Critical Geographies* 5, no. 2 (2006): 300–327.

Newkirk, Ingrid. *Free the Animals: The Amazing True Story of the Animal Liberation Front.* New York: Lantern Books, 2000.

Niebuhr, Reinhold. *Moral Man and Immoral Society: A Study in Ethics and Politics.* Scribner Library of Contemporary Classics. New York: Scribner, 1960.

Noddings, Nel. *Caring: A Feminine Approach to Ethics and Moral Education.* Berkeley: University of California Press, 1984.

Norton, Bryan G. *Ethics on the Ark: Zoos, Animal Welfare, and Wildlife Conservation.* Zoo and Aquarium Biology and Conservation Series. Washington, D.C.: Smithsonian Institution Press, 1995.

Oates, John F. *Myth and Reality in the Rain Forest: How Conservation Strategies Are Failing in West Africa.* Berkeley: University of California Press, 1999.

Orlans, F. Barbara. *In the Name of Science: Issues in Responsible Animal Experimentation.* New York: Oxford University Press, 1993.

Patterson, Charles. *Eternal Treblinka: Our Treatment of Animals and the Holocaust.* New York: Lantern Books, 2002.

Pearce, John M. *Animal Learning and Cognition: An Introduction.* 3rd ed. Hove: Psychology Press, 2008.

Pepperberg, Irene M. *Alex and Me: How a Scientist and a Parrot Discovered a Hidden World of Animal Intelligence—and Formed a Deep Bond in the Process.* New York: Collins, 2008.

———. *The Alex Studies: Cognitive and Communicative Abilities of Grey Parrots.* Cambridge, Mass.: Harvard University Press, 1999.

Petrini, Carlo. *Slow Food Nation: Why Our Food Should Be Good, Clean, and Fair.* New York: Rizzoli Ex Libris, 2007.

Pollan, Michael. "Engaging with the Omnivore: The *Satya* Interview with Michael Pollan." *Satya,* September 2006, 46–49.

———. *In Defense of Food: An Eater's Manifesto.* New York: Penguin Press, 2008.

———. "My Letter to Whole Foods." June 14, 2006. www.michaelpollan.com/articles-archive/my-letter-to-whole-foods.

———. *The Omnivore's Dilemma: A Natural History of Four Meals.* New York: Penguin Press, 2006.

———. "The Way We Live Now: 4-22-07; You Are What You Grow." *New York Times Magazine,* April 22, 2007, 15.

Potter, Will. "Green Is the New Red." 2009. www.greenisthenewred.com/blog.

Preece, Rod, and Lorna Chamberlain. *Animal Welfare and Human Values.* Waterloo: Wilfrid Laurier University Press, 1993.

Prince-Hughes, Dawn. *Songs of the Gorilla Nation: My Journey through Autism.* New York: Harmony Books, 2004.

Probyn, Elspeth. *Blush: Faces of Shame.* Minneapolis: University of Minnesota Press, 2005.

———. *Outside Belongings.* New York: Routledge, 1996.

Rabinowitz, Alan. *Jaguar: Struggle and Triumph in the Jungles of Belize.* New York: Arbor House, 1986.

Rachels, James. *Created from Animals: The Moral Implications of Darwinism.* Oxford: Oxford University Press, 1990.

Regan, Tom. *The Case for Animal Rights.* Berkeley: University of California Press, 1983.

———. *Empty Cages: Facing the Challenge of Animal Rights.* Lanham, Md.: Rowman and Littlefield, 2004.

Rifkin, Jeremy. *Beyond Beef: The Rise and Fall of the Cattle Culture.* New York: Dutton, 1992.

Rollin, Bernard E. *Animal Rights and Human Morality.* Rev. ed. Buffalo, N.Y.: Prometheus Books, 1992.

———. *The Unheeded Cry: Animal Consciousness, Animal Pain, and Science.* Expanded ed. Ames: Iowa State University Press, 1998.

Rothfels, Nigel. *Representing Animals.* Theories of Contemporary Culture. Bloomington: Indiana University Press, 2002.

Rowan, Andrew N. *Of Mice, Models, and Men: A Critical Evaluation of Animal Research.* Albany: State University of New York Press, 1984.

Rowe, Martin. *The Way of Compassion.* New York: Stealth Institute, 2000.

Rowlands, Mark. *Animals Like Us.* Practical Ethics. London: Verso, 2002.

Rudacille, Deborah. *The Scalpel and the Butterfly: The War between Animal Research and Animal Protection.* New York: Farrar, Straus and Giroux, 2000.

Saint-Exupéry, Antoine de. *The Little Prince.* New York: Reynal and Hitchcock, 1943.

Sanders, Clinton. *Understanding Dogs: Living and Working with Canine Companions.* Animals, Culture, and Society. Philadelphia: Temple University Press, 1999.

Sandoval, Chela. *Methodology of the Oppressed.* Theory out of Bounds 18. Minneapolis: University of Minnesota Press, 2000.

Savage-Rumbaugh, E. Sue, and Roger Lewin. *Kanzi: The Ape at the Brink of the Human Mind.* New York: Wiley, 1994.

Schlosser, Eric. *Fast Food Nation: The Dark Side of the All-American Meal.* Boston: Houghton Mifflin, 2001.

Schwartz, Marion. *A History of Dogs in the Early Americas.* New Haven: Yale University Press, 1997.

Scully, Matthew. *Dominion: The Power of Man, the Suffering of Animals, and the Call to Mercy.* New York: St. Martin's Press, 2002.

Sedgwick, Eve Kosofsky. *Epistemology of the Closet.* Berkeley: University of California Press, 1990.

———. *Tendencies.* Series Q. Durham, N.C.: Duke University Press, 1993.

———. *Touching Feeling: Affect, Pedagogy, Performativity.* Series Q. Durham: Duke University Press, 2003.

———, Adam Frank, and Irving E. Alexander. *Shame and Its Sisters: A Silvan Tomkins Reader.* Durham, N.C.: Duke University Press, 1995.

Serpell, James. *The Domestic Dog: Its Evolution, Behaviour, and Interactions with People.* Cambridge: Cambridge University Press, 1995.

Shepard, Paul. *Coming Home to the Pleistocene.* Edited by Florence R. Shepard. Washington, D.C.: Island Press, 1998.

————. *Encounters with Nature: Essays.* Edited by Florence R. Shepard. Washington, D.C.: Island Press 1999.

Shiva, Vandana. *Earth Democracy: Justice, Sustainability, and Peace.* Cambridge, Mass.: South End Press, 2005.

Siebert, Charles. "Watching Whales Watching Us." www.nytimes.com/2009/07/12/magazine/12whales-t.html?pagewanted=1&_r=1&ref=magazine. Accessed July 17, 2010.

Silko, Leslie Marmon. *Ceremony.* New York: Viking Press, 1977.

Simon, Michele. *Appetite for Profit: How the Food Industry Undermines Our Health and How to Fight Back.* New York: Nation Books, 2006.

Sinclair, Upton. *The Jungle.* New York: Doubleday, Page, 1906.

Singer, Peter. *Animal Liberation.* New York: Avon Books, 1975.

————. *Practical Ethics.* 2nd ed. Cambridge: Cambridge University Press, 1993.

————. "Singer Says: The *Satya* Interview with Peter Singer." *Satya,* October 2007, 8–14.

————, and Bruce Friedrich. "The Longest Journey Begins with a Single Step: Promoting Animal Rights by Promoting Reform." *Satya,* September 2006, 12–13.

————, and Jim Mason. *The Way We Eat: Why Our Food Choices Matter.* New York: Rodale, 2006.

Smith, Julie Ann. "Beyond Dominance and Affection: Living with Rabbits in Post-Humanist Households." *Society and Animals* 11, no. 2 (2003): 181–97.

Sperling, Susan. *Animal Liberators: Research and Mortality.* Berkeley: University of California Press, 1988.

Spiegel, Marjorie. *The Dreaded Comparison: Human and Animal Slavery.* Rev. and expanded ed. New York: Mirror Books, 1996.

Sternberg, Sue. *Successful Dog Adoption.* Indianapolis: Howell Book House, 2003.

Stolzenburg, William. *Where the Wild Things Were: Life, Death, and Ecological Wreckage in a Land of Vanishing Predators.* New York: Bloomsbury, 2008.

Sunstein, Cass R., and Martha C. Nussbaum. *Animal Rights: Current Debates and New Directions.* Oxford: Oxford University Press, 2004.

Sutherland, Amy. *Kicked, Bitten, and Scratched: Life and Lessons at the World's Premier School for Exotic Animal Trainers.* New York: Viking, 2006.

Tattersall, Ian. *Becoming Human: Evolution and Human Uniqueness.* New York: Harcourt Brace, 1998.

Thurston, Mary Elizabeth. *The Lost History of the Canine Race: Our 15,000-Year Love Affair with Dogs.* Kansas City, Mo.: Andrews and McMeel, 1996.

Tuan, Yi-fu. *Dominance and Affection: The Making of Pets.* New Haven, Conn.: Yale University Press, 1984.

Uexküll, Jakob von. "A Stroll through the Worlds of Animals and Men." *Instinctive Behavior: The Development of a Modern Concept.* Translated and edited by Claire H. Schiller, 5–80. New York: Intentional Universities Press, 1957. A new translation of this essay was recently published as *A Foray into the Worlds of Animals and Humans,* translated by Joseph D. O'Neil (Minneapolis: University of Minnesota Press, 2010).

Waldau, Paul, and Kimberley C. Patton. *A Communion of Subjects: Animals in Religion, Science, and Ethics.* New York: Columbia University Press, 2006.

Walt Disney Productions. *Bambi.* Videorecording. Burbank, Calif.: Walt Disney Home Video, 1997.

Warner, Michael. *Fear of a Queer Planet: Queer Politics and Social Theory.* Cultural Politics. Minneapolis: University of Minnesota Press, 1993.

Wasserman, Edward A., and Thomas R. Zentall. *Comparative Cognition: Experimental Explorations of Animal Intelligence.* Oxford: Oxford University Press, 2006.

Webber, Bill, and Amy Vedder. *In the Kingdom of Gorillas: Fragile Species in a Dangerous Land.* New York: Simon and Schuster, 2001.

Welty, Jeff. "Animal Law: Thinking about the Future." *Law and Contemporary Problems* 70, no. 1 (2007): 1–8.

White, Lynn. "The Historical Roots of Our Ecological Crises." *Science* 155 (1967): 1203–7.

Winne, Mark. *Closing the Food Gap: Resetting the Table in the Land of Plenty.* Boston: Beacon Press, 2008.

Winograd, Nathan J. *Redemption: The Myth of Pet Overpopulation and the No Kill Revolution in America.* Los Angeles: Almaden Books, 2007.

Wirzba, Norman. *The Essential Agrarian Reader: The Future of Culture, Community, and the Land.* Lexington: University Press of Kentucky, 2003.

Wise, Steven M. *Rattling the Cage: Toward Legal Rights for Animals.* Cambridge, Mass.: Perseus Books, 2000.

Wishart, Adam. *Monkeys, Rats, and Me.* 2006. www.adamwishart.info/2007/01/monkeys_rats_an.html.

Wolch, Jennifer R., and Jody Emel. *Animal Geographies: Place, Politics, and Identity in the Nature-Culture Borderlands.* London: Verso, 1998.

Wolfe, Cary. *Animal Rites: American Culture, the Discourse of Species, and Posthumanist Theory.* Chicago: University of Chicago Press, 2003.

Wynne, Clive D. L. *Animal Cognition: The Mental Lives of Animals.* Basingstoke: Palgrave, 2001.

INDEX

Adam (farmer), 82
Adams, Carol, 35
affect, 189–97; in animal advocacy, xiii, 10, 23, 25, 152, 187–204, 198, 202; in animal experimentation, 157, 174; in animal stories, xx, 26, 111, 193, 199, 201–4; clothing metaphor of, 188; corporeal aspect of, xvii–xviii, 107, 181, 188, 193; discourse on, 26; effect on pleasure, 15; effect on policy change, 24; in evaluation of morality, 15; in human–animal relations, xvi–xxx, 22, 24–25, 144, 180–85, 192–93, 197, 198; in human–canine relations, 68, 70; in the humanities, 189; as knowledge, 189; language of, 193; as noun, 189; in political realm, 189; reason in, xvi, xvii, 192; in research animal relationships, 170–73, 178, 196;

rights and, 191; role in selfhood, 192, 194; role in social change, 7; role in subject formation, xvii, 192, 203, 215; role of food in, 181–83; role of language in, 185; sacredness in, xviii–xx; sentimentality in, xvii; spirituality in, xviii–xx; transformative power of, 26; as verb, 189. *See also* love
affirmative action, 7
Agamben, Giorgio, 229n27
agribusiness, American, 74–75, 86–93; chemical use in, 89–90, 92, 105, 108; Fordist approach to, 87; government subsidies for, 91; social opposition to, 105
AIDS epidemic, 105
Alex (parrot), 179
American Anti-Vivisectionist Society: research guidelines of, 175
American Kennel Club, 46; breeding

247

Kathy Rudy is associate professor of women's studies at Duke University. She began her career researching reproductive ethics, religious ethics, sexuality, and feminist theory and now focuses on animals and ethics, nature, food politics, ecology, and ecofeminism. She is the author of *Beyond Pro-Life and Pro-Choice: Moral Diversity in the Abortion Debate* and *Sex and the Church: Gender, Homosexuality, and the Transformation of Christian Ethics.*